Other Titles by William Pfaff

*Fear, Anger and Failure: A Chronicle of the
Bush Administration's War Against Terror,
from the Attacks of September 11, 2001 to
Defeat in Baghdad* (2004)

*Barbarian Sentiments: America in the
New Century* (2000)

*The Wrath of Nations: Civilization and the
Furies of Nationalism* (1993)

*Barbarian Sentiments: How the American
Century Ends* (1989)

Condemned to Freedom (1971)

with Edmund Stillman:

*Power and Impotence: The Failure of
America's Foreign Policy* (1966)

*The Politics of Hysteria: The Sources of
Twentieth-Century Conflict* (1964)

*The New Politics: America and the End of the
Postwar World* (1961)

T. E. Lawrence

Gabriele D'Annunzio

Ernst Jünger

Willi Münzenberg

André Malraux

Arthur Koestler

Vladimir Peniakoff

Benito Mussolini

Filippo Tommaso Marinetti

Che Guevara

Charles de Foucauld

Simone Weil

The Bullet's Song

Romantic Violence and Utopia

William Pfaff

SIMON & SCHUSTER

New York   London   Toronto   Sydney

SIMON & SCHUSTER
Rockefeller Center
1230 Avenue of the Americas
New York, NY 10020

Parts of Chapters 3, 8, and 10 appeared originally in a different form as
"The Fallen Hero," *"L'Homme Engagé,"* and "Terrorism" in *The New Yorker.*
Part of Chapter 11 appeared originally in a different form as "Progress"
in *World Policy Journal*, Vol. XII, No. 4 (Winter 1995–96).

For information about special discounts for bulk purchases,
please contact Simon & Schuster Special Sales at
1-800-456-6798 or business@simonandschuster.com

Designed by Jeanette Olender
Manufactured in the United States of America

1   2   3   4   5   6   7   8   9   10

Library of Congress Cataloging-in-Publication Data
Pfaff, William, 1928–
   The bullet's song : the romance of violence and utopia / William Pfaff.
      p.   cm.
   Includes bibliogaphical references and index.
      1. Social history—20th century.   2. Intellectuals—Political activity—
History—20th century.   3. Radicalism—History—20th century.   I. Title.
HN16.P483   2004
303.6'094'0904—dc22   2004049167

ISBN 0-684-80907-9

To my beloved wife, children, and grandchildren.

This is what I can leave you.

Ce monde est une porte fermée. C'est une barrière et en même temps, c'est le passage.

SIMONE WEIL, *Cahiers*

CONTENTS

Introduction

CHAPTER ONE

———

ROMANTICISM AND VIOLENCE

This book tells a story about the twentieth century, which has in it a lesson for the twenty-first—one that I would think unlikely to be learned, since it is a moral lesson, concerning the role of virtue in human existence, and we know about moral lessons.

My book deals with certain aesthetic and intellectual forces implicated in the great shift that took place in the West's moral and historical assumptions before and during the 1914–1918 war, and that produced the twentieth-century crisis, its totalitarian regimes and wars, and the armed utopian movements in Italy, Germany, and Russia that in interaction with the responses to them of the liberal West dominated international affairs from the 1920s to the 1990s and the end of the cold war.

My argument first concerns the loss of a code of national and personal conduct we can summarily call chivalry. This loss was one consequence of the appeal made to intellectuals and other members of the European elite in the nineteenth and twentieth centuries by political romanticism and the idea of redemptive, utopian violence (moral violence as well as physical). The appeal of violence was a powerful, sometimes overt, sometimes subterranean force in political society throughout the period, and is certainly not exhausted yet. Utopian violence is the subject of the second part of the book.

3

The story is a good one, about intelligent people, filled with romance and adventure, surely to twenty-first-century taste, while revealing tragic illusions about history, not yet renounced. From it, private as well as public lessons are to be drawn.

◦

Chivalry had been a part of the European order since the Middle Ages and remained an important force in the nineteenth century, until it was decisively undermined by the events of 1914–1918. I use the term *chivalry* as shorthand reference to an extensive code of behavior and expectations among the middle and upper classes of the major Western nations that had an important practical effect on human and societal conduct during the period before 1914.

This code acknowledged the individual Western nations as legitimate powers inhabiting a shared moral universe, and imposed implicit limits on the conduct permissible in international relations. It regarded national rivalries as normal and open to negotiation or, if necessary, determination by war, but it also considered war as a national recourse which was limited, tolerable in its employment of violence, a legitimate if extreme instrument of national policy that nonetheless posed no threat to the existence of states or to the nature of society. "Total" war did not arrive, conceptually at least, until 1914 and after.

The cosmopolitan German patron of arts, connoisseur, unofficial diplomat (and reserve officer) Count Harry Kessler wrote in 1914 to his sister in Paris, married to a Frenchman about to be called up, to wish his brother-in-law luck. "We must all bear up and not give way to nerves or sentiment. . . . I do not think that, anyhow, the war can last very long, the war itself perhaps two to three months, the peace preliminaries another three or four months; all should be over by next spring."

The chivalric code's importance can be seen in the lives of individuals. The chivalric framework of values included a conception of war as, in individual terms, a test of valor, rewarded by "honor." Europeans who believed this then found themselves in a convulsion of objectively purposeless and eventually suicidal national struggles, in which modern industrial technology was employed to cause immense human suffering, social and material destruction, and moral disorder.

✦◦

The origins of chivalry are medieval, originally concerning a hereditary military class which understood war as a politically necessary and potentially ennobling activity whose essential barbarism was limited through a commitment by elites to certain norms of behavior. These, as Mark Girouard has written, "derived from an amalgamation of Christianity with pre-Christian traditions of the warrior bands of northern Europe; they were adapted to the social structure of feudalism and amended by the cult of courtly love as it developed in the rich and sophisticated courts of southern France." It was a code, and produced a literature, which made a powerful and lasting appeal to the generations that followed, "gradually developing until it becomes one element of the accepted code of conduct for gentlemen" in nineteenth- and early-twentieth-century European (and by derivation, American) civilization.

In England its extreme, and superbly absurd, manifestation is generally acknowledged to have been Captain Robert Falcon Scott's incompetently prepared and badly executed race to the South Pole in 1912. Scott arrived there thirty-five days after the efficient and classless Norwegian Roald Amundsen had already been and gone. All Scott's men perished on the journey back, the captain painstakingly recording each death in his journal as that of "a brave man and an English gentleman. We all hope to meet the end in the same spirit. . . ."

This was a tradition whose cultural power was by no means con-

5

fined to England and France. Girouard writes of "the influence of chivalry on German attitudes before and during the Great War or on the kind of American gentlemen who died with such style on the *Titanic*." He says,

> The Kaiser talked about putting on "shining armour" and the war posters of Germany and her allies contain far more chivalric images than the English ones. America at this period had a flourishing boys' movement called the Knights of King Arthur; most of the popular editions of Malory* in circulation in late Victorian and Edwardian England were written by Americans; England had nothing as ambitious as [Edwin Austin] Abbey's great sequence of Arthurian paintings in the Boston Public Library; and chivalry was sufficiently strong for Mark Twain to deliver a vicious attack on it in *A Yankee at the Court of King Arthur*.

Whatever the sentimentality, or kitsch, of its popular manifestations, the chivalric code held that what an individual or a society could licitly do to another was limited by a morality linked to the essential values of Western civilization. The First World War ended this, replacing it with a nihilism that men subsequently reacted to through codes of individual transcendence and collective will on the one hand, and on the other by utopias based on historical fictions. The fundamental problem remains unresolved today, and in some respects worsened when the dominant liberal democratic state became the international military hegemon, acting under the influence of a myth of national mission.

---

* Sir Thomas Malory, whose fifteenth-century *Morte d'Arthur* was the first literary rendering of the Arthurian legend.

My second concern is with the ideological manifestation of political romanticism, largely post-1918 in its consequences, that led serious, intelligent, and "moral" people to commit themselves to betrayal, murder, torture, or terror in the service of utopian fictions. This was the most important disruptive force in international politics from 1918 to 1989, and has reappeared today in official and unofficial circles.

On the left, violence in the service of utopian projects was rationalized as a higher form of realism ("what vileness would you not commit to exterminate violence...," as the German Communist poet and dramatist Bertolt Brecht demanded). On the right it inspired a theory that because the violence of war could raise heroes from ordinary people, a collective project of heroism could heal human mediocrity and change society and history. Such ideas were overtly at work in twentieth-century wars, and were a subterranean force in peacetime political life. I would think their attraction not yet exhausted, although temporarily out of intellectual fashion.

The individuals who figure in this book are intellectuals or artists, most of whom played significant political roles during their lives, but none of whom were major political figures (other than Benito Mussolini, who makes an appearance in one part of my story). They imposed themselves upon the author as living evidence of the inner history of the modern crisis—its moral history, so to speak: a matter of inexhaustible interest. These people in their lives and public experience provided individual accompaniment to the political history of the century. It was my interest in them as individuals, whose lives in some cases indirectly affected my own, and in their works, in the case of those who were writers, that led to my book and my conclusions.

All believed themselves committed to progressive causes (it is unfashionable to point it out today, but Fascism, to Fascists, was a progressive cause).* All but one ended in disillusionment, or stoicism, irony—or murdered; or in one case, in religious conversion.

Three of my principal subjects took part in the First World War, the most important event of the twentieth century. Three of them fought in the war of 1939–1945. The others (like myself) were people of the cold war. Each tried to make more of war than war, an effort that came spontaneously to them, as most were artists, or artists manqué.

At the origin of the book was my adolescent interest in T. E. Lawrence ("Lawrence of Arabia") and the French novelist André Malraux (the "Byron" of the 1930s), prototypical romantic figures of their periods. Two other early interests were also important: military matters, particularly the First World War, and painting, including Futurist painting.

Lawrence as hero was, as one discovers, a creation not only of historical circumstance but of his own deliberate falsifications. He conducted what he believed was a successful revolt by an oppressed people, the Bedouin Arabs, which proved a political failure and ended in their betrayal. He subsequently joined the British enlisted military service under an assumed name. Lawrence as an RAF airman accomplished little that was tangible, yet through his example

---

* Renzo De Felice, author of the most comprehensive and complex consideration of Mussolini yet published, is quoted as describing Fascism as "a forward-looking totalitarianism of the Left with ideological and moral roots sunk in the humus of the French revolution." The abominable Heinrich Himmler himself said: "We are original in one important point, our measures are the expression of an idea, not the search for any personal advantage or ambition. We desire only the realization on a Germanic scale of a social ideal and the unity of the West. We will clarify the situation at whatever cost." He also said, "It is the curse of greatness that it must step over dead bodies to create new life. Yet we must create new life, we must cleanse the soil or it will never bear fruit. It will be a great burden for me to bear."

and his writings he was to have an unforeseeable and significant influence on the twentieth-century moral sensibility, as well as on the political and strategic phenomenon of later twentieth-century guerrilla warfare.

Filippo Tommaso Marinetti and the members of the artistic movement he created, Futurism, advocated war as "the world's only hygiene." They subsequently were neglected or disparaged outside Italy for many years, and their accomplishments ignored, because of such outrageous statements and because most became personally compromised by Fascism. Their influence upon art in the twentieth century and on the cultural circumstances from which Fascism emerged has been discounted. The peculiar historical role played during and after the First World War by the "Arditi," Italian storm troops, in whose ranks many of the Futurists chose to serve, has also been neglected.

The Italian poet, writer, and war hero Gabriele D'Annunzio's Fiume adventure was a Futurist episode if ever there was one. An immensely popular romantic and "decadent" novelist and playwright until the First World War, D'Annunzio then re-created himself as a heroic warrior, if a faintly absurd one, and led a postwar nationalist seizure of territory denied Italy during the Versailles negotiations, inventing in the captured city of Fiume (now Rijeka in Croatia) an original, romantic, "playful," populist, and eventually sinister regime that greatly influenced Fascism—which in turn, thanks to the socialist Benito Mussolini's crucial merger of the ideas of nationalism and socialism, became the most influential political innovation of the century.

Ernst Jünger was, like Lawrence, a man who entered the world war with the chivalric and romantic assumptions of the Edwardian period. He was to become an officer of German storm troops and a great war hero, and later an artist and scientist, but he reacted to the fateful break between the values of the pre-1914 elite and the nihilism that followed by becoming the self-conscious celebrant of an intensely romantic interpretation of violence, a fervent nationalist, and an enemy of the Weimar Republic. He saw his romantic project of a reconstructed Reich actually attempted by Hitler, whom he despised and eventually conspired to overthrow.

◦⌒◦

The Right, in the 1920s and 1930s, promised a radiant future, just as did the Left; it too believed in the illusion of human progress. The utopianism of the Left led to Stalinism, but before and long after the enigmatic and terrible career of Stalin, Communism claimed the support of millions, through its promise of justice for the masses. Its cause was promulgated in the world outside Russia through the Comintern, whose propaganda genius, Willi Münzenberg, was an important influence in the adherence to the myth of liberating revolution of such writers and intellectual figures as André Malraux and Arthur Koestler—two people who eventually turned against the lie that the myth had been.

Willi Münzenberg's accomplishments as a Comintern propagandist, like Malraux's fabulations as "homme engagé," helped persuade a generation in Europe and America to believe lies about the future. He, Jünger, and Koestler turned back from the brink, just in time; although the last-named never shook off his sense of an impending political apocalypse.

André Malraux's purpose was to become a great man and immortal writer, and if that could only be done fraudulently, or not be done at all, at least to attach himself to a genuinely great man, in the event, Charles de Gaulle. Malraux was influenced by D'Annunzio, who also wanted literary immortality, and to be a Superman as well; and who really did liberate a place, a city, and tried to turn that into a liberation of the oppressed everywhere—the cause of the Left, not of the Right, even though D'Annunzio was one of those who inspired Fascism. For Marinetti, the Futurist, the goal was to overturn Italy's antique inheritance and make the world new; for Jünger, adventure, and after he had become a killer, to find a philosophy to justify what he had done. For the secret agent Münzenberg it was

revolution; eventually, for Koestler, it was counterrevolution—
before it was too late.

＊◯

My people were not only implicated in violence that served national and international causes but exploited it for themselves, in
fulfilling themselves, looking into it for the extremity of themselves, as well as seeking to reveal the innate *form* the artist looks for
in his regard of his subject. For most, their undertakings produced
creative individual transformation, and from many of them literary
or intellectual works of merit. For some, their action took place in a
suspension or absence of moral code. Jünger came to consider the
First World War itself in terms of a zoological evolutionary struggle. D'Annunzio, according to a biographer (John Woodhouse),
"despite his great intelligence and his creative genius . . . never
seemed to develop beyond adolescence. . . . There is no evidence
that D'Annunzio ever showed regret or compassion or even consideration for others once they had gratified a temporary whim;
selfish egoism governed his every action."

After the world war, and under the influence of Leninism (and
for a later generation, Maoism), the conflation of revolutionary
commitment with liberating violence made the chivalric hero ob-
solete and substituted the selfless and ruthless Comintern agent, Jesuit of revolution, and the intellectual or artist "éngagé" who
celebrated him.

Eventually terrorism, a phenomenon of the nineteenth-century
breakdown and an evidence of political despair, made its return.
The international terrorists of the early twenty-first century, out-
raged by the condition of the modern Middle East and the crisis of
Islamic civilization, at this writing remain in pursuit of an evanes-
cent triumph of true religion over "crusader" America, the Palestinian cause an open wound. The Western terrorists of the 1960s
and 1970s, motivated by Vietnam, as well as the fate of the Pales-
tinians, and by the perceived mediocrity and injustice of European

and American society, were eventually confounded by their hubristic pursuit of social transformation and political redemption by means of bombing and murder. Before, terrorism had been associated with retrograde nationalism and utopian anarchism, as in a certain sense it became again in the 2000s, under different gods, in a reactionary Islamic mutation of what began as Liberation.

❧

My individuals all saw in violence or its intellectual counterpart, manipulation, means to redemptive political change and the possibility to impose through action as well as art *significant form* upon historical materials and experience (borrowing the term from the aesthetic writings of the philosopher Jacques Maritain).

Most of my subjects were also engaged in re-creating themselves as someone they were not, or as Arthur Koestler said, in finding "the him in me who is more me than myself." This at its most vulgar could simply mean manipulating one's reputation, as Lawrence, D'Annunzio, and Malraux notoriously did; but there is anguish attached even to that. Where war and death are concerned, the search acquires an inevitable and perhaps unexpected moral dimension.

Their excess has drawn me. The result of what they did was, for most, personal as well as political failure—which is even more interesting, as is why they had to fail, which has an explanation toward which we will advance in the pages to follow.

❧

There are no Americans among my principals, other than when I write about the cold war, mainly because America largely excluded itself from the inner history of the twentieth century, which was written in Europe, and mostly at Europe's expense. America intervened in this history in 1917 (temporarily) and 1940 (lastingly) only as a reluctant outsider. One might think Ernest Hemingway belongs here, because of his romanticism about war and death. But while he wrote two great American novels and made a permanent mark on the American language, he remained an isolated American, and as a moral figure he was, as we Americans are disposed to say, a phony; or in personal terms a tragedy, victim of the American disease, celebrity. Neither intellectual detachment nor irony is in the American style.

The Americans I do mention, mainly people who were implicated in the Comintern and Soviet intelligence services, including Whittaker Chambers, Michael Straight, Noel Field, and undoubtedly Alger Hiss, appeared at the time of the revelation of their secret roles as themselves victims, usually bathetic rather than heroic or sinister—even the self-consciously Dostoyevskian Chambers seeming a City College intellectual who had lost his way.

Chivalry was an intellectual construction and moral system with several forms of modern influence. The chivalric romanticism of the nineteenth century was mostly extinguished in Europe by 1918, Churchill and de Gaulle providentially anachronistic survivors, and in the United States by the 1960s. An American looks back today with admiration and consciousness of loss to the patrician reformism and belief in public obligation displayed by such American figures as Robert E. Lee, Theodore Roosevelt, and George Marshall (who refused a million-dollar offer for his memoirs after the Second World War, saying that one does not enrich oneself from public service).

The implication of the United States in pre-1940 contemporary history began with the brief American intervention in the First World War, a matter of nineteen months and 53,500 fatal casualties in a war in which, overall, an estimated ten million died. Britain lost a million men, and was one of the more lightly affected societies. France is estimated to have lost one in twenty-eight of its entire population. The chivalric romanticism, destroyed by the war, that Europeans had shared with an anglicized American elite, afterwards enjoyed a half-life in certain circles in the United States, which occupied, so to speak, a different cultural time zone. I was part of the generation in between, which is a reason for this book, and for a personal digression. There is a sense in which these people selected me.

◦⌒

My father was still in army officer candidate school in November 1918. His older brother had been in the National Guard, and had been mobilized to ride with "Black Jack" (General John J.) Pershing to pursue the Mexican revolutionary Pancho Villa into Mexico in 1916, and when the United States entered the world war, he became an artillery observation balloonist. A maternal uncle was gassed in France but survived, nonetheless to die an early death. My mother's and father's families thus were more touched by the war than most American families, but even so, for my parents the 1920s were a time of fun and prosperity, ending only in mid-Depression.

I was born at the end of 1928, and my boyhood was one for which warfare meant Lafayette Escadrille, the "Lost Battalion," and the romanticized battles of Chateau-Thierry and Belleau Wood. My magazine reading was all about flying aces and derring-do. The model airplanes I built were Spads, SE5's, Sopwith Camels, Fokkers. The movies I eagerly watched were *Dawn Patrol*, *The Fighting 69th*, and such sagas of Hollywood imperialism as *Four Feathers* and *Gunga Din*.

My father solemnly took me to *All Quiet on the Western Front*, to show me what war really was about. But my indiscriminate reading remained romantic adventure, even going back to G. A. Henty (a supply of whose books, many set on Britain's nineteenth-century imperial frontiers, was in my grandmother's attic, she having had four sons).

The Civil War was still a presence, especially in the South, where the deaths of veterans of "The War Between the States" were still being reported and eulogized in the 1940s. My mother's older sister wrote a charming, much-anthologized story in the 1920s about a Boy Scout who was grudgingly persuaded to miss the Fourth of July parade in order to look after the old man next door. The latter proved to have been a Union drummer boy present at Lincoln's Gettysburg Address, and gave the Scout a button from Lincoln's coat, presented to him by the great man himself.

After Pearl Harbor, which occurred when I was thirteen, we spent the war years (and after) in an army town in Georgia, where Fort Benning housed the Infantry School itself and the elite parachute and Ranger schools, and where at the peak of the war soldiers outnumbered townspeople three to one. I put on an American uniform at the age of fourteen, in the high school Reserve Officer Training Corps (and took it off, leaving the active Army Reserve, at thirty).

The ideas acquired from this experience were largely egregious fantasy, as I was to learn. But if I lived under the influence of the past, *that past had really existed.* Thanks in part to an exceptional (in the United States) classical and religious education that insisted upon the tragic dimension of existence, emphatically validated by the history of the twentieth century, I was at the same time learning something about what the world and war were really about.

As an adult, the political horrors of Eastern Europe under Soviet control, and of the Soviet Union itself, the war in Korea, the cold war political and cultural wars, the misconceived disaster of the Vietnam struggle, and wars in the Balkans, in all of which I was to have some active or passive professional engagement, taught me something more, this time about the ability of secular utopian thought to inspire a lethal dogmatic idealism served by an intense cruelty. I was nonetheless left with a peculiar combination of romanticism and realism, in that I could do quite foolish and romantic things while making a detached judgment of what I was doing. Thus for the subjects of this book I feel both empathy and distance, interest and a certain emotional engagement, while feeling far enough from them to be able to "place" them in the history of my century, in whose tragedy we were all implicated.

Violence is a product of human volition as well as an activity in which men find affirmation and pleasure. This usually is denied. The statement that violence is an aspect of humanity itself invites sterile and reductive argument about the definition and immutability, or otherwise, of human nature—topics of greater interest to certain physiologists and behavioral scientists than to those professionally involved with the permanent realities of politics and history (or to the men and women who make their way in the domain of common sense). I believe it better that a moral vocabulary is used, and that we agree that violence and war are aspects of the tragedy of human existence, more profitably considered by way of art and philosophical or theological reflection than by science.

I would think it obvious that it is essential to human equilibrium and a true engagement with reality to acknowledge that tragedy is the defining part of human life, and to accept the limits (and opportunities) this imposes, both individual and political. The effort to deny tragedy was among the fundamental factors responsible for what happened in the twentieth century. Utopianism defies tragedy—and fails. My book includes accounts of the attempt to deny tragedy and substitute a faith in progress, in flight from the reality of the human predicament. Each version of this faith promised a final solution—of one or another sort—to the condition of humans in history.

Two of the individuals most important to my discussion, T. E. Lawrence and Vladimir Peniakoff (otherwise known as "Popski," who once had a private army), found a kind of serenity in resolute acceptance of and engagement with the violence in our nature, deriving from it what I would call the only true solution, the classical one, identified by Aristotle as the pursuit of virtue, the only proper pursuit for a human being.

Such is an uncomfortable route toward a solution since it demands individual self-examination and renounces the consoling ideologies and utopian illusions of a collective resolution of the human problem. Virtue is an all but totally ignored conception today, when narcissism and the (futile) pursuit of self-esteem are the prevailing counterfeits of individual worth and achievement, with death denied in the search for the therapy of immortality.

✧

The past dealt in death as the most important fact in life. Horace taught a classically educated generation that it is sweet to die for one's nation, *dulce et decorum est pro patria mori;* and the elites of European society went to war in 1914 with that conviction. Another classical writer, Grimmelshausen, the seventeenth-century author of the great novel of the Thirty Years' War, *The Adventures of Simplicissimus*, observed that "the splendid deeds of the heroic would be glorious to celebrate if they had not been achieved by other men's ruin and loss." This is decidedly relevant to the twenty-first century, when the Machiavellian/Clauswitzian paradigms concerning the political use of violence no longer describe our condition.

It has been the American as well as a certain French intellectual fashion in recent years to assert that "truth" is a text, and human history a textual construction. This nihilistic ontology has represented an intellectual attempt to dispense with the past and claim the power to do away with the constraint of reality. On the other hand, modern governments, led by the United States, increasingly act within the dimensions of a virtual reality their own propaganda or ideology has created, so that such constructs as "Asian Communism" (in the 1960s) or later, "rogue states," "Islamic terrorism," or indeed "terrorism" itself, treated as an autonomous phenomenon, acquire a power over political imagination and discourse, and official decisions, that is infrequently questioned.

Those who have been truly successful rulers and "makers" in history recognized the realities of past or present as essential ingredients in what was to be constructed. A man who served de Gaulle in London in 1941 and 1942, and in Normandy after the 1944 landings, François Coulet, once remarked to me that he had "always re-

17

spected the distinction the general carefully drew between 'la France' and 'les Français.' " Charles de Gaulle famously said, in the opening sentence of his memoirs, that he had all his life possessed "a certain idea" of France. He created this France in London in 1940, sustained it against all opposition, imposed it upon the "real" France to which he returned in 1944, reimposed it when he regained power in 1958, and held this imaginative creation in being until 1969, when his departure allowed the French people, with relief, to resume being themselves.

It is significant that de Gaulle was an artist, as his memoirs demonstrate, and so was Churchill. They were artists, but politics (and history) was their medium. The aesthetic impulse is a permanent force in politics and political thinking, neglected to our risk, since it is not always positive in effect. (Hitler was also an artist, an architect who had first to clear his site.) If politics is integrally related to aesthetic forces and vision, as it is in the greatest political leaders, whose action may be governed by aesthetic perceptions and imperatives, we need to abandon certain conventional ideas. We see that the arguments between those who believe humans inherently cooperative as well as rational, and those who think men naturally competitive and combative, are beside the point.

There are men and women with neither cooperative nor competitive philosophies, but with more complex visions of society and history, who believe violence is not only inevitable but essential. Jünger, after four years as a storm-troop officer, thirteen times wounded and given the highest German military decoration, wrote gnomically, in an essay published in 1922, that the war had no ordinary cause but was the expression of an "idea" which the process of the war itself revealed, yet to which the war would prove only a prelude.

CHAPTER TWO

OVERTURE

Historians and political scientists deal in economic and demographic forces, class interests and struggle, national interest and national aggrandizement, commercial interest and rivalry, all of them factors in international life. Yet history is fundamentally driven by ideas, and as the British historian Lewis Namier has said, "to treat political ideas as the offspring of pure reason would be to assign them a parentage about as mythological as that of Pallas Athene." He goes on, "What matters most are the underlying emotions, the music, to which ideas are a mere libretto, too often of a very inferior quality."

This is revealed in art itself: attentive to the dissonance that entered into the music of the times in the nineteenth century. Romanticism implied an alternative interpretation of humanity's political possibilities to that of the pragmatic politician, the historical conservative, or the philosophical realist.

Romanticism was a seventeenth- and eighteenth-century German reaction to the inferior intellectual as well as political position in which Germany (the German states, more than a thousand of them at the time, all part of the old Holy Roman Empire) found itself following the wars of religion, by comparison with the centralized and successful French and English nation-states. This, Isaiah Berlin has said, was true particularly vis-à-vis the French, this brilliant glittering state which had managed to crush and humiliate them, this great country which dominated the sciences and the arts, and all the provinces of human life, with a kind of arrogance and success unexampled hitherto. This did plant in Germany a permanent sense of sadness and humiliation which may be discovered in the rather doleful German ballad literature and popular literature of the end of the seventeenth century, and even in the arts in which the Germans excelled. . . . There is no doubt that if you compare composers like Bach and his contemporaries, and Telemann, with French composers of that period, then, although Bach's genius is incomparably greater, the whole atmosphere and tone of his music is much more, I will not say provincial, but confined to the particular inner religious life of the city of Leipzig . . . and was not intended to be an offering before the glittering courts of Europe, or for the general admiration of mankind.

The Germans took recourse first in pietist religion, spiritual life, contempt for ritual and form, pomp and ceremony. This led to a cultural movement of opposition to the classicism and rationalism of France. This movement, Berlin says, eventually became an attempt "to impose an aesthetic model on reality, to say that everything should obey the rules of art."

This was Romanticism, and held that creation emerged not from reason but from polarity and tension, fusion following break and pain. The historian J. L. Talmon says "the most real thing in the universe was thus the fact of becoming, and not of being, of activity and not completion, of endless longing . . . ," or as Novalis, one of the early German romantics said, "thinking is only a dream of feeling, an extinct feeling, only gray, weakly living."

Romanticism flourished during the crack in time between religion's intellectual dominance and the scientific rationalism of the nineteenth century. It held that truth is not objective and that the great answers to life, and indeed life itself, need to be invented.

These "are not something found, they are something literally made."

This was taken to apply to political affairs and history quite as much as to art. In fact the possibilities of art for art's sake came to seem less interesting than those of making history, which in the nineteenth century sent Byron to Greece. It appeared that the historical order in which men and women lived was as open to creative action as was the substance of art and could itself be made into a form of work of art. The creative act itself was as important as, or indeed more important than the end; thus the romantic insistence upon vital expression and novelty, upon immanence becoming the flow of experience. Truth itself, accordingly, was not objective but was to be invented in terms of experience. The romantics believed in the goodness of man. All of this was in violent opposition to such conservative or classical notions as natural philosophy, natural order, good sense as the master of life, government as "the greatest happiness of the greatest number" (as the eighteenth-century economist and jurist Cesare Beccaria had argued). Harold Nicolson, the English diarist and diplomat, conservative and snob, makes the romantics seem absurd: "they ceased to think in logical terms, relied more on the heart than on the head, rejected the rectilinear in favor of the serpentine, favored the display of personal emotion, wept copiously. . . ." They also changed modern history.

The romantic aims at a generalized liberation and expresses a desire for transcendence, to re-creation of society by imposing upon it a vision of new institutions (or of no institutions at all, in the anarchists' case) and new structures of values. The romantic's attack on established or "establishment" values has too frequently in practice invited their replacement with something worse. In the case in point, most today look back at the emergence of European middle-class society in the nineteenth century as the foundation of modern liberal political civilization. It was just that society which came under assault in 1914. Liberty depends on the existence of what since 1990 has been called civil society but then was called bourgeois civilization, respectful of the social value of individual human relationships, and of practical tolerance, common sense, and compromise in the common life of a community. Bourgeois society was also materialistic, conformist, and often intellectually and socially stultifying, complacent about its faults as well as its qualities. It nonetheless made a liberal politics possible.

Political romanticism is quite the opposite. To quote Berlin again, it offered "something literally novel, self-subsistent, self-justified, self-fulfilling." Romanticism emphasized "the subjective and ideal rather than the objective and real . . . the process of creation rather than its effects . . . motives rather than consequences, and as a necessary corollary of this . . . the state of mind or soul of the acting agent." The history of the twentieth century thus was delivered over to fundamentally nonreasonable or unachievable political ideas and ambitions.

The First World War was beyond doubt the most important event of the twentieth century. It was a product of a European crisis of political culture which still has to be fully explained. Why should there have been frenzied enthusiasm for war after an incident in the Balkans not unlike other incidents in the Balkans? There had already been two Balkan wars since 1912 (and as our generation knows, there were to be more).

Today one must say that a new war responded to no rational interest. The nineteenth century and the early twentieth, up to 1914, were for continental Western Europe, not to speak of Britain and the United States, times of unprecedented general prosperity, material improvement, and well-being. Wars had been infrequent and, for the most part, brief. The mass of people had improved their lives. The material indexes show no breakdown of society or of its structures.

If one speaks about Central Europe, where the political authority of the Austro-Hungarian Empire had in the later nineteenth century splintered under the force of romantic nationalism (a product of writers and intellectuals), or about Turkey or China, where very old political structures were faltering because of their inability to deal with the competitive threat and example of the western European powers, one can reasonably say that a breakdown was taking place. But in western Europe?

The breakdown was in the mind and spirit. The intellectual structure that had rested on practical confidence in religion's propositions had been lost. The loss was caused by the advance in scientific thought, leading to an attempt to find equivalent reassurances and new values in a scientific interpretation of historical development, parallel to that proposed by evolution in the animal kingdom. A "science" of progress in society and economy was sought. This was not found. Science itself eventually yielded what had seemed certainties to probabilities, relativism, a very principle of uncertainty, and the discovery of further mysteries as the explanation of apparent mysteries. The desire to find a postreligious moral explanation for life was responsible for the question posed much later by Albert Camus: "Is it possible to become a saint without believing in God?"

The uneasiness felt during the late nineteenth and early twentieth centuries about the replacement of old assumptions was accompanied by violent condemnations of the latter by estranged or prophetic elements in the intelligentsia and among artists. The catastrophic culmination was the First World War—so casually entered into, in obedience to the conventional assumptions of the day, and producing not only human but political carnage. War had been widely anticipated for reasons at the same time inexplicably deep and essentially frivolous, of which simple boredom (or longing for sacrifice or drama—for something *interesting*) was one.

When it came, war was welcomed with expectations of individual fulfillment and chivalric affirmation. Such ideas prevailed among the elites of society on both sides of the 1914 battle lines, except for those few, like the Polish banker Ivan Bloch, who bleakly imagined where industrial warfare could lead. (His contemporary, Norman Angell, wrote in 1910 that modern industry and the commercial and financial interdependence of the great powers would prevent war because people would see how unreasonable it would be, and his book *The Great Illusion* was an international success.)

"Never had times seemed so rich in hope, nor destinies so malleable," a contemporary wrote of the eve of the First World War. Then came (I quote a letter of Henry James's) "the plunge of civilization into this abyss of blood and darkness; a thing that so gives away the whole long age during which we have supposed the world to be, with whatever abatement, gradually bettering, that to have to take it all now for what the treacherous years were all the while really making for a *meaning* is too tragic for any words."

There were possibilities of life that simply were ended. Paul Fussell has written movingly of the changes that illustrate this in English poetry between 1914 and 1918. In 1914, the language was elegiac and pastoral, using a vocabulary of chivalric comradeship and honor. Wilfrid Gibson wrote of those about to die, for example, that in their eyes "a sudden glory shone, / And I was dazzled by a sunset glow." By 1917, Wilfred Owen was writing, "If you could hear, at every jolt, the blood / come gargling from the froth-corrupted lungs, / Obscene as cancer, bitter as the cud / Of vile . . ."

Before 1914, it was plausible to plan to become a hero, and men did so. Winston Churchill had sought "the bubble reputation / Even in the cannon's mouth." No one who took part in it finished the First World War with anything remotely resembling so innocent a view of heroism. The poets Robert Graves and Sigfried Sassoon, the novelists Erich Maria Remarque, Ernst Jünger, Pierre Drieu la Rochelle, Henri de Montherlant, Louis-Ferdinand Céline—all might have said what Jünger subsequently wrote: that this war had proved man "the most dangerous, the most bloodthirsty, and the most goal-conscious being" on earth, and that "the dynamic of the cosmos exists in tension, battle, and unrest."

The First World War put an end to the perception of individual heroism as a social ideal, an exemplary proposal of the way a man ought to conduct himself. Heroism, after all, is an artifice, or, to be exact, a complicated moral stance, in which some combination of moral courage, staunchness, idealism, fraternity, love of fellows, recklessness, nihilism, morbidity, a suicidal will, simple stupidity, or insensibility before danger triumphs over the powerful natural impulses of fear and the urge to survive. It can be argued that T. E. Lawrence was the last hero, and that European civilization afterwards had no place for heroism. It was considered delusion, hysteria—instance of political exploitation. (The exemplary difference between Ernst Jünger in 1914 and the same man in 1940 is described in chapter four.)

In 1914, a belief in heroism was not only possible but indispensable.* The idea of achieving heroism rationalized going to war, a de-

---

* Certainly to a European (or American) gentleman. (Service in the American Field Ambulance Service, or enlistment in the Lafayette Escadrille or French Foreign Legion, the Canadian air force or a Canadian regiment were the choices made by many privileged young Americans, often intellectuals or writers, before the United States declared war in 1917.) One can question how deeply such a sentiment went among ordinary people and the working classes, although even for the latter it may initially have seemed to offer glamorous relief from the drudgery of life; the figures cited later on volunteer service in Britain and the very low evasion of national service in France are significant in this respect.

cision that had its essential origins in other factors at work in both the cultural and the political situation of Europe before 1914, as well as in qualities of the human personality itself. H. Stuart Hughes writes of French and German intellectuals in 1914: "The more bellicose felt at last within their grasp the life of action for which they had longed. The more reflective welcomed it as a deliverance from unfruitful anticipation."

Afterwards, the embittered and disillusioned thought chiefly in terms of catastrophe—of the violent breakdown of the civilization they had known, but also of a violent historical renewal. Some believed that the essentials of the broken civilization must swiftly be replaced, even by revolutionary means, and continued to believe in action and progress. A conception of revolutionary heroism, of the homme engagé, was proposed, which had great influence in the 1930s, even though it was sometimes narcissistic and politically exploitative. However, most of the morally articulate recoiled in loathing from the society that had conceived, produced, and prosecuted such a senseless war.

Roland N. Stromberg's intellectual history of the European pre-1914 and wartime experience suggests that the belief in an enemy threat validated a popular desire for restored community and for reunion with "the organic roots of human existence." War inspired "sacred unity" of the nation and provoked "spiritual awakening," an escape from "narrowness and pettiness."

A drawing together in time of risk is a phenomenon of nearly all wars, at least initially. In 1914 this amounted to a rejection of the most important intellectual currents of the preceding decades, when the new modern movement had attacked tradition, conventional community, and patriotism.

The military historian Sir Michael Howard cites Hew Strachan's argument in the latter's book *The First World War* that the war for the Germans really was one of ideas. "Ultimately the Germans were not fighting to retain Alsace-Lorraine, or to extend their rule into Eastern Europe, or even to create a Weltreich (world-state). They were fighting for a way of life, a Kultur, that they believed to be threatened by the demoralizing creeds of the West, whether the superficial rationalism of the French or the crass materialism of the Anglo-Saxon, which if they triumphed would destroy the virtue, the Tugend, of which the German nation was the divinely inspired bearer; a virtue expressed as much in the heroic values of war as in the disciplined bonding of peace. It was not in itself an ignoble cause," Howard concludes.

Enthusiasm for the war in 1914 was overwhelming on both sides, in total contrast with the demoralization and disillusionment that followed 1918 and prepared the crises of 1933 and 1939. An observer in Berlin in August-September 1914 said that if Social Democratic deputies—previously enemies of nationalism, committed to international working-class solidarity—had not voted war credits they "would have been trampled to death in front of the Brandenburg Gate." The nineteen-year-old Ernst Jünger went to Hanover to enlist, where he saw women passing through the ranks of a marching regiment, garlanding the troops. "Since then, I've seen many inspired crowds, but no inspiration was deeper and mightier than on that day. It was an impression of blood, roses, and splendid tears that went to the very core of oneself." Charles Péguy, the Catholic socialist, Dreyfusard, militant republican, and poet and journalist, wrote in 1913, "Blessed are those who have died in great battles / Lying on the ground in the sight of God," and nine months later he was dead on the Marne. Rupert Brooke notoriously wrote in the summer of 1914, "Now God be thanked Who has matched us with His hour / Honour has come back. . . ." This was chivalry become hysteria. The poets later changed their tune.

Max Weber, Thomas Mann, Freud, Durkheim, Plekhanov, the scientists Röntgen and Max Planck in Germany and Haldane and Cavendish in Britain, Rilke, Claudel, Bergson, Proust, Thomas Hardy, Arnold Bennett, Galsworthy, even Henry James (who petitioned for British nationality to demonstrate his solidarity with Britain), as well as Mohandas Gandhi (who recruited in India for the British forces), the English suffragists, and the English Quakers—all were enthusiastic for war. Stuart Hughes writes that "it is curious to find that even at these rarified levels of thought, the attitudes of the intellectuals so closely parallel those of the population at large."

There was actual hysteria. The chief of municipal police in Stuttgart, second city of imperial Germany, circulated the following alert to his forces:

> The population has gone mad. The streets are filled with hysterics of both sexes whose behavior dishonors them. Each sees in his neighbor a Russian or French spy, and thinks he should attack him or her. . . . The clouds are seen as enemy airplanes, the stars are dirigibles. People think that in the center of Stuttgart bridges and telephone lines are about to be blown up. . . . One might as well be in a lunatic asylum. . . . Officers! Stay calm! Keep your sang-froid!

The French novelist and political intellectual Romain Rolland (Nobel Prize for Literature in 1916) was in Switzerland when the war broke out. He wrote an anguished article for the *Journal de Gèneve* called "Above the Mêlée" in which he deplored (with little exaggeration) that "among the elites of each country there is not one who does not proclaim and is not convinced that the cause of his people is the cause of God, the cause of liberty, and even of human progress." (He also said of British and French use of colonial troops from Asia and Africa, "the sight of a great European people facing these savage hordes is impossible for me to tolerate without revolt." The "savage hordes" included, of course, individuals who were to become leaders of the Asian and African nationalist movements of the 1930s and 1940s, having learned all about European savagery.)

The enthusiasm for the war lasted, even though from 1915 on it should have been clear that continuing the war was for any of the participants their worse option. Until the mutinies of 1917, the French army's desertion rate remained at only one percent. Britain did not have to install conscription until the third year of the war. Before then, there were a million volunteers—as Stromberg observes, "the greatest expression of enthusiasm for war in all history."

Pre-1914 social thought had described a loss of purpose and solidarity in society, of gemeinschaft. The prewar period was argued to have been one of deracination and alienation. Marx had written of society dissolved into "atomized and mutually hostile individuals." The mass enthusiasm for war provided an unexpected and spontaneous correction to all that. The war seemed "a kind of triumph of spirit over matter." It was a popular triumph of romanticism about violence. The war, Stromberg says, "for most intellectuals, for the university youth who rushed to join it, was a revolutionary act."

Art had opened the way. There had been a revolution in perception and representation, and since the romantic movement's emergence in Germany, a disruptive change in the social role and condition of the European artist had taken place. Previously art existed on a continuum that included crafts, decoration, building, and artisanship, all part of the world of work and well-made things. Romanticism made the artist a prophet, which indeed he proved to be.

Futurism was a movement that remains today in some disrepute because of its involvement with Fascism, but should be of the greatest interest for just that reason—as well as for its prodigious originality. Incorporating an absurd romanticism about violence, it contributed crucially to the kind of politics that emerged in Italy in 1919 and after.

A convention of modernism in the twentieth century was the celebration of sensualism and undisciplined energy, even when they led, as Susan Sontag approvingly wrote of what she identifies as the century's major works, to "anguish, cruelty, derangement." The Dionysian search for action, destruction, speed, war, and even derangement is by no means recent; it was a specialty of the Futurists. Unlike the postmodernists of the present day, and the "decadents" who had preceded them (and whom they repudiated), the Futurists were political and moral optimists. They believed that the world could be remade, having no inkling of how in fact it would be remade after 1914 by those who believed, with them, that violence is liberating.

A fundamental change in artistic perception and purpose took place in western Europe in the later nineteenth century, when objective representation was abandoned (to photography), replaced by the attempt to paint the inner reality of objects, originally by way of the impressions imposed upon the observer's mind by the object, subsequently by reseeing the object itself. (Later came painting as an act with its own justification, unrelated to external object, the "action painting" of the New York School.) All this was subversive of the conventional notion of world and society as themselves unassailably objective, rationally definable, "out there." The interior of the mind, the interior angles and atoms of light in what was perceived, its "spiritual" reality, took the place of the physical reality of what before had been painted.

This change took a particular and politicized form in Italy, where the Futurist artists claimed revolutionary politico-social ambitions, expressed with considered bombast as the "reconstruction of the universe."

The Israeli scholar Zeev Sternhell, in writing about the origins of Fascist ideology, "reminds us, once again, of the vital intellectual life of Italy at the turn of the century" (I am quoting a writer in *The Review of Politics*, A. James Gregor).

For more than half a century, American academics, to a surprising extent, have succeeded in repressing the recognition that Italy at the turn of the century was the home of some of the most exciting intellectual currents of the twentieth century. Revolutionary syndicalism and futurism burst on the horizon in Italy during the first decade of the twentieth century, and both shaped the thought of Mussolini, the ideology of the Fascist movement, and the history of Europe in the interwar years.

Mussolini's Fascism, "not to be identified with the pathologies of Hitler's national socialism . . . was 'a very specific . . . synthesis of organic nationalism with the antimaterialist revision of Marxism' . . . of contemporary relevance, if not in central and western Europe then certainly elsewhere." An anonymous reviewer in the *Times Literary Supplement* (of H. R. Kedward's 1969 *Fascism in Western Europe, 1900–1945*) cited Kedward as identifying Fascism as "a reaction of irrationalism against the belief in the virtue and value of reason which was established in the eighteenth century, and perhaps affected the nineteenth century even more profoundly. Fascism was originally, that is to say in Italy, associated with the Futurists and the great break with traditionalism in the arts which took place immediately before the outbreak of war in 1914."

Futurism was the first great art movement (after religious art) to self-consciously direct itself to a mass audience, and its founder, the writer, painter, and polemicist Filippo Tommaso Marinetti, was a genius of publicity, exploiting outrageousness and absurdity to his purpose.

This purpose—apart from the celebration of his own ideas—was first of all the rescue of Italy from its "smelly gangrene of professors, archaeologists, ciceroni, and antiquarians. . . . The numberless museums that cover her like so many graveyards." It was, however, to have an importance to modern European art, as well as to Europe's political development, which is only now being adequately recognized.*

---

* A turning point having undoubtedly been the brilliant exhibition on Futurism that was organized in Venice in 1986 by Pontus Hulten.

It would be impossible to argue that the Fascism which emerged in Italy after 1918 was consciously created with a vision of where it was going. Nor did anyone anticipate the effect that Fascism was to have in Germany and Eastern Europe, and to a lesser extent in Britain and France, as a method for structuring the confusing, anguished, and inchoately revolutionary reaction to the collapse of prewar society, the squandered lives and sacrifices of the war, and the emptiness of the postwar period. Nonetheless, Mussolini and those associated with him were acting within a particular cultural situation in which dominant figures included the poet Gabriele D'Annunzio and Marinetti and his fellow Futurists.

Marinetti was a wealthy member of a North Italian family with business connections to Egypt, where he was born in 1876, in Alexandria. He attended the Jesuit college there and at seventeen went to Paris for university studies. Italy, newly united, nonetheless remained without a single center of intellectual and artistic life, and in both respects remained strongly influenced by France, where many of its writers spent much of their careers. To go to Paris was normal enough for an ambitious and brilliant young Italian. There, Marinetti made an undistinguished beginning as poet and playwright but eventually discovered his real talent, which was as a combative politico-aesthetic theorist and polemicist of revolutions, transformations, destructions of the past, and assaults upon the future. André Gide wrote of him,

He taps his foot; he makes the dust fly; he swears, curses and demolishes, he organizes contradictions, oppositions, cabals, triumphantly emerging from them. As well, he's the most charming man in the world, if I except D'Annunzio; full of verve in the Italian manner that often takes verbosity for eloquence, show for riches, agitation for movement, febrility for inspiration. He came to see me some ten years ago and deployed such unbelievable courtesies that they drove me to leave immediately afterwards for the country. If I had seen him again it would have been too much for me, and I would have ended up taking him for a genius.

His Futurism, Marinetti held, was the art that would transform art by depicting speed and motion, capturing the uniqueness of the machine age, and remaking Italy—if not the universe.

As the Oxford historian James Joll has written, the main themes of Futurism were already in the air—"violence, destruction, hatred of the past and its values, and, at the same time, intense excitement about the prospects of the new century that was just beginning, an awareness of the beauty of machines which could replace the more traditional objects of aesthetic satisfaction, and a realization of the heightening of experience which new sensations of speed and mechanical power could give." He goes on:

> The admiration for destruction was common enough at a moment when Nietzsche's influence in France and Italy was at its height, and when Georges Sorel was elevating violence into a political doctrine. Indeed, a group of minor writers and artists, who had founded in Paris a group called Compagnons de l'action d'Art, based on a mixture of anarchist and Nietzschean ideas, had already gone so far as to publish a Manifesto in 1907—two years before the Futurists—in which they proclaimed the necessity of resorting to violence to preserve the dignity of art, declared the inequality of man, and exclaimed "Long live violence against all that makes life ugly!" And, as many of Marinetti's contemporaries were pointing out, Walt Whitman, Zola, Verhaeren and others had already been concerned to glorify "les villes tenaculaires." ... As early as 1904, ... [the eminent critic Giovanni Papini] had written: "When lives have to be sacrificed we are not saddened, if before our minds shines the magnificent harvest of a superior life that will arise from their deaths. And while the lowly democrats cry out against war as a barbaric residue of ferocious ages, we believe it is the greatest awakener of the weak, a quick and heroic instrument of power and wealth."

Marinetti was to make these ingredients into a peculiarly explosive mixture by adding to them Italian nationalism, in parallel with Mussolini's admixture of socialism with nationalism.

Futurism's debt to the Romantic movement of the nineteenth century is unmistakable, acting upon Romanticism's valuation of fear and violence (as Edmund Burke put it) as of "sublime effect." The inventor of Futurism argued that an aesthetic "revolution" is capable of creating a political revolution, an idea which had consequences not only for Fascism but eventually found other expressions in dissident Marxism and in the western European and American student rebellions of the late 1960s.

Marinetti's Futurism, closely implicated in the origins of Italian Fascism, found that Fascism in power provided the Futurist theorists and artists with ample action and destruction. Marinetti was to describe Mussolini as a "lyric child with a marvelous intuition . . . a Futurist temperament." He became himself a Fascist candidate for parliament in 1919 (as did the conductor Arturo Toscanini—later an enemy of Fascism and exile in America). Mussolini called Marinetti "the innovator poet who gave me the feeling for the ocean and the machine." The two had in common notions about heroism and the man of action, exemplified by the storm troops, the Arditi (the bold ones), in which many of the young artists associated with Futurism enlisted when Italy entered the war.

Art and war, a Futurist manifesto said in 1913, "are the great manifestations of sensuality." It said: "We will glorify war—the world's only hygiene—militarism, patriotism, the destructive genius of freedom-bringers, beautiful ideas worth dying for, and scorn for women."

Marinetti wanted "great crowds excited by work, by pleasure, and by riot; we will sing of the multicolored, polyphonic tides of revolution in the modern capitals . . . of the vibrant nightly fervor of arsenals and shipyards . . . greedy railroad stations that devour smoke-plumed serpents . . . factories . . . deep-chested locomotives . . . the sleek flight of planes . . ." This is from Marinetti's original Futurist Manifesto, improbably published on the front page of the most important conservative daily newspaper in France, *Le Figaro*, in 1909.

Futurism was the painting of movement rather than rest. It painted "sounds, noises, and smells." It anticipated action painting in the 1940s, kinetic art, programmed art, video art, neoconstructivism, tactile art, and most of the rest of what followed during the later twentieth century. There was Futurist music of noises ("ancient life was all silence. Today, noise triumphs"). Futurist radio drama made use of "found sound" and positive silence. A noise machine was invented, and a chromatic piano which played light. There was Futurist drama, architecture, sculpture, and Futurist clothes ("asymmetrical, daring clothes, with brilliant colors and dynamic lines . . . made to last for a short time only in order to encourage industrial activity." The modern fashion industry unknowingly is Futurist.)

The Futurists deliberately manipulated publicity, not merely to épater les bourgeois but for aesthetic purposes, and even playfulness. The aesthetic of New York in the 1950s and 1960s—action painting, op art, machine and light sculpture, John Cage's music, and Andy Warhol's exploitation of publicity (not to mention the skyscraper skyline that went up in the 1920s and 1930s)—bears striking resemblances to what already existed or was anticipated in Italy before the First World War and during the Fascist years that followed. The most famous of Marinetti's statements—his demand for a "non human" model of man, produced through war—was also fulfilled; he lived to 1944, long enough to see it realized.

The manifestos that followed Marinetti's original manifesto included those of the Futurist painters (1910), musicians (1910), a "Technical Manifesto of Futurist Sculpture" (1912), "The Art of Noises" (1913), "The Painting of Sounds, Noises, and Smells" (1913), "The Futurist Manifesto of Men's Clothing" (1913),

"Chromophony—the Colors of Sounds" (1913), Marinetti's own "The Destruction of Syntax—Imagination Without Strings—Words in Freedom" (1913), "The Futurist Manifesto of Lust" (1913), the manifestos of architecture (1914) and the stage (1915), "Warpainting" (1915), "The Futurist Cinema" (1916), and "The Futurist Reconstruction of the Universe" (including discussion of the Futurist Toy and "Metallic Animal") in 1915—followed, in 1918, by "The Futurist Universe."*

The politico-social content of these manifestos included demands for heavy taxes on inherited wealth (even though Marinetti supported the movement with inherited wealth), the socialization of land, mineral resources, and church property; the eight-hour day, free legal aid, consumer protection, equal pay for women, easy divorce, and the gradual dissolution of matrimony as preparation for free love and state responsibility for children (even though the Futurist Manifesto of 1909 had notoriously included "contempt for women" as part of its "insolent challenge to the stars").

The Futurists envisaged a parliament consisting of "industrialists, agriculturalists, engineers and tradesmen." If parliament proved inadequate—they assumed this often would be the case—they wanted expert, technocratic, rule, "by twenty experts not over thirty years old." This elitism was their real inclination, and a principal reason why most of the Futurists became Fascists in the 1920s and 1930s.

The political commitment of Futurism nonetheless antedated Fascism, evident in its early manifestos. The fortnightly cultural newspaper *Lacerba* was published first on January 1, 1913, claiming to be "the spokesman of all the principles of irrationalism." It won a sizable working-class readership in Milan and Turin, becoming a

---

* W. S. Di Piero has written that the "most abrasive and rudely endearing Futurist manifesto" in the Futurists' campaign "to redeem themselves from the wasteful obedience to, and worship of, past forms," was the one called "Let's Kill Moonlight."

political force of some consequence. Marinetti's genius as propagandist and self-publicist made Futurism known throughout Italy, even to ordinary people, whether or not they had a very clear idea of what it meant.

The Futurists themselves saw their movement as a source of moral energy "capable of playing a role in the management of civil affairs, to such an extent that no productive element of the environment should remain untouched by it." (When France's Socialist culture minister of the 1980s, Jack Lang, called an assembly of the world's artists and intellectuals in Paris in 1983 to find solutions to the international economic and social problems of the day, it was an unavowed Futurist gesture.) The Futurists said that art is a branch of knowledge, and sensation is related to ideas, being merely different modes of perception.

The Futurist painters said their purpose was "to put the spectator in the center of the picture." To do so, the Italian critic Umbro Apollonio has written, was to make the observer

> the pivot of all contemporary artistic activity, no matter in what form it is carried out. Bodies and objects are no longer opaque, no longer immobile. Light permeates objects, emanates from them or constructs them. Creative development takes place on the level of their basic structures. A whole new world of art has grown up. And those who have since tried to reject the implications of Futurism, referring the origins of modern art to some point or other in the past, have wasted their time. As has happened often in history, a new path had been taken. . . .

There were Futurist measurements, Futurist toys (teaching the child "spontaneous languages . . . maximum elasticity . . . imaginative impulses . . . infinite stretching and animation of the sensibility . . . physical courage . . . fighting and war. . . . The Futurist toy will be of great use to adults too, since it will keep them young, agile, jubilant, spontaneous, ready for anything, inexhaustible, instinctive and intuitive"). There was a Futurist destruction of syntax and a Futurist reconstruction of the universe, "by making it more joyful, in other words by an integral re-creation. We will give skeleton and flesh to the invisible, the impalpable, the unponderable and the imperceptible. We will find abstract equivalents for all of the forms and elements of the universe, and then we will combine them according to the caprice of our inspiration, to shape plastic complexes which we will set in motion."

Talk of war as a purge of civilization and source of renewal, executioner of a boring, trivial, materialistic society, was easy for those who knew war not. But the Futurists proved as good as their word. They had said that they wanted war, and when it came they rushed off to fight. According to Marinetti, thirteen members of the Futurist movement were killed and forty-one injured in the course of the war. Of the major group, in Milan, eight volunteered in 1915 for a cyclist battalion—the speediest force they could find. They subsequently were transferred to an Alpine regiment; three were killed and four wounded.

The Futurists were not disillusioned by the war. They had said they wanted action, speed, and violence, liberating them from the past, re-creating sensibilities, clearing ground for the revolutionary future. They found war an arena for high drama, gesture, self-realization, and self-re-creation—"a wonderful, marvelous, terrible thing. And in the mountains it seems like a battle with the infinite. Grandiose, immense, life and death. I am happy." That was the painter Umberto Boccioni, who volunteered at thirty-two and did not survive. The last thing he wrote was "I shall leave this existence with a contempt for all that is not art. There is nothing more terrible than art. . . . Only art exists."

It was indeed a way of "overcoming . . . trite and imbecile everyday life" (as the painter Geraldo Dottori said), but the outcome was unsatisfactory when trite and imbecile life resumed. Italy was more than ever a land of cemeteries. Before the war it had been possible to talk, write manifestos, paint, and to describe the imagined society that art would create. War had been held to be the indispensable prelude to human reconstruction, but the reconstruction did not follow. Nonetheless the words had been taken seriously. Flamboyance before the war had been paid for by flamboyant action in the war, at the risk, or cost, of the artist's life. The war had taken Futurism out of the mind and into the lives of individuals, a serious affair. It opened eyes to the potentialities of further action and violence. Benito Mussolini was one of those who understood.

⟊

Mussolini began as a socialist intellectual. He translated Sorel and Kropotkin into Italian. Like Marx and Trotsky, he was originally a journalist. The political movement he inspired was, like theirs, romantic and visionary in character. The vainglorious image he subsequently acquired was in part a propaganda invention. Later generations have mostly seen Mussolini as Charles Chaplin and Jack Oakie reinvented him in Chaplin's film *The Great Dictator*, caricaturing Mussolini's own presentation of himself as a heroic figure in flamboyant uniforms, with outthrust chin and dramatic gestures. Actually he was so serious that his merger of socialism with nationalism, emulated in much of Europe and eventually elsewhere, provoked uprisings and wars, eventually sweeping Mussolini himself to destruction.

When the Italian socialist movement split in 1912 between revolutionaries and reformists, he became editor of the revolutionaries' newspaper, *Avanti*, which he made the most successful popular paper in Italy. He resigned from the Socialist Party when he was unable to convince it to support Italian intervention in the world war against Austria and Germany. When intervention indeed occurred, he enlisted, served in the elite Bersaglieri, was wounded, and was invalided out in 1917.

39

He reentered politics with a new newspaper and a neosocialist program, as demobilized soldiers returned to a worsened economic situation, and people disappointed by the war began demanding the territorial rewards Italy had been promised in the 1915 secret treaty with the Allies. It was then that he added nationalism to his socialism, a dynamic innovation. Nationalist socialism was to dominate European politics for the next forty years. As the historian John Lukacs has remarked, its potential has yet to be exhausted.*

The weakness of democratic socialism was that it was rational. It purported to provide a scientific analysis of history, from which a rational program of action was derived. Mussolini wrote that "socialism, if it is not to die, must have the courage to be barbarous." He tapped into the powerful subterranean human impulse to violent collective action for a utopian goal. Fascism seized the emotions. That is why Russia's Bolshevism, after it took power, imitated Fascism. Stalin, a party functionary, donned military uniform, which Lenin had never worn. (Fidel Castro was never to take his uniform off.) It explains the military (and militarized civilian) pageantry of Soviet bloc May Day parades, and the military vocabulary of Communism, which conducted "struggle" and "combat" on "fronts" to achieve "breakthroughs" in production and cultural "victories." The "scientific" Marxism that Lenin took from Switzerland to Saint Petersburg—until then an intellectuals' affair—adopted a militarized apparatus to evoke the irrational and emotional forces that nourished Fascism, and later Nazism. Mussolini appropriately said that "revolutions must be considered the revenge of madness on good sense."

* *Fascii*, bundles of rods—a Roman symbol of authority and discipline—had been used as a symbol by the interventionist movement of 1915, the "Fascio d'Azione Rivoluzionario" (the Band of Revolutionary Action).

In 1918 and 1919, not even Mussolini had seriously thought out what his movement could become. It could easily have evolved into something historians today would identify as left-wing. Its aim was non-Marxist revolution, but beyond that its ideas were confused and even contradictory. Antonio Gramsci, co-founder and theorist of the Italian Communist Party, demanded "Nothing less than the destruction of the present form of civilization. . . . [This] means the destruction of spiritual hierarchies, prejudices, idols, traditions that have become rigid. It means to be unafraid of what is new and daring. . . ." This could as well have been said by Mussolini. It was said, in substance, by Marinetti (one of Mussolini's original Fascist parliamentary candidates), whom Gramsci, at the time (like Mussolini), considered an ally.*

Mussolini admired Marinetti but grew wary of the extravagance and fantasy the latter brought to Fascism. Marinetti attacked monarchy, the Pope, and bureaucracy, announcing that in "Futurist democracy" ordinary morality would make way for "the morality of danger: elastic liberty with neither prisons nor carabinière." By 1920, Mussolini, the practical politician, was attempting to accommodate Fascism to church and monarchy, and this effort eventually led him to disavow the Futurists, as well as the anarchists and syndicalists who had been Fascism's fellow travelers in its formative stage.

Before Marinetti allied himself with the Fascists, he had created a Futurist political party of his own, whose program in many respects

---

* Luigi Barzini, who knew him, has described Mussolini as a great instinctive popular journalist who exploited every event to his own political ends, grasping what people wanted to hear. He invented his personage as "Il Duce," the brilliantly uniformed and posturing dictator remembered today—pivoting, as Barzini says, "on one spurred boot heel as if he were always trailing a long purple cloak behind him." An intelligent friend of Mussolini's said in the 1930s, "I cannot help thinking, when I see him, how much his face must ache at night when he retires."

anticipated many of the "events" of Paris 1968, although in place of the romantic Left's faith in popular power it defended the notion of government by an elite.

Marinetti's party recruited many of its early activists from the Arditi, storm troops kept apart from ordinary army units, whose mission (unlike that of the commandos or special forces of a later period) was the shock frontal assault. As the elite of the Italian army the Arditi attracted an exceptional body of men, including intellectuals and artists, as well as common-law prisoners given the choice of service in this corps as alternative to the penitentiary. The Futurists in the force initially called themselves the Fasci Futuristi.

The nature of the Arditi and their mission imposed upon its members a true resignation or fatalism in the face of the probability that they would die, and this prompted an intensity about the life that precariously remained to them and an indifference to the mundane preoccupations of ordinary existence. They lived in the rarefied atmosphere of imminent death, like the eighteen- and nineteen-year-old fighter pilots of the time, bearing (as Alan Clark wrote) "that same distant look which haunts the gaze of all those aces who allowed themselves to be photographed late in their career." (In Vietnam this was known as the thousand-yard stare.)

A highly romantic description of the Arditi was provided in the journal *Roma futurista* in January 1919: "Aristocracy of character, muscles, faith, courage, blood, brains. Patricians dismounted from their chargers, aviators from their planes, intellectuals removed from their ideologies, sophisticates from their salons, mystics disgusted with churches, students avid of life, and youth—youth who would conquer all or lose all, who want to give wholeheartedly, with sanity, the energy of their nineteen years generously and lovingly to Italy, to all the beautiful things of Italy, the lovely land, the beautiful women, the beautiful cities, the future they see as marvelous." Emilio Gentile comments that here D'Annunzian theses met those of Futurism, and the myth of dynamic youth, insolent and arrogant, then became "practically the prerequisite, the condition for being Fascist."

✂

The Arditi, at war's end, were peculiarly undemobilizable. What could they do in peacetime that compared with what they had experienced during the war? Peace was trivial, dominated by cowards who had evaded the war, avarice, and pettiness. The intellectual volunteers shrank like seminarians from the coarseness and selfishness of ordinary life. Like seminarians and monks they had withdrawn from the world for lives of renunciation and spiritual intensity. One of them wrote in 1918: "with the end of the war we are precisely those who have no direction any more, those surrounded by the abyss, those without bread. Every one of us . . . is obliged to exclude the possibility of picking up our lives at the point at which they had been interrupted in 1915." (There is a clear parallel with the experience of many American soldiers in Vietnam, worsened in the latter's case by finding themselves scorned or repudiated by the civilian society that had sent them to war.)

The Arditi had acquired the idea that if they stayed together in peacetime they might attempt somehow to carry out a purification of Italian political society. One of them wrote that they might "take apart, clean, lubricate, and modernize all the parts of the complicated political-bureaucratic-judicial Italian machine, or finding it out of service, hurl it into the melting-pot of revolution." Politicians and the government feared precisely that, and wanted the Arditi disbanded. Then the idea occurred to the government that such a disciplined force could be a useful instrument at a moment of increasing political unrest, and also that keeping the Arditi together could stop them from passing over to the revolutionary Left. Their revolutionary ideas were not those of the socialists. In one notorious affair a band of Arditi systematically wrecked the Milan offices of the Socialist paper, *Avanti*, which Mussolini had edited. The

socialists had abandoned their prewar pacifism and internationalism, and after the war were promoting anti-capitalist and anti-
landowner uprisings.

❧

Renzo De Felice, the historian of Italian Fascism, says the Arditi's
essential accomplishment was the militarization of Italian politics.
They took what had been an affair of programs, rhetoric, manifestos, and electoral campaigns, and "put political conflict on a new
plane, organizing it according to military criteria." They mostly
ended in Mussolini's new party, and were responsible for much of
its violence.

The exploitation of this militarized form of political organization and action was Mussolini's second vital innovation, meant to
re-create, in the compromised and corrupting conditions of peace,
the solidarity and purity of purpose men had experienced in the
trenches. It proved to be one of the First World War's most significant political consequences. "The future will bring something
quite new to us, such as we have never seen before. Something
stronger, more beautiful, will be born from all this blood and sacrifice. All forms of art and politics will be overthrown; the new ones
will be healthier." That is the Italian poet and dramatist, Gabriele
D'Annunzio.

The Arditi's contribution to Fascism was an attempt to continue
and extend into civilian life—that place (as their English contemporaries said) of slackers and hard-faced men who had done well
from the war—the purposefulness and intensity of feeling that had
been discovered in the experience of the war.

It was an international phenomenon. Oswald Mosley, who also
fought in the war, wrote of Armistice night:

> I passed through the festive streets and entered one of London's
> largest and most fashionable hotels, interested by the sounds of rev-
> elry which echoed from it. Smooth, smug people, who had never

44

fought or suffered, seemed to the eyes of youth—at that moment age-old with sadness, weariness and bitterness—to be eating, drinking, laughing on the graves of our companions. I stood aside from the delirious throng, silent and alone, ravaged by memory. Driving purpose had begun; there must be no more war. I dedicated myself to politics, with an instinctive resolution which later came to expression in my speeches: "Through and beyond the failure of men and parties, we of the war generation are marching on and we shall march on until our end is achieved and our sacrifice atoned." What did it mean? What end? What atonement?—this sentiment of youth, which was then only instinct without shape? . . . We later gave form to instinct. . . .

That was written fifty years later, in justification of a political career that led Mosley from the Conservative to Labour benches in the House of Commons, where both parties considered him a future prime minister, to the impatient formation of his own "New Party," which eventually became the British Fascist Party. Yet there is no reason to think the sentiments expressed are false. Ernst Jünger's commitment to the so-called national movement in Germany similarly envisaged an alliance of former soldiers with factory workers.

A writer and contemporary of Mussolini's, Mario Carli, called his alliance of Futurist artists, storm-troop intellectuals, disabused official socialists and new reform socialists, republican antimonarchists, and trade unionists "our bolshevism," and had believed that it would make a revolution. The revolution followed, when Mussolini took power in 1923, but it assuredly was not the one Carli wanted, nor was it like the one the Bolsheviks in Russia actually carried out. But like Bolshevism, Fascism proved a utopian enterprise the world would have grievous cause to regret.

PART ONE

Chivalry

CHAPTER THREE

THE FALLEN HERO

The influence of T. E. Lawrence on the Western mind in the twentieth century is very large and very strange, since superficially his appeal would seem to be to adolescent romanticism in one or another version, mainly Anglo-American, often sexually immature or ambiguous. Yet his literary and intellectual effect has been international, deeply influencing hundreds if not thousands of individual lives.

I met Lawrence in the summertime heat of the stacks of the old Columbus, Georgia, public library, when I was fourteen or fifteen and took down from the shelf *Seven Pillars of Wisdom*. I had vaguely heard of "Lawrence of Arabia"; beyond that, the names, events, references were wholly strange. The personality of the man writing—however overwrought his prose, epic in intent, intensely romantic—gripped me from the start, and did not let go for a very long time.

His influence could well have left me dead, given the choices it dictated to me in military life during the Korean War. It sent me to the combat theater as a "rifleman volunteer" (to share the experience of my generation, I said; a well-disposed Providence and an inefficient adjutant general's office spared me the logical consequence), and afterwards into one of the early U.S. Army Special Forces formations. It could have put me into even more trouble than I actually had with Egyptian, Lebanese, and Indian police during another career, as a political warfare operator. It sent me off to become an "engaged" intellectual in the painful foreign policy controversies of the 1950s (and since), at a time when nearly everyone else I knew wanted to be a university teacher, if only, like Harvard professors, to get a job in Washington. My efforts to do otherwise finally ended in intellectual journalism, a moribund trade, at least in the United States.

However, my encounter with Lawrence was a pathetically small-bore version of what others experienced (although here I am, still writing about it). André Malraux was obsessed with Lawrence, trying to appropriate him, writing in his autobiographical books about heroes who went off to liberate the East, and might or might not be real, or might be Lawrence, or might even be Malraux himself. He invented for himself an identity as a revolutionary leader in Asia that had not the slightest truth to it. In the Second World War Resistance, which he only belatedly joined (a *résistant de la dernière heure*, as the French classified such people), he gave himself the wartime pseudonym "Berger," the name of a guerrilla hero in his own books, who was modeled on Lawrence. He falsely claimed to have known Lawrence and wanted to be taken as his successor. These pretensions eventually compelled him, in self-respect, or acceptance of a self-invoked destiny, to assume the qualities and conduct of his invented personage and become a hero in Spain, during the Civil War, and then in the Second World War.

The British traveler, war correspondent, and sometime intelligence agent Gavin Young wrote that "the Lawrence of Arabia bug got its teeth into me, and refused to let go" in Basra, in Iraq, at the beginning of the 1950s, when Young was "a clerk at £5 a week" at an international trading firm, which had taken him on after he had finished national service and was an aimless young man in all respects other than his desire to travel.

The Laurencian passion led him to Wilfred Thesiger, the last of the great Arabian explorers, and Thesiger led Young to the Marsh

Arabs of Iraq (a society nearly destroyed as a consequence of the Iran-Iraq and Gulf wars, and Saddam Hussein's repression). Young lived among them for two years, and then went on to the south-western Arabian desert, life with the Bedouin, to the Algerian war, to newspaper correspondence for London's *The Observer*, the Congo, the Nagas in India, Vietnam, the pursuit of the shade of Joseph Conrad in the Pacific—to an entire life, a vocation, so to speak.

The most recent English-language biographer of Lawrence, Michael Asher, who became an explorer and geographer, intro-duces his book by saying that *Seven Pillars of Wisdom* "is permeated by a sense of spiritual awe which is, for me, the essence of human experience in the desert. T. E. Lawrence has affected my life with particular power. Without Lawrence I would probably not have be-come an Arabic speaker and a camel rider, would not have . . . made the first ever west-east crossing of the Sahara. . . . Without Lawrence I would probably not have served with the Special Air Service Regiment, simply because without Lawrence there would probably have never been an SAS."

Many other intelligent people have been caused by Lawrence's influence to do foolish things when wars were available, and some-times when they were not. The Libyan desert in the 1940s, behind the Italian and German lines or deep on their flank, was cluttered with British, Australians, and New Zealanders playing Lawrence. The war diary of the Long Range Desert Group, which conducted topographical, reconnaissance, and intelligence work deep in the southern desert, complained that it was expected to provide a trans-portation service for "a stream of commandos (European and Arab) . . . bogus Germans, lost travelers, escape-scheme promoters . . . , etc., etc."

All that nonetheless remains part of the adolescent adventurer side of things. The moral issues of violence, masochism, and fabu-lation which Lawrence posed have to be discussed, and also the question of art, which was central to Lawrence.

✐

I begin with him because he was formed by and remained faithful to a chivalric conception of society that prevailed among the elites of Edwardian Britain and other Western countries until the First World War, and that now is as remote from us as the medieval world which was its source.

He maintained these values during the world war because the circumstances of his Arabian campaign allowed it, while nihilism came to prevail on the western and eastern fronts, where the world war became a matter of mechanized and hypertrophic violence for goals that increasingly lost rational definition. One reaction to that, as I will argue later, was the vitalism and cult of heroism articulated by Ernst Jünger, foreshadowing Nazism. Lawrence's other contemporaries, the Futurists, had foreseen and invoked this violence with profound but sinister frivolity, and found themselves implicated in Fascism. Lawrence is distinguished by the fact that while others looked in politics or revolution for a justification or recompense for the war, he simply assumed responsibility for it, or for what he had done in it, and allowed that to shape the life he afterwards lived. It was a life of sacrifice, or even of a kind of secular sanctity, although he would never have conceived of it in such terms; he was a survivor of the prewar moral order and progenitor of the one that followed, in a situation of moral tension that is one reason for his interest today, although not the only one.

✐

The attraction of Thomas Edward Lawrence—"of Arabia"—(1888–1935) to isolated and puritanical adolescents such as myself, or to other unsettled and idealistic young men, is easy to understand, since Lawrence himself remained to the end of his life adolescent in a crucial respect, having failed to resolve adolescent problems of sexual identity and having declined to integrate himself into the adult world of family and career.

His retirement from enlisted service in the Royal Air Force in

1935 was to his cottage, "Clouds Hill," in Dorset, near his last RAF station. It was the refuge of an intellectual and puritan adolescent: a plain cottage with books and records, a bedroll for a visitor—all this finite and controllable—with, standing outside, a powerful and meticulously kept motorcycle, a means of physical and symbolic liberty.* It was on the motorcycle that he was killed.

The psychological interest and lasting attraction of Lawrence derive in part from the tension between the romantic form adopted by Lawrence the writer to describe his experience in Arabia, the romantic persona he assumed at that stage in his life, and the drama and harshness of the true events in which he was a leading actor— a tension reflecting an equivalent failure of reconciliation in Lawrence's own life, during both wartime and postwar years, until his death. Lawrence was an authentic hero, and had made himself one, consciously, even cunningly, by exploiting the fortunes of his own war according to the norms of Edwardian society, discovering that this was an artificial and "literary" conception of heroic conduct, but one that was lethal in consequences for him and for others as well.

The appeal of heroism is that it represents the same impulse to unreasonable perfection which leads men and women into monasteries and convents, or, on the other hand, to improbable physical feats in sports, or into lives in the classical ballet: that one can pare from

---

* He described Clouds Hill in a 1934 letter: "I have had great satisfaction and some exasperation in building everything that goes into the place. Fenders, chairs, tables, couches. It has two rooms and two of everything, accordingly; the whole place is designed for just the single inhabitant! It has neither rugs nor paint nor plaster nor wallpaper. Panelling; bookshelves; bare wood and undyed leather. A queer place, but great fun. No pictures and no ornaments." The author of a 1975 "portrait" of Lawrence, Flora Armitage, says: "With Clouds Hill he made his ultimate gesture to the Pre-Raphaelite Hall, and hall or cottage, surely no dwelling place ever reflected so strongly the personality of their owner. . . . a masculine stronghold: an emphatic denial of the existence of the female, a cancelling out, on the personal level at least, of the irrefutable fact of humanity's cleavage into two mutually-complementary, mutually-antagonistic elements: a well-calculated snub for Adam's rib, and for Adam himself, cold disapproval that he should ever have desired the cleavage for the sake of love and multiplicity."

oneself everything unnecessary, vulgar, self-indulgent, and become one of life's exceptions, so as to achieve a kind of immortality.

Heroism's link to violence is part of its appeal. To kill and not be killed is—emotionally, not logically—evidence of worth and intimation of immortality. If I am not killed but he is killed, I am affirmed by his negation. War is usually welcome enough, although this is usually not admitted, because it offers a holiday from ordinary life, and also because it provides that encounter with death which most men postpone until decrepitude and senility. Why not test life and death in one's youth and the fullness of one's powers? War offers heroism on the cheap, making potential heroes of us all—a reason to like war. The experience of Vietnam only temporarily obscured this sentiment among Americans, although such military adventures as the clownish Grenada and sordid Panama affairs did not restore it, nor the Afghanistan and Iraq interventions. However, it will eventually return, being a phenomenon of human nature.

Fascists understood the thirst for heroism better than anyone else. While conventional thinkers, liberal or conservative, look for national interest, an idealistic cause, and high political purpose in war, the Fascists understood that war is about death, and that when people's lives are sterile they consciously or unconsciously welcome war (which, among other things, provides gratification for both masochistic and sadistic impulses, a consideration of perhaps neglected importance). As sensible a man as the former British prime minister Harold Macmillan, who was gravely wounded and permanently disabled at the Battle of the Somme in 1916, said in North Africa, where he was Churchill's resident minister at Allied headquarters in 1942–43, "I enjoy wars. Any adventure's better than sitting in an office." Churchill's relish of war was notorious, a product of the same impulse many lesser men have felt: to find in war, regular or irregular, a liberation from the boredom of life.

T. E. Lawrence made of himself, as did Macmillan, an Edwardian hero, a type that was shortly to be eliminated from history. Edwardian society proposed a nominally exalted standard of rectitude, honor, and chastity, albeit with an extensive unacknowledged secondary society of license set apart from the first by hypocrisy, sometimes principled, sometimes not, with savage punishment when hypocrisy was renounced. Lawrence's parents were people who defied the code. The story is now well known. His father, Thomas Chapman, was of the Anglo-Irish baronetcy, and abandoned his wife and four daughters for a girl, herself illegitimate, who had come from Scotland to look after the Chapman children. Chapman's new family lived the rest of their lives under an assumed name in several places, finally settling in Oxford.

They were shadowed by the hostility of the Chapman relatives and dominated by the guilt felt by Chapman's new consort, Lawrence's mother, an Evangelical Protestant who, after Thomas Chapman's death (in April 1919), went to China as a missionary. Lawrence's elder brother also became a missionary. None of the family was capable of an acceptable hypocrisy. Lawrence himself, having found that his were false credentials, after the war signed his abridgment of *Seven Pillars of Wisdom*, *Revolt in the Desert*, in quotation marks—"T. E. Lawrence"—and subsequently changed his name to Hume, then Ross, and finally to Shaw, for anonymous enlistments in the military ranks, insisting that he be accepted as the nameless man he seemed to feel himself to be. He thought the credentials of his heroism equally fraudulent. He had gone abroad to act according to the norms of his society in a war put forward as glorious, had killed and betrayed in its name, and, in the event, had found that here, as in his family's life, what had been done was falsehood.

More than two hundred complete or partial accounts of Lawrence's life have been published in English, German, French, Italian, other European languages, Japanese, and Arabic, including Richard Aldington's 1955 biographical inquiry, the first of several works accusing Lawrence of being a fraud, and others concerning his masochism, possible sadism, and undoubted, if probably unrealized, homosexuality.*

There also are several volumes of letters, a general collection, the *Home Letters* to his mother and his brothers, and separate volumes of his correspondence with Robert Graves, Basil Liddell Hart, E. M. Forster, Bruce Rogers, E. T. Leeds, and others. Still other correspondence, including that with George Bernard and Charlotte Shaw and with the family of his last commanding officer, Sydney Smith, as well as with Winston Churchill, Augustus John, and others, appears in other volumes. The centenary year of his birth, 1988, brought yet another selection of correspondence with the family.

Friends and those who served with him in Arabia, Arabs as well as British and French, and old companions in the Tank Corps and in the RAF, have published their recollections. His own books have been translated into virtually every modern language. "Lawrence Studies" now exists as an academic enterprise in which scholarly careers are built.

He has been the subject of poems by W. H. Auden, Robert

---

* Of the many biographies, beginning with those of Robert Graves and Basil Liddell Hart, with whom Lawrence himself collaborated (and are for that reason less than completely reliable), the most recent and comprehensive in English are those of Michael Asher (in 1998), a former soldier (British army Parachute Regiment and SAS), a desert traveler and indefatigable investigator, who is also the biographer of another Lawrence-like English eccentric, the explorer and traveler Wilfred Thesiger; the authorized biography by Jeremy Wilson, written with the collaboration of Lawrence's youngest brother, Arnold, published in 1989; an iconoclastic work of great interest by the late Desmond Stewart in 1977; and the sympathetic Harvard psychiatrist John E. Mack's 1976 biography. For the postwar years of enlisted military service, H. Montgomery Hyde's 1977 *Solitary in the Ranks* is indispensable, making use of Lawrence's correspondence during his RAF years with Air Marshal Sir Hugh Trenchard, another mentor and friend. Stephen E. Tabachnick and Christopher Matheson published a volume in 1988 combining photographs from the latter's Lawrence archive with valuable essays on the principal "images" and controversies concerning Lawrence. The authorized biographer, Jeremy Wilson, provided a 248-page catalog for an exhibition of Lawrence portraits and memorabilia at London's National Portrait Gallery in 1988.

Graves, Archibald MacLeish, and others, and of several novels, including a thriller (about his supposed murder by the British Secret Service, to prevent him from becoming a leader of British Fascism and threat to the Crown). As played by Peter O'Toole, he was, of course, the subject of a flamboyant biographical film by David Lean, based on Anthony Nutting's 1961 biography. He is the hero of Terence Rattigan's play *Ross* and Auden's *The Ascent of F-6*, and a central figure ("Private Napoleon Alexander Trotsky Meek") in George Bernard Shaw's *Too True to Be Good*.* Tourist agencies in Jordan (when regional conflict permitted) have offered The Lawrence of Arabia Excursion.

Why? Lawrence's celebrity followed from his having played a brave and romantic role in the First World War, wearing romantic garb, on a front remote from the carnage of the western front. He contributed to his own celebrity through his predilection for self-dramatization and mystification, a combination of self-promotion and evasiveness only later seen by most as connected with the illegitimacy of his birth and the unresolved conflicts of his sexual ideals and experiences. The American journalist Lowell Thomas first made him famous by lecturing in London and in the United States about "the uncrowned king of Arabia" and his role in the Allies' capture of Jerusalem and Damascus from the Turks. Lawrence was taken up by influential people, entranced by his force of personality and his intelligence. Nonetheless, the military affair in which he had been engaged was, as he said himself, a sideshow of a sideshow. The campaign in the Middle East against Ottoman Turkey did little to damage the Central Powers, and of all the Allied Eastern offensives, at Gallipoli and in Mesopotamia as well as into Palestine and Syria from Egypt, the last offered the smallest possibility of

* The young Auden compared Lawrence to Lenin and said that he exemplified "most completely what is best and significant in our lives, our nearest approach to a synthesis of feeling and reason, act and thought."

making a serious difference to the outcome of the war, though it did prove the most successful in military terms. In that offensive the part played by the Arab Revolt, and by Lawrence himself as adviser to its military leader, the Hashemite Prince Faisal, was entirely subordinate to a conventional campaign carried on by regular forces under General Sir Edmund Allenby.

Lawrence, however, is remembered. He is remembered because he was authentically a hero in circumstances that were unreproducibly pre-modern and that revealed to the generations that followed how heroism in war ceased to be innocent in Western culture. His account of his adventure, modeled in its prose upon the mannered and pseudomedieval *Arabia Deserta* of Charles Doughty, and devised with the ambition of equaling Dostoyevsky and Melville, was subtitled "A triumph" but nonetheless began by speaking, in modern phrases of pain, of "the evil of my tale." That was in the very first sentence. "Pray God," it continued, a little way into the first chapter, "that men reading the story will not, for love of the glamour of strangeness, go out to prostitute themselves and their talents in serving another race. A man who gives himself to be a possession of aliens leads a Yahoo life, having bartered his soul to a brute-master. He is not of them."

The bones of his story, as they bear on the major issues of his adult life, are as follows.

Sarah Lawrence was eighteen in 1879, when she took employment with the family of Thomas Chapman, a wealthy landowner in County Westmeath, Ireland. She was the illegitimate daughter of an alcoholic mother, who died when Sarah was nine, and a shipwright father who abandoned her. She was brought up in the Highlands and on the Isle of Skye by a minister of the Episcopal Church of Scotland (the so-called Wee Frees) and his wife. Her new employer in Ireland was the grandson of a baronet, educated at Eton and Cirencester, the eighth generation of landlords originally given their Irish properties under the patronage of Sir Walter Raleigh, a relation.

Thomas Chapman had four young daughters in 1879 but an un-happy marriage. He fell in love with the beautiful, energetic, and capable Miss Lawrence. In 1885 she became pregnant and went to Dublin, where Chapman set up a home for her and where he visited her. Their first son, Robert, was born in December. Thomas Chap-man asked his wife for a divorce, which she refused. He left his wife and took Sarah and the child to Wales, where their second son, Thomas Edward ("Ned") was born on August 16, 1888. Two other sons followed. The family eventually moved to Oxford in 1896, where a fifth son was born.

The father's settlement with the family he had left behind in Ire-land left a sufficient income for his new family to live in comfort-able circumstances and seeming respectability as Mr. and Mrs. Thomas Lawrence and sons. Their secret enjoined discretion and an introspective family life. A neighbor said that "the family did not go about much . . . but they had some very true friends. They were always happy [with] a lot of fun and silly jokes, but of course Mrs. Lawrence managed them all." So she did, as every account agrees. She was a brilliant but inflexible manager of her home and servants, a plantswoman and gardener of encyclopedic knowledge, the moral authority in her family, deeply committed to the fundamentalist and puritanical views of the Wee Frees, teetotal, disapproving of dancing and theater (other than Shakespeare), hospitable, gener-ous, and emotional. She could also be overpowering and terrifying, according to those who knew her. David Garnett, the friend who later edited and published Lawrence's letters, and compiled from them and his other writings *The Essential T. E. Lawrence* (1951), called her "a terror," a person who devoured people "like a lion."

❦

Her own situation was undoubtedly responsible for her devotion to the doctrine that God hates the sin but loves the sinner. She never referred to Mr. Lawrence as "my husband" but always as "Tom" or "the boys' father." The two oldest boys became Sunday School teachers. She wanted them all to become missionaries. The family read from the Bible mornings before school, held domestic prayers at home on Sundays, and the parents were prominent at Oxford's St. Aldate's Church, whose rector was a leader of the nineteenth-century Evangelical Revival.

The father was described by friends as diffident and shy, although he seems to have possessed the ultimate decision in family crises, and sometimes surprised people by displaying an unexpected authority in dealing with strangers. He was interested in cycling, occasional sailing, carpentry, photography, shooting, and architecture, passing most of these enthusiasms to his sons. Years later, in 1927, Lawrence wrote to Charlotte Shaw (wife of George Bernard Shaw and Lawrence's closest woman friend in later life) that his father "was on the large scale, tolerant, experienced, grand, rash, humoursome, skilled to speak, and naturally lord-like. He had been 35 years in the larger life, and a spendthrift, a sportsman, and a hard rider and drinker. My mother, brought up as a child of sin in the Isle of Skye by a bible-thinking Presbyterian, then a nursemaid, then 'guilty' (in her judgement) of taking my father from his wife. . . . To justify herself, she remodeled my father, making him a teetotaler, a domestic man, a careful spender of pence. . . . [T]he inner conflict, which makes me a standing civil war, is the inevitable issue of the discordant natures of herself and my father, and the inflammation of strength and weakness which followed the uprooting of their lives and principles. They should not have borne children." A neighbor described the father as "a tall slender man, very distinguished looking, looking rather like Bernard Shaw, I should say." One of the young Lawrence's teachers wrote that he was "one of the most charming men I have known—very shy, very kind." Lawrence was later to say that he saw his father as a friend rather than as a figure of authority; in later life he cultivated the friendship of older and powerful men who became his patrons, and who were, as all of his biographers suggest, father replacements.

Corporal punishment was the manner of the times and place in disciplining the boys, and this was left to Sarah, who followed the strict precedents of her puritan foster parents. The boys were whipped on their bare buttocks "for disobedience, willfulness or dishonesty." Ned seems to have been the principal victim; the youngest brother, Arnold, recalled having been beaten only once. He said, though, that his mother's beatings of Ned "seemed to be given for the purpose of breaking [his] will." Lawrence's psychiatrist biographer, John Mack, quotes Mrs. Lawrence in later years as remarking "that the reason Lord Astor's horses never won was because he wouldn't whip them." She was vigilant in watching for the appearance of adolescent sexuality, and according to a friend "never wanted any of the sons to marry." None but the youngest, Arnold, did, and the mother's influence can be understood from the fact that when he made up his mind to do so he announced it in a letter mailed from Athens. On the day that he calculated she would receive the letter he awoke in a daze, forgetting where he was, staggered outside, and recovered himself only with difficulty. Asher writes, "he knew that Sarah was violently opposed to his marriage and he felt that her influence had 'absorbed' him even at that distance."

Ned, the second oldest, resolved early on to resist this suffocating influence, doing so through an emotional withdrawal that extended not only to his mother but, throughout his life, to others as well, allowing him to become genuinely close to very few people. "His schoolmasters noticed that he was silent, self-possessed and inscrutable, and gave a hint of latent power, just out of reach."* Asher attributes to his relations with his mother his lifelong fascination with the machinery of siege warfare. "She is always ham-

---

* The daughter of a neighbor, a great friend of the Lawrence boys, Janet Laurie, said that even at six he could be "frightfully bossy; he used to order us about, but in a very nice way." He exerted "quiet authority." Lawrence later was to propose to Janet Laurie, who was two years older than he, when he was still an undergraduate. She thought at the time that the proposal was serious but was so astonished at its coming without preliminaries of any kind that she laughed. She later told Mack that he said, "Oh, I see," or "All right," and never spoke about it again.

mering and sapping to come in . . . I always felt she was laying siege to me and would conquer if I left a chink unguarded," he long after wrote to Charlotte Shaw. The great intellectual interest of his adolescence and the subject of his university thesis (which influenced his later practice of guerrilla warfare) was the military architecture of the Crusaders.

The struggle with his mother was provisionally settled, or stalemated, in 1905 when he rejected a mathematics scholarship at Oxford, resolving to study history. Sarah sensed in this a move away from her influence, and Asher presumes that she "tried her old tactics—bluster, violence, manipulation." Lawrence responded by leaving home and secretly joining the army (he was seventeen).* He was shipped to a Royal Garrison Artillery station in Cornwall, where his military fantasies quickly encountered the brutal reality of enlisted life in the pre-1914 British regular army. He broke, and let his father know where he was, and Thomas bought him out. His brief experience with the army nonetheless made his point to his mother. The episode, Asher maintains, contributed to a sense of inadequacy with respect to other men which persisted in adulthood, and which Asher maintains lay behind much of Lawrence's lifelong dissimulation and mystification, contributing to fantasies that fed a nascent masochism.

Contemporaries at Oxford speak, however, of good-natured intelligence and humor, as well as of a talent to charm. An American Rhodes scholar from Kansas, also reading medieval history, recalled Lawrence as having put himself out to be kind to the foreigner. "No other person took the trouble he did to be kind." The charm was employed from early on toward older people in a position to help Lawrence find the distinction he clearly sought. He also "discovered early that mystery was news," as his friend, the

* Tabachnick connects this to the discovery of his illegitimacy.

diplomat and writer Harold Nicolson, later said. He got attention by brief revelations, or inventions, of supposed contradictions in his personality, earning for him an early reputation as a poser and calculator (which persisted to the end of his life). Asher writes:

> On the surface he seemed a fiery iconoclast, with what he called his "knight errant way of tilting at all comers," and Edward Leeds [a young keeper at the Ashmolean Museum at Oxford, who became a friend] noted "the fearlessness with which he attacked the views and theories of other writers." Yet Lawrence's revolt was frequently revolt into style, for he had an uncanny knack of telling those in authority what they most desired to hear.

Winning First Class Honors, he embarked on a postgraduate thesis on the origins and development of medieval pottery in England, and with the support of D. G. Hogarth, Keeper of the Ashmolean Museum, obtained a junior research fellowship at Magdalen College. That same autumn, however, he convinced Hogarth to let him join an exploratory season of excavations at Carchemish in northern Syria, initially as an unsalaried assistant. He had earlier traveled in the region, in connection with his university thesis on Crusader castles.

⌒

This archaelogical work at Carchemish was to go on until the war's outbreak in 1914, and provided perhaps the happiest period of Lawrence's life. He immediately demonstrated a remarkable ability to handle the local workforce. Asher writes:

> His first response to the Arabs . . . was aesthetic: they were fine-looking chaps, he thought, though most were thin as rakes, and few were taller than himself. He was fascinated by their culture and set himself the task of learning all about their customs and language. Not only did he learn the names of all the workers, he quickly assim-

ilated the names of their tribes and families, and the nature of their relationships.

He quickly grasped that in the Arab world family and kinship ties define an individual. He was able to use this knowledge in dealing with the workers, pointing fun at individuals and cajoling others by bringing up some skeleton in the family closet. Asher says that

> within months of his arrival Lawrence had become a sort of unofficial arbiter of disputes, sorting about the jealousies among pickmen, shovellers and basketmen, separating members of families with blood-feuds between them, settling fights, castigating the water-boys for falling short, advising a man on the payment of a bride-price, bailing another out of prison. . . . He even took pride in doctoring their injuries, treating scorpion-stings and dressing cuts they had received from tools or falling rocks.

The biographer says that he had begun to act and think "like the model British District Officer in a backwater of the Empire, administering 'his' natives. . . . He might have been echoing any decent-minded British colonial official carrying 'the White Man's Burden' when he told his mother: 'Our people are very curious and very simple, and yet with a fund of directness and child humor about them which is very fine.' Before his eyes, the Arabs had been transformed into noble savages. . . ."

This explains something about the nature of the "liberation" Lawrence later envisaged for the Arabs. During the Arab Revolt he intended that the Hashemite princes acquire a kingdom free of Ottoman control but he did not imagine that theirs would become a wholly sovereign nation, any more than contemporary Egypt was wholly sovereign. Desmond Stewart quotes a letter written at the time in which Lawrence said, "My own ambition is that the Arabs should be our first Brown Dominion." Asher writes that "the result of Lawrence's style of colonialism would be a people with their own

distinct cultural patterns, firmly but covertly under British dominion. . . ." Lawrence particularly deplored French colonialism,
which held France's civilization to be superior to that of the Arabs
and an example to be emulated, and taught Arabs French, which in
his eyes deprived the Arabs of their own authenticity, turning them
into a "vulgarized" people who could never be really French, or
meet the norms of European civilization, but would no longer be
themselves.

Lawrence's intimacy with the Arab workforce was responsible for
an episode crucial in his life. He met Salim Ahmad, a young water
boy, nicknamed Dahoum—the "dark one," according to Jeremy
Wilson. (The name could also have been given ironically, since by
most accounts he was unusually light in coloring; he was also "not
particularly intelligent," according to Lawrence's uninfatuated fellow archaeologist, Leonard Woolley, "but beautifully built and
remarkably handsome.") Lawrence fell in love with Dahoum,
although he undoubtedly could not or would not at the time have
acknowledged that this was the case. He made Dahoum his protégé
and taught him, he said, "to use his reason as well as his instinct," in
the course of an effort to educate the illiterate boy (while simultaneously deploring the influence of missionary schools in "spoiling"
the Arabs).

Dahoum became his assistant and traveling companion during
his years in Syria. He even took him on a visit to Oxford. This association has naturally been much discussed by his biographers, who
seem generally convinced, because of Lawrence's own inhibited nature as well as the norms of respectable Arab society, that it remained a nonsexual, or asexual, relationship. Asher writes, "to the
boy he must have appeared almost a wizard from a far-off land. . . .
The relationship was not and could never be one of equality: socially they were as far apart, almost, as medieval serf and master—at
least, this is the way Lawrence himself imagined it; 'Dahoum is very

useful now, though a savage,' he wrote [during his second year in Syria]; 'however, we are here in the feudal system, which gives the overlord great claims: so that I have no trouble with him.' "

After leaving Syria in 1914, Lawrence presumably never saw Dahoum again (who is thought to have died in 1916). However, *Seven Pillars of Wisdom* begins with a dedicatory poem, "To S.A.," saying, "I loved you, so I drew these tides of men into my hands / and wrote my will across the sky in stars / To earn you Freedom. . . ." This is usually thought to have been addressed to Dahoum.*

In 1914, before the war broke out, the British authorities in Egypt wanted a military mapping survey of Turkish-held Sinai. This was carried out in the guise of an archaeological expedition sponsored by the Palestine Exploration Fund, conducted by Lawrence and his Carchemish colleague Leonard Woolley, providing cover for a survey party from the Royal Engineers.

When the war began, Lawrence was at Oxford. Because of his efforts in the Sinai survey he initially found war work in London with the Geographical Section of the War Office, where for military convenience he was given a direct commission without medical ex-

---

* Desmond Stewart believes that "S.A." actually refers to Sharif Ali ibn al-Hussain, a comrade of Lawrence's during the Arab Revolt, or possibly that the initials link the two men. "This would make the kind of involved sense that fits a cipher" (a "cipher" is what Lawrence said the poem was, according to Robert Graves). The sharif, a handsome young aristocrat, ten years younger than Lawrence, a relation of the Hashemites, served with Faisal and Lawrence to the end of the Arab Revolt, afterwards joining Faisal in attempting to save Damascus from the French when the war settlement placed Syria under French Mandate. Eventually he became disillusioned with the Hashemites and allied himself with the Wahhabite Ibn Saud who ousted them from Arabia in the 1920s (and whose descendants rule Saudi Arabia today). Stewart is convinced that Lawrence loved Sharif Ali and had a physical relationship with him, possibly masochistic in character. Lawrence had Eric Kennington make Ali's portrait in 1921; it appears on page 187 of the 1926 New York Doubleday edition of *Seven Pillars of Wisdom* (identical to the limited British Subscribers' Edition).

amination as a "temporary second lieutenant interpreter" (and went out to buy a uniform off the rack at the Army & Navy Stores). He was soon transferred to the Intelligence Department in Cairo, where he joined many of the people he had known in the Middle East, including Hogarth.

He became one of several officers working for British political warfare and military intelligence who saw in the Hashemite claim to power in Arabia a possibility of mounting a useful guerrilla adjunct to the campaign by regular British troops against Turkey, ally of Germany. He met, in 1916, the Hashemite Prince Faisal, whose father, the Sharif Hussain, had proposed a revolt against the Ottoman Turks by the Arabs, provided that an independent Arab state could result which would include virtually all of the Arab dominions of the Ottoman Empire. The British authorities in Cairo, who considered Hussain a minor chieftain, thought this approach to them near-effrontery until they discovered that Hussain, as Emir of Mecca and Protector of the Holy Places, had been given a mandate to speak for nationalist figures in Syria and Iraq as well, including Arab officers in the Turkish army who in 1915 had secretly signed the so-called Damascus Protocol, a document that set the frontiers of a future independent Arab state, in which all privileges for foreigners would be abolished, but which would accept a defensive alliance with Britain.

The British resisted these terms, as London envisaged a future division of Ottoman Arabia with France (as actually happened). On New Year's Day 1916 Hussain made a fateful, and as it proved, fatal decision, so far as independence for the Arabs was concerned. Confident of "English standards of honorable dealing"—as he later told the Arab historian George Antonius—he offered to waive full discussion of the frontier question until after the war. The Arab Revolt was launched, but the prospect of an autonomous Arab nation, encompassing Arabia, Syria, Iraq, Palestine (including present-day Israel), and what now is Jordan, was extinguished a month later by the Sykes-Picot agreement, signed by Britain and France in February

1916. Much later, Lawrence wrote that when he learned of this agreement, and realized the duplicity involved in his own position, "in revenge I vowed to make the Arab Revolt the engine of its own success, as well as handmaid to our Egyptian campaign: and vowed to lead it so madly in the final victory that expediency should counsel to the powers a fair settlement of the Arabs' moral claims. This presumed my surviving the war, to win the later battle of the Council Chamber—immodest presumptions, which still balance in fulfillment." (This was written for the 1926 Subscribers' Edition of *Seven Pillars*.)

~◦

As advisor to Faisal, the only one in his immediate entourage possessing a general acquaintance with the strategic situation and the international political context, and as it turned out, possessing a real instinct for guerrilla tactics, Lawrence assumed a leading role in the uprising that followed. He is generally credited with developing the original and ultimately successful program of systematic attacks on the Hejaz railroad, which ran eight hundred miles south from Damascus to Medina, location of the Prophet's Tomb. It was the single important means of transportation, and hence of Ottoman power projection, in Arabia. Its effective interdiction cut off the Ottoman forces there, culminating in their destruction and the capture of Damascus, taken by the Arabs jointly with British regular forces in December 1917.*

---

* Conventional military thought at the time held to the Clausewitzian principle of closing with the enemy at his strongest point, since, arguably, only there could he be decisively beaten. This at the time is what the Allies and the Central Powers thought they were doing on the western front (and what the Central Powers actually did on the eastern front). Lawrence immediately understood that the Arabs would be destroyed in any direct confrontation with the Turkish regular army (which had just inflicted a humiliating defeat on French and British imperial forces at Gallipoli, throwing the Allies' invasion back into the sea after inflicting a million casualties). He said (in *Seven Pillars*), "we might . . . develop a habit of never engaging the enemy." The Arabs' assets were speed, surprise, possession of the initiative—and the desert, where they

The Arabian campaign, like most guerrilla campaigns, had not been decisive. The political calculations behind it were hypocritical to the extent that no responsible British officer expected a fully independent Arabian kingdom to be set up. The British assumptions were still those of empire and paternalistic power. Eventual creation of a Jewish National Home in Palestine (become, today, Israel), in which the promise was made to guarantee the rights of the Palestinian Arabs, was for expedient reasons conceded in the middle of the war (in the Balfour Declaration). Lawrence did not know of this agreement until 1917, but he certainly understood that the political assurances he gave the Hashemites risked going beyond what Britain would really concede.*

Lawrence returned to London soon after the war ended. He attended the Versailles negotiations as translator and adviser for Faisal, attempting on his own initiative as well as in Faisal's interest to counter the decision taken by the British and French governments to divide Arabia and place it under their own effective control. Later he was to work through Winston Churchill, when Churchill was colonial secretary in the 1920s, to give Faisal and the Arabs a part of what had been promised them.

Acknowledging what he had done to mislead, or even betray, the Arabs among whom he had lived, he honorably attempted to do what was in his power to make up for it. He did not, however, forgive himself for his use of the Arabs and their revolt, the killings in which he took part while reinventing himself as "Lawrence of Arabia," the identity he subsequently came to detest, or fear.

---

were unseen by the enemy, and independent of bases and conventional communications. As Asher writes, "Lawrence saw with visionary clearness that the desert was his great ally: he had discovered 'desert power.' "

* The 1916 Sykes-Picot agreement assigning Syria to a French sphere of interest was responsible for Lawrence's conviction, subsequently expressed, that "it was not the Turks but the French who were the real enemies in Syria."

~⊃

Lawrence later wrote that the final distribution of Ottoman lands and Arab princes, carried out by the British authorities at a Cairo meeting in 1921, including confirmation of Britain's promise that a Jewish National Home could be created inside Palestine, "made straight all the tangle, finding solutions fulfilling (I think) our promises in letter and spirit (where humanly possible) without sacrificing any interest of our Empire or any interest of the people concerned.* So we were quit of our war-time Eastern adventure, with clean hands, but three years too late to earn the gratitude which peoples, not states, can pay." The Arab historian George Antonius has said that this is a statement "so palpably untenable as to cast serious doubt on Lawrence's understanding of the issues involved." However, as it was actually written in a footnote added to the 1935 edition of *Seven Pillars*, long after the deeds were done (and the wenches dead; indeed in the same year of Lawrence's own death), one might assume that Lawrence understood very well the

* Faisal was originally offered the throne of Syria, but when Syria was mandated to France in 1920 he was ousted from Damascus by French forces. He eventually became king of the new British Mandate state of Iraq, set up by the Treaty of Sèvres in 1921. His brother, Abdullah, became king of a new Trans-Jordan state, today's Jordan, formerly included in Syria. (Abdullah was assassinated soon after Jordan became independent in 1951. Its present king, Abdullah II, is Abdullah's great-grandson.) Faisal was murdered in the course of an anti-Western military coup in Iraq in 1958, which proclaimed a republic. The Hashemites were themselves ousted from Arabia in 1924 by the Wahabi fundamentalist movement led by Ibn Saud (hence Saudi Arabia), whose descendants rule Arabia today—although exempting themselves personally from some of the exigencies of fundamentalism, and inviting into their country the influence and troops of the infidel United States (to their subsequent bitter regret, since this provoked dissident Saudis to condemn their association with the United States and organize the New York and Washington terrorist attacks of September 11, 2001, with all that followed). The American bases established in Saudi Arabia at the time of the Gulf War were shut down by Washington immediately after the defeat of Iraq's army in summer 2003. This had been demanded by Osama bin Ladin, and was his—unacknowledged, to be sure—victory over Washington.

issues that had been involved, but which were by 1935 settled, for better or worse.

⊷

Lawrence's ambition was to write an account of the Arab Revolt, combining fact with epic elaboration, turning what had occurred into a saga. This was to become *Seven Pillars of Wisdom*, first published in a limited Subscribers' Edition privately distributed in 1926, followed by his own popular abridgement, *Revolt in the Desert*, meant to pay for the lavishly designed and illustrated private edition.* He began making descriptive notes of persons and places in 1917. He wrote the book in 1919 and 1920.

He seems to have believed at the time that he might fulfill his prewar ambition—derived from his admiration for the artist, designer, and bookmaker William Morris—to found a private press to publish fine books. He hoped to print the Subscribers' Edition of *Seven Pillars* himself. This did not work out, but the ambition to make the limited edition a work of bookmaking art remained, and he commissioned Eric Kennington and other artists (including William Nicholson, William Rothenstein, John Singer Sargent, Paul Nash, and Augustus John) to provide portraits of the principals in his story, including himself.† (According to Rothenstein, in contemporary painting he had "a marked preference" for Futurism and its English counterpart, Vorticism, as for Vorticism's leader, the painter and novelist Wyndham Lewis; and William Roberts and

---

* A 1922 version of the manuscript of *Seven Pillars*, considerably longer than the final published version, was issued in 1998 in a limited edition in two volumes, with a third volume of illustrations and annexes, edited by Jeremy Wilson.

† Rothenstein subsequently wrote that Lawrence himself "seemed to like being painted . . . he never seemed to object to standing for hours together—once, when I was painting the folds of his outer garment, he remained standing for two hours without a rest!" He also sat for portraits of himself by Kennington and Augustus John, remarking to Robert Graves that he "hoped this could uncover a personality which puzzled its owner as much as anyone."

Frank Dobson, associated with Vorticism, were involved in preparing the Subscribers' Edition.)*

His outlook and essential ambition were those of an artist. Morris, his most powerful early influence, had been a writer and social reformer, as well as artist. William Morris founded the Kelmscott Press in 1890 to make fine books, for which he designed the type, pages, and bindings. Lawrence went back to his lifelong ambition to establish a hand press of his own after leaving the RAF, planning to establish it at his cottage, Clouds Hill, where he would bring out a limited edition of his account of enlisted military life, *The Mint*, followed by the work of "some good but obscure poets."

He wished to leave behind works of art: his monumental book on the desert campaign; a translation of the *Odyssey*, which was published in 1932 (Irving Howe said, "He turned the *Odyssey* into firm, often pungent English prose—some classicists have balked, but it is a living book"); and *The Mint*, written in 1927 (but withheld, eventually published in 1955). Art was what he had believed in before he became involved in prewar military intelligence, in the course of his archaeological work, and before the war itself came into his life. It was to art that he returned when these were behind him.

He had, in *Seven Pillars of Wisdom*, dealt with his Arabian experience in a manner that reflected the influence of Malory's *Morte d'Arthur* and the medieval romances and epic poetry that had played a large role in his childhood imagination, and of his earliest scholarly interest, the Crusaders. "Remember that my period was the Middle Ages, always," he wrote to Basil Liddell Hart. Liddell Hart obliged (in the biography he published in 1934) by portraying

---

* The planners of the National Portrait Gallery exhibition of 1989, Robin Gibson and Honor Clerk, wrote that "Lawrence's patronage of artists, especially for the illustrations for *Seven Pillars of Wisdom*, is one aspect of his life which is often overlooked, and he can be regarded as one of the few important private patrons in Britain in this [twentieth] century."

the Bedouin as being led out of the Arabian desert by Faisal and Lawrence of Arabia to break the power of the Ottoman Turks and conquer the Crusader cities of Jerusalem and Damascus, the first step in achieving an ambition that consisted, even when Lawrence was a schoolboy, "of hustling into form, while I lived, the new Asia which time was inexorably bringing upon us." Lawrence said, "Mecca was to lead to Damascus; Damascus to Anatolia, and afterwards to Baghdad; and then there was Yemen."

The Mint was of an entirely contrasting matter-of-factness in dealing with the then unexplored subject of the enlisted man's life in the regular military. Its "realism," which is to say its severe, scrupulously detached honesty about the sexuality and scatology of the barracks, made it, in his opinion, unpublishable except in a private edition.* Needless to say, the literature of the Second World War and since has made it an honorable curiosity in the literature of realism.

Lawrence's postwar career was sensational. In 1922 he gave up archaeology and the academy (he had been made a Fellow of All Souls at Oxford) and abandoned government service (Winston Churchill had made him an adviser in the Colonial Office) to enlist (with Trenchard's complicity) in the ranks of the Royal Air Force as an airman under the assumed name of "John Hume Ross." When this became publicized, he was forced out, and in 1923 enlisted in the

---

* His admirer and patron, Air Marshal Sir Hugh Trenchard, founder of the Royal Air Force, after reading the manuscript, wrote to him, "I understand everything you put down at the time and your feelings, but I feel it would be unfair to let this loose on a world that likes to blind itself to the ordinary facts that go on day after day. Everything you have written—I can see it happening—the way you have written as if it was happening, but the majority of people will only say, 'How awful! how horrible! how terrible! how *bad!*' There are many things you have written which I do feel we know go on and we know should not go on, though what you have written does not hurt me one bit—far from it, and yet, if I saw it in print, if I saw it being published and being misunderstood by the public, I should hate it, and I should feel my particular work of trying to make this force would be irretrievably damaged and that through my own fault."

Tank Corps as "T. E. Shaw." Once again, as in 1905, he recoiled from the servitude and purposeless brutality of enlisted army life, and in 1925, after hinting at suicide, he was allowed back into the RAF, which because of its novelty and technical demands attracted a better educated and better motivated body of recruits. He served there until February 1935. His departure was followed by his death, in May, in a motorcycle crash.

Newspaper notoriety pursued him. It is not yet exhausted. In 2001 the novelist Tariq Ali published an article in *The London Review of Books* (of all places) reviving the long-discredited claim that Lawrence's 1927–28 RAF posting to what now is Pakistan's northern frontier was cover for a still undisclosed Secret Service mission. Ali added to that his claim to know that, while there, Lawrence married a Pakistani girl—which would be news indeed, if true.*

The revelation, in the 1960s, of his sad and complicated compulsion to have himself beaten as penance for fantastic and fictional offenses against an imaginary uncle—the story he told the young soldier he engaged to administer the whippings—made a series of London newspaper articles and another book.

The truth about a central episode in *Seven Pillars of Wisdom*, in which, spying in the town of Deraa, he was captured by the Turkish authorities and was beaten and raped, was much debated for years, although it might have been thought settled in the 1980s by the publication of a 1927 letter to E. M. Forster, after Forster had sent him an "unpublishable" homosexual short story. Lawrence replied, "I suppose you will not print it? Not that it anywhere says too much: but it shows far more than it says: and these things are mysteries. The

---

* Lawrence's posting was actually because *Revolt in the Desert* was about to be published, and after its earlier experience with Lawrence and the press during his 1922 enlistment, the RAF wanted him as far from reporters as possible. His post was an isolated one near the Afghanistan frontier. His main non-RAF occupation there was his translation of the *Odyssey*. A London newspaper, *Empire News*, nevertheless invented a story that Lawrence "the secret agent" was in India, operating in the disguise of a holy man. Reprinted in India, it led, according to Asher, to disturbances in which a real holy man was beaten nearly to death. Lawrence was then hastily returned to Britain.

Turks, as you probably know (or have guessed, through the reticences of the 'Seven Pillars'), did it to me, by force: and since then I have gone about whimpering to myself Unclean, unclean. Now I don't know. Perhaps there is another side, your side, to the story. I couldn't ever do it. I believe the impulse strong enough to make me touch another creature has not yet been born in me. . . ."

His biographers nonetheless remain divided as to whether the Deraa episode actually happened. Wilson and Mack are convinced that it did. Asher, analyzing the travel circumstances, Lawrence's war notebook, the dates, and the *Seven Pillars* text in detail, concludes that the episode probably was an invention and is masochistic fantasy, although undoubtedly linked to real experiences, probably including a manhandling by Turkish police when Lawrence was traveling in Syria in 1912.

Desmond Stewart thinks the Deraa story an invention but agrees about its psychological relevance, saying that the war experience and Lawrence's encounter with Sharif Ali ibn el Hussain had combined to arouse him from the "asexuality" of the prewar years, and that in interaction with his puritanical upbringing the result was a subsequent search for physical punishments for sexual transgressions.* Mack, the psychiatrist, says flatly,

---

* Stewart also claims that Lawrence, after the war, "had unwisely attended flagellation parties in Chelsea conducted by an underworld figure known as Bluebeard, and Bluebeard's impending divorce case threatened to release lubricious details concerning Lawrence and one of his aristocratic friends which had already been hinted at in a German scandal-sheet." Lawrence supposedly wrote to the Home Secretary asking for Bluebeard's expulsion and a ban on the German magazine. Stewart attributes this information "to one of the few students of Lawrence's life who have been given access to certain otherwise embargoed papers in the Bodleian Museum." Hyde discloses that this individual was the *Sunday Times* journalist Colin Simpson, and that Simpson subsequently was unable to produce his notes concerning the Home Office letter, the original of which Hyde, with access to the Bodleian papers, was unable to find. With no better source, the suggestion remains unproven, and seems implausible given Lawrence's physical fastidiousness and demonstrated discretion concerning his intimate life; but the story was undoubtedly part of homosexual community gossip about Lawrence from the 1920s to the 1970s, when Stewart wrote.

I have found no evidence that Lawrence ever as an adult entered voluntarily into a sexual relationship for the purpose of achieving intimacy or pleasure.

He goes on,

This applies equally to heterosexual and homosexual relationships. There are a few passages in his letters and notes which indicate a longing for sexual experience, but no evidence that he could act on these longings, and much evidence that he could not. The evidence certainly does not support the view that Lawrence was "asexual," but rather that his early development brought about a deep need to reject and devalue all intimacy between the sexes, and gave rise to intense fears and inhibitions that prevented action.

The clearest statement of Lawrence's sexual puritanism, inhibition, and conflict occurs in a letter to Mrs. Shaw in 1925: "I'm *too shy* to go looking for dirt. I'm afraid of seeming a novice in it, when I found it. That's why I can't go off stewing in the Lincoln or Navenly brothels with the fellows. They think it's because I'm superior, proud, or peculiar or 'posh,' as they say: and it's because I wouldn't know what to do, how to carry myself, where to stop. Fear again: fear everywhere."

⊷

Mack seems right about this, as about the influence of Lawrence's illegitimacy, another matter of disagreement among his biographers. Richard Aldington was the first to reveal the circumstances of Lawrence's birth in his 1955 "biographical enquiry," in which he wrote that he became "more and more convinced that sometime in [Lawrence's] early life he had been dealt a terrific blow by Fate, some humiliating and painful wound which he was always trying to compensate [*sic*]." Lawrence himself claimed that before the age of ten he had known he was illegitimate, but his friend and mentor David Hogarth later said that he thought the young Lawrence had only a garbled version of the story, in which his father had married his mother only after he and some other of the boys were already born. Lawrence claimed that he "hadn't given a straw about the matter." As far as the evidence of his contemporaries indicates, he never mentioned the matter to childhood friends or fellow students at Jesus College. He seems to have first spoken of the subject during the war.

Asher thinks that Lawrence's biographers have mistakenly "attempted to turn his story into a tale of existential guilt over his family circumstances. Apart from some play over his name, and an assertion of his 'Irishness' which was new, though, the revelation came too late either to mould his character or to affect his career: when he learned the truth in 1919, he was already on the way to becoming a national hero." Asher believes that Lawrence throughout his life was driven by fear of physical pain and a conviction of his own inadequacies, and by his determination to overcome both at whatever cost, but he does not explain the source of this felt inadequacy, other than Lawrence's short physical stature (attributed by some to a childhood accident). This seems wholly unsatisfactory as explanation for a lifelong combination of self-abasement with exhibitionism.

As late as 1927 Lawrence said in a letter, with more apparent bitterness than humor, "My 'Lawrence' label (an invention for his own reasons, of my father's late in life) is worn out." That same year, his placing his name in quotation marks when *Revolt in the Desert* was published cannot have been other than an act of cruelty to his mother, who apparently never spoke to her sons of their illegitimacy. At the time of the Aldington book's publication, in 1955, when she was ninety-five, friends tried to keep her from the radio when the book was about to be discussed in a broadcast, but her oldest son (Robert, who had always refused to believe the accusation) led her into the room while the program was on the air. She sat through it without moving or speaking, and at the end "got up and walked stiffly out of the room without comment."

Lawrence's youngest brother, Arnold, was to write: "The strongest impression I have is that his life has been injured by his mother." Lawrence himself said (to Charlotte Shaw), "One of the real reasons . . . why I am in the service is so that I may live by myself. [My mother] has given me a terror of families and inquisitions. And yet you'll understand that she is my mother, and an extraordinary person. Knowledge of her will prevent my ever making any woman a mother, and the cause of children. I think she suspects this: but she does not know that the inner conflict, which makes me a standing civil war, is the inevitable issue of the discordant natures of herself and my father, and the inflammation of strength and weakness which followed the uprooting of their lives and principles. They should not have borne children."

Lawrence's character was surely deeply marked by his illegitimacy, which was the crucial factor in his mother's struggle to impose on her sons the virtue she conceived herself as having lost through her sin with their father. She wanted an inhuman perfection from them. Hers was a peculiarly intense version, involving expiation of her own guilt, of the perfectionist demands of other charismatic mothers, who justify their own lives through those of their children; and whose inescapable message, throughout the lives of those children, is that whatever the child does can never be good enough.

An internalized message that nothing is ever good enough for the person whom you have most loved can dominate a lifetime, inspiring astounding accomplishments—and despair. Lawrence resisted his mother's influence throughout his life, but vainly; it was an influence founded in his puritanical religious formation, which assumed secular form when religion itself was consciously repudiated. His brother Arnold said of his flagellations, "His subjection of the body was achieved by methods advocated by the saints whose lives he had read."

✦

The mature personality is able to grasp its sources and its limits, even if it does not much like what it finds. Lawrence seems never to have forgiven himself for his sexual nature, or for the pleasure he had taken in war, the personal rewards he had found in the use and exploitation of others, and the role he had taken in an Arab "awakening" that was betrayed in the peace settlement.

He had used war and the qualities of war—its idealism, but also its limitedness, its comprehensibility, its terrible simplifications, its elimination of all the ordinariness of ordinary life, of the ordinary human relationships of family and conventional friendship, its dramatic gratification of the pleasures of destruction—to reinvent his own life.

His use of others did not consist simply in making political promises his government did not or could not keep. He used them in a purely personal enterprise, the transformation of the bastard Thomas Edward Lawrence, short and physically unprepossessing archeologist and student of Crusader military architecture, sometime intelligence gatherer in the amateur style of pre-1914 Oxford and Foreign Office, who in the ordinary course of things was destined to academic obscurity, into a model of modern chivalry, "the uncrowned King of Arabia," a modern crusader in the modern cause of national self-determination, a would-be liberator of the "new Asia": a hero, the only real popular hero to emerge from the war— Lawrence of Arabia, "A triumph." He made certain of that creation by fixing it in *Seven Pillars of Wisdom*, privately printing the book in an elegant edition not to be circulated in his lifetime, thereby guaranteeing for it maximum attention. His abridgment, *Revolt in the Desert*, half the length of the original, was meant to pay for the unabridged edition. He gave the profits to an RAF charitable fund.

Lawrence was a victim of the collapse of the pre-1914 assumptions about the relationship of Europe to what were, or had been, its colonial peoples: a collapse that he deliberately contributed to, only to find himself, as he later said, imprisoned in a lie. He was a major actor in what another generation would call the decolonialization of the Arabs, by bringing to an end their domination by Turkey, and was then instrumental in their provisional recolonization by both France and Britain, and the beginning of the Palestinian Arabs' dispossession by the Zionist movement, which was installing itself with the intention of making Palestine a Jewish state. His imprisonment in lies is the reason usually given for his postwar renunciation of a conventional career.

Having done what he could, he retreated into what was certainly a penitential life—of "brain sleep," as he said, and gratification of his masochism, "to make me impossible for anyone to suggest for a responsible position . . . self-degradation is my aim." He continued to apply to himself the ethical judgments of his puritan formation, effectively concluding that because his reinvention of himself had proved a failure he deserved the elected prison of enlisted military service, the renunciation of honor, the catharsis of whippings. The ethical and political norms of the society that formed him had proved unsustainable. The realities of guerrilla war among an Islamic people against the Ottoman state—desiccated survivor of a Central Asian nomad empire, incapable of competing with the new European industrial society—were beyond the moral resources of that English conception of life and conduct by which he had set out to live, and this incapacity he internalized.

Lawrence could never afterwards repair the damage to himself that had been done. Something, he said, was broken, and it appears that he never fully understood what it really was that had broken. His postwar life was dominated by penance for crimes for which he had no, or very limited, responsibility (his birth, his personality and sexual nature), or where his own influence, however large, could never have been decisive (the political outcome of the war). One gathers, from what he later wrote to Charlotte Shaw, that he could never put behind him his responsibility for killing not only some of his own wounded, for whom no possibility of treatment or evacuation existed, and prisoners, who could not be guarded or transported, but also for killing his enemies themselves.

Yet these penitential efforts gave his postwar life a hardness and shapeliness beyond those of virtually any other contemporary public life. This was achieved by his retreat from large engagement. Unable to deal with the external consequences of the collapse of the cultural standards that had formed him, he chose austerity, remoteness from all but the most strictly controlled companionships, and yet a genuine charity and abnegation.

His close relationships were with Charlotte Shaw, Bernard Shaw's wife—conducted almost entirely by letter and thereby distanced; with the wife and family of one of his last RAF commanding officers, Wing Commander Sydney Smith; and with several Air Force comrades, uneducated men with whom he could be close on his own terms, without revealing any more than he wished to reveal. He used the means provided by enlisted military life to give his postwar existence severity and concentration. He was the victim of a mutation in contemporary culture by which chivalry ceased to be possible, or even imaginable, at exactly the moment when he had made of himself that figure of chivalry, "Lawrence of Arabia."

To invent a life is not so rare. Lawrence's reinvention of himself, in the 1920s and '30s, was achieved, like all good art, by minimization, rejection of the nonessential. He reduced his life to simplicity, when he had the possibility of power and complexity; for a considerable time he had possessed power, and been urged by Churchill and others to keep it, to pursue a political career. His choice was a consequence of personal forces, formed by the cultural circumstances of the time in which he lived, but it was also a consequence of political and military events that had ended one period in modern history and begun another.

In *Studies in a Dying Culture*, Christopher Caudwell, a Marxist and a poet, said of Lawrence,

> Only in the ranks of the Army he found a stunted version of his ideal, barren of fulfillment but at least free from dishonor. In the Army, at least, though men have taken the King's shilling, it is not the search for profit that holds the fabric together; but it is based on a simple social imperative and wields a force that never reckons its dividends. Like a kind of Arabian desert in the heart of the vulgar luxury of bourgeoisdom, the bare tents of the Army shield a simple comradeship, a social existence free from competition or hate. It is both survival and anticipation, for on the one hand it conserves old feudal relations, as they were before bourgeoisdom burst them, and on the other hand it prophesies like a rudimentary symbol the community of tomorrow united by ties of common effort and not of cash.

That is a romantic and ideologized view of the military as it existed before World War Two, but there is undoubtedly something in this, although it is not the full explanation.

"There seemed a certainty in degradation, a final safety," Lawrence wrote in *Seven Pillars of Wisdom*. "Man could rise to any height, but there was an animal level beneath which he could not fall."

✦

Neither of the methods for dealing with the trauma of 1914–1918 that was adopted by most of his sensitive younger wartime contemporaries was available to him. (Lawrence was twenty-six when the world war broke out.) The dominant intellectual reaction among the younger wartime generation was recoil from the civilization that had produced the war, condemning European liberal politics and society as sham, "gone bust"—a great swindle by which they and their friends had been victimized. For most of these men one answer was abandonment of public life (or retreat into the nihilism and pleasures of the 1920s), regarding politics with indifference or contempt. Some turned to revolutionary political romanticism of the Left or the Right. Thus, Fascism had its season of favor in Britain and France as well as in Italy, Germany, and Eastern Europe, and revolutionary Communism later had, particularly in the democracies, a large and enduring influence on writers and artists as well as on the politically active.

The dominant post–Great War theme, however, was attack upon the society that had produced the war: an attack reflecting the impotence that men had felt as victims on the western front. Beneath that, an enduring and compensatory, if hysterical, optimism could often be discerned about what some apocalyptic change might bring. Lawrence, on the other hand, who had experienced command, accomplishment, unparalleled success, took upon himself as personal penalty the failure of the culture into which he had been born.

Thus the "Prince of Mecca" (his own claim), master spy of the British Secret Service (a belief widely held outside England, where his postwar military enlistment was popularly considered a subterfuge), a man admired or feared by some in Britain as a potential Fascist and even as a dictator. His fatal motorcycle accident occurred as he returned from sending a telegram confirming a proposed visit by his friend Henry Williamson, a novelist whose war experience had produced an intense commitment to reconciling the war generations of Germany and Britain in order to prevent a new war. This was a theme of the British Fascist movement of the time. Williamson wanted to put Lawrence together with Oswald Mosley, the Fascist leader, in the belief that Lawrence might join Mosley's cause. Another friend, Robert Graves, has said that had Lawrence not been killed "he would have found the temptation to strong political action almost irresistible," which is speculation. Lawrence knew nothing of Williamson's plan, and had earlier, to others, ridiculed the notion of a connection with the Fascists.

The link with Fascism is nonetheless significant. Lawrence himself expressed no Fascist sympathies, nor were his mind and temperament, on the evidence of all that he wrote and of what those who knew him said about him, in the least disposed that way. I met Oswald Mosley when he was old, a magnetic, arrogant man, limping badly (from a flying accident that had left one leg shorter than the other), an intellectual bully, a charmer. His dominant and fatal quality was humorlessness. (A menacing wit, he possessed.) Mosley was unquestionably brilliant, the only British politician of his day to grasp the sources of the economic crisis of the 1930s and to propose original ways of dealing with it. He understood Keynes, and initially attracted to himself such intelligent men as Harold Nicolson and John Strachey, but his arrogance and humorlessness drove them off, and he ended his political career in exile in Paris, powerless, and despised by his fellow countrymen. The contrast with Lawrence's intellectual detachment, practical intelligence, and human sympathies could not have been greater.*

Even so, there is something about Lawrence that makes people think of Fascism. Fascism's rhetoric was that of heroism, and he was a hero. He was apolitical, and Fascism, at the time, purported to be beyond politics: an affair of strong men, the war's survivors, sweeping politicians aside. Those are superficial reasons; there are better ones. Lawrence was a destroyer of prewar assumptions not only about colonialism and the "guardianship" of empire but about the structures of political power and the limits of war. He took power in his own hands and dreamed of "the new Asia." He was an irregular, a guerrilla, a subverter of empires—of his own empire. He was a

---

* Mosley himself, in his autobiography, *My Life*, expressly denied that he had ever met or had any communication with Lawrence, "despite many later rumors to the contrary."

subverter of class and social convention, abandoning class, and power as well, for anonymity among a wretched, Depression-era military proletariat. He was a man of the shadows, an armed idealist. He committed atrocities in the service of an idea of his own. He helped destroy the wartime conventions of a civilization engaged in destroying itself. People have naturally associated him with the Fascists, who later, in Britain, gave a large political formulation to all this, glorifying it, without recognizing that Lawrence, having done it, had retreated from it all. "By our own act," he said, "we were drained of morality, of volition, of responsibility, like dead leaves in the wind."

While others planned new political careers for him, Lawrence wrote, just after his discharge from the RAF, to his friend Eric Kennington, "You wonder what I am doing? Well, so do I, in truth. Days seem to dawn, suns to shine, evenings to follow, and then I sleep. What I have done, what I am doing, what I am going to do, puzzle me and bewilder me. Have you ever been a leaf and fallen from your tree in autumn and been really puzzled about it? That's the feeling." The image of the dead leaf recurs. He was emptied. Possibly the penance was completed. Robert Graves wrote, "The least and most that can be said about Lawrence is that he is a good man." A moralist would say that he had answered Camus's question as to whether it is possible to become a saint without believing in God. However, the mature Lawrence once said that a belief in God was all that remained with him of his mother's religion.

He interests us because of his political ambiguity, a chivalric Edwardian who adventured into, and was caught by, modern forces: of nationalism, liberation movements, and even proto-totalitarian mass politics. Like the German Ernst Jünger, he was a man trapped in a cleft in the twentieth century, when middle-class civilization yielded to the destructive forces it had rashly evoked from within itself. He could not resolve such contradictions (as Jünger was eventually able to do). He endured them and fashioned a modest post-war life in which he did small goods and avoided further evils.

He served usefully at several air stations. He found pleasure in mechanics and speed. He had the opportunity to work with the British seaplane entry in the 1929 running of the Schneider Races, won by the Supermarine Rolls Royce S6, which evolved into World War II's Spitfire. He was involved in developing the high-speed air-sea rescue motorboats that presaged the torpedo boats of the later war. His interest in fast boats led him to off-duty experiments with early forms of hydrofoil and air cushion hulls, powered by aero engines.*

He used his high contacts to improve the conditions of enlisted life in the RAF. He was a good friend and mentor to a number of uneducated men, introducing them to books and music. His Harvard biographer, John Mack, writes of "the subtler influence he seems to have exerted at virtually each station at which he served. It is hard to convey this quality. His commanders have characterized it as a morally uplifting influence, a subtle force that raised the standards of efficiency, improved the quality of work, and had a beneficial effect upon the tenor of relations on the base and upon morale generally. In some instances Lawrence's influence remained, like a

---

* One of his commanders, J. F. Manning (later Air Commodore) wrote that "of all the interests that Shaw [Lawrence] had in his rather unusual life, his last six years in the Air Force represented a haven, represented an object of great devotion, gave him a technical challenge which he couldn't have believed would arise. . . . Purely by chance, arising out of the rescue operations associated with a flying boat crash in Plymouth Sound in 1929, his long association with motor boats began. Once involved, entirely unprofessionally at first, he soon became deeply committed to a personal crusade of technical improvement of RAF safety launches. In retrospect we know that his contribution to the development of new boats of revolutionary design was immense. My own view is that he was one of the prime architects of our Air-Sea Rescue Service. Although he did not live to see this service grow beyond its adolescence, I feel sure that had he lived to see the 64-foot launches in operation during the last war, and had he known of the thousands of lives they helped to save, he would have felt both contentment and pride in his achievement; something that Lawrence appeared not to experience after his Arabian venture."

legend, bringing about change at a particular station long after he was gone."

✦

His were not bad choices to make in a difficult life, and, as he said, cannot be called "an ordinary effort." Nevertheless, the effect of his successes in Arabia and of the glamour he artfully attached to them contributed to the destruction of the limits on warfare that were generally respected in his time. His manipulation of the Hashemite princes in the service of his own dream of Asia's liberation prefaced and influenced the national-liberation movements and struggles by irregular forces to follow, each of them glamorous in its time, most of them cruelly murderous, few of them actually liberating. He anticipated, as well, the Arabs' systematic exploitation in our day by external powers.

Lawrence's was not a modern personality, even though he was a protomodern figure, scouting out what is most sinister in what the modern world has become. Even in his time, he was an anachronism. His puritan inability to forgive himself, his attachment to chivalry, the punishing asceticism he imposed upon himself—this might as well be medieval for all it has to do not only with the present day, surfeited with guiltlessness, but with the 1920s and 1930s, when Nietzschean rejection of Christian civilization and affirmation of a "heroic" model of human action and Freudianism became major intellectual and moral influences. There was in Lawrence a hardness with self, an unforgivingness, a stoicism, a refusal of indulgence.

Not a modern personality at all, he was unwittingly a maker of the modern age, linked by direct and often decisive influence to the revolutionary hommes engagés who followed in Europe, and later in Asia and Latin America, committed to irregular and unrestrained war against unjust institutions, bringers of their own exculpatory injustices, dreamers like Lawrence, rebels against what is, victims of progress.

CHAPTER FOUR

THE WARRIOR

With Ernst Jünger one moves to the terrible core of the war of 1914–1918, where romantic gesture and frivolous nationalism were ground into mutual slaughter by the three most powerful—and civilized—societies on earth, Great Britain, France, and Germany.

Jünger experienced, acted out, articulated, and then attempted to remedy the destruction of chivalry and the arrival of totalitarian violence in Germany. He initially tried to reestablish the chivalric ethic in a way that could incorporate the experience of his generation, but there was an obvious edge of hysteria in his effort, which postulated a new aristocracy of warriors whose ordeal had made them superior beings.

It was a common theme of protofascist thought to expect a Leader (sought by the Arditi, the legionnaires of D'Annunzio's League of Fiume, and by the intellectuals who eventually backed Oswald Mosley in London, as well as by certain figures on the contemporary Left). Jünger was simultaneously exemplar and theorist, but unlike some of the others proved too intelligent not, in time, to see through what he had done. He eventually joined the effort to kill the Leader: "the Führer."

He nonetheless remained in some disrepute until the end of his long life, even though he had become the familiar of German chancellors and French presidents, the most read of modern German novelists other than Thomas Mann, and in France a favorite in literary circles and of the reading public, despite having as a soldier twice invaded France.

He was despised by liberal Germans, who considered that he had "several ideological incarnations, all of them pernicious and contemptible," a man "without whom Hitler would never have come to power." This is the view of Konrad Kellen, an early exile from Germany, friend and sometime secretary to both Thomas Mann and Alfred Einstein, veteran of the American army and its political warfare organizations, who ended his career at the Rand Corporation. Jünger's ideal of society in the 1920s, according to the British scholar Noël O'Sullivan (writing in his 1983 book, *Fascism*), was "to extract the worker from Marxist theory and remodel him instead in the totally different image of Freikorps adventurer. Upon this image, drawn from . . . Jünger's own personal experience, were superimposed an impersonal cult of the machine age, on the one hand, and an extreme cult of suffering and Angst, on the other."

O'Sullivan goes on:

> He always denied that the policies of the Nazi regime, when once Hitler came to power, corresponded to his idea of total mobilization . . . but what is beyond doubt is the fact that his doctrine of total mobilization readily lent itself to an extremist interpretation of the Nazi type, since Jünger himself had openly proclaimed his indifference to truth or falsity on moral and political matters; "the important thing," he said after the first world war, is "to sacrifice oneself for a faith, regardless of whether that faith embraces truth or error."

He was not an attractive figure, on first intellectual acquaintance. He is significant to my argument in this book because he existed, acted, and exerted enormous influence in Germany at the exact moment when the tradition of European chivalry was turned into a nihilistic counterfeit of chivalry, appropriated by Hitler, his SS, and subsequently by Fascist or quasi-Fascist parties from Romania to

Ireland and Australia. Jünger's effort to maintain that tradition was exploited by the Nazis, although it also underlay his eventual effort to rid Germany of Nazism.

◦

Consider the testimony of August von Kageneck, born in the Rhineland in 1924. It is an afternoon in 1937 or 1938 (he is not sure). He remembers lying on the bed in his mother's room reading a book that dramatically answered the questions that seemed posed to a young German, and which changed his life. He was reading Ernst Jünger, writing about the moment before a First World War infantry assault.

> Supreme instant. Life suspended. What will fate say, once out of the trench? When does death come? How? Will it be painful? Will the man next to me be killed? Afterwards? Will there be an afterwards? ... The air so charged with joyful heroism that one weeps without knowing why. That men's hearts can feel this! Ecstasy! This state which saints, great poets, great lovers achieve—it's revealed in courage as well.*

This celebration of the "voluptuousness of blood, eroticism of blood, purity of blood; blood and earth; race of warriors, race of no-

---

* Compare this with a passage from Hélie de Saint Marc (many years later a friend of Kageneck's), a Frenchman sent to Buchenwald at twenty-one as a résistant, who when liberated in 1945 was unable to remember his own identity. He subsequently was commissioned at Saint-Cyr, served three assignments to Indochina, was in Algeria from 1957 to 1961 and took part in the parachutists' anti–de Gaulle putsch of 1961, and was imprisoned for military mutiny from 1961 to 1966. "Those who claim to love war must do so far from the carnage of the battlefield, the scattered corpses and the disemboweled women. War is an absolute evil. There is no joyful war nor sad war, beautiful war or dirty war. War is blood, suffering, burned faces, eyes staring with fever, rain, mud, excrement, filth, rats running over the bodies, monstrous wounds, women and children turned into carrion. War humiliates, dishonors, degrades. It is the horror of the world assembled into a paroxysm of filth, blood, tears, sweat, and urine."

bles, lords of death; man pushed to the extreme, only there finding himself" conveyed to Kageneck "the image I adopted for myself, my brothers and my parents . . . of struggle as principal purpose of life, action supreme, unique."

He continues, ". . . [to understand my reaction you have to know] what had been going on around me for two or three years. . . . There were constant appeals to sacrifice, heroism. The entire people were permanently appealed to for solidarity, self-sacrifice, comradeship, ending social barriers. Was that not what Jünger called for in his books?"

The fatherland? Bizarrely, the word did not appear in what Jünger wrote, or appeared but rarely—on the margins. His subject, Kageneck goes on, was the "community of men who lift themselves above the baseness of the bourgeoisie, above the 'scrapings of café-waiters' as he contemptuously described those incapable of sacrifice. 'An entirely new race,' Jünger wrote in *Combat Viewed as an Interior Experience* [1921], 'men such as the world has never known have come out of the material battles of the first world war, energy become flesh, charged with unequaled power. . . . ' "

Kageneck himself went on to follow the Jüngerian example that had been offered him. He became a Panzer officer, serving on the eastern front—where eventually, he bitterly writes, "we learned that the fatherland was lost, the community of men torn apart, heroism turned to derision; but to the end we remained faithful to Kniebolo." (That was the contemptuous name, denoting a frenzied and evildoing clown, that Jünger gave to Hitler in his Second World War journals.)*

---

* Kageneck, whose father was an aide-de-camp of William II, later wrote three books about the eastern front, one of memoirs; a history of his regiment, defending the honor of his Wehrmacht companions against accusations of atrocities; and in 1996, a work entitled (in its French edition) *Examen de conscience*, reconsidering his own experiences in the light of the evidence produced in Germany in the 1990s of the Wehrmacht's actual implication in atrocities, and reexamining the Wehrmacht command's rationalizations and actions to conceal atrocities and silence protesting officers. In this

The scholar Ernst Kahler, author of *Man the Measure*, has said that Jünger bears "the greatest responsibility for preparing German youth for the Hitler state." The historian Walter Laqueur denies that this is so (in his book *Weimar Culture*). However, the witness of Kageneck can be taken as evidence that if Jünger did not prepare the way for the Hitler state, he certainly prepared the way for Hitler's war, through the intellectual and emotional influence his writing had upon the young men who were to fight that war—which of course is not the same thing.

Notions of manly fulfillment in sacrificial death in a national cause are not only totally unfashionable today but nearly incomprehensible to the contemporary reader. The intelligent writer Ian Buruma, recounting an interview with Jünger in 1993, in *The New York Review of Books*, could make no sense of him at all and was reduced to condescension and ridicule of how frightfully elitist it all was (elitism being the taboo of the 1990s). However, this is one reason precisely why Jünger is important. He represents still another aspect of the decline and demise of the pre-twentieth-century ethic in its most dramatic form. He provided a particular and fatefully influential German response to the violence that accompanied and accomplished that decline.

The national character of Jünger's response was emphasized by Paul Fussell in his marvelous book *The Great War and Modern Memory* (1975), discussing the theatricality of the war's conduct. He reports a British account of the German machine gunner who fired an entire belt without stopping at two minutes before eleven

---

book he also reflected on the roles of his own class, the old aristocracy, and the traditional army leadership in supporting Hitler's ascension, and their lack of civic courage when he was in power. Kageneck subsequently took part in "voyages of reconciliation" by former German soldiers to the cities of Eastern Europe and the former Soviet Union overrun by the German army.

o'clock on the morning of the eleventh of November, 1918, the moment of armistice. The gunner was "then seen to stand up beside his weapon, take off his helmet, bow, and turning about walk slowly to the rear." Fussell says,

> The machine gun actor taking his final bow may have been German, but the eye that noticed and the hand that recorded were British. Instead of reaching toward the cool metaphor of stage plays, [Erich Maria] Remarque, [in *All Quiet on the Western Front*], and Jünger, in *In Storms of Steel*, invoke overheated figures of nightmares and call upon the whole frenzied machinery of Gothic romance. Chapter 4 of *All Quiet* enacts a mad and quite un-British Gothic fantasia as a group of badly disorganized German troops is shelled in a civilian cemetery. Graves are torn asunder, coffins are hurled in the air, old cadavers are flung out—and the narrator and his chums preserve themselves by crawling into the coffins and covering themselves with the stinking cerements. This will remind us less of *Hamlet* than of, say, *The Monk*. In a similar way, Jünger, seeking an imagery adequate to his feelings as the German bombardment reaches a climax before the great attack of March, 1918, conjures up all the traditional violence of Gothic and Renaissance Europe that a Romantic imagination can conceive and packs it into one sentence. After asserting that "the tremendous force of destruction that bent over the field of battle was concentrated in our brains," he writes: "So may a Cellini have raged or werewolves have howled and hunted through the night on the track of blood." As imagery this is disastrous: it sounds worse than war. The British way is more phlegmatic and ironic, more conscious that if the war is not real, it must be not real in a more understandable, social way.

The poet Wilfred Owen called the idea that it is honorable to die for one's nation "the old lie," but it was why the public schools of England were emptied by the rush to enlist in 1914. One reason the idea of a Lost Generation had so powerful and even crippling an effect in Britain after the Great War—even though British casualties were proportionately lower than the German, French, or Russian—is that Britain's elite had so conspicuously sacrificed itself in the very first weeks and months of the war.

Some of the survivors, most of them probably, afterwards felt bitter anger at the waste and final purposelessness of the First World War. In the English-speaking world Robert Graves's *Goodbye to All That* and (in translation and film) Erich Maria Remarque's *All Quiet on the Western Front* were undoubtedly the most influential literary expressions of that sentiment. The idea that ex-soldiers "could make a better job of it" than the politicians was also common, but this took serious revolutionary form only in Italy and Germany. I have already quoted Oswald Mosley's angry rumination on the armistice, but Mosley bore no essential resemblance to Jünger, or to the Arditi, as he had never been in their existential situation. His war service had been brave but conventional.*

Jünger's war was not democratic war for a better world, nor mass war that seemed all waste. It was ennobling war, in which a self-elected elite had for reasons of honor personally taken upon themselves potentially suicidal commitments, leaving the rest of the war to those "sweepings of café-waiters" whose fate was to become, as Jünger also wrote, the "iron-laden day laborers of death."

The moral strategy of the intellectual soldier who embraces violence as part of the reality of existence and embraces it as chivalric duty and obligation of honor ends logically in a political elitism that sets apart men who have risked their existence, cleansing from themselves the selfishness of living. They have not done so as pub-

---

* Mosley was on active service for less than a year, four months as an air observer, and in the trenches for less than five months. The limp that contributed to his saturnine postwar glamour came from a leg injury in an air crash while showing off for his family. It subsequently failed to heal, and caused him to be sent home from France in March 1916, which probably spared him for the Fascist political adventure that followed.

lic duty, as such, since while national authorities may have employed them in a national cause, they made their personal commitment as a moral choice. The political consequences of this in the nationalist movements that followed the Great War have already been seen in the case of the Arditi.

The world war discredited the notion of war as a limited and reasonable instrument of state, which had prevailed from the end of the wars of religion in the Settlement of Westphalia in 1648, establishing the modern state system, until the twentieth century.

The First World War began on the assumption that it would be limited and decisive, it but evolved—to the confusion, dismay, and disorientation of all its participants—into something that had no intrinsic limit or rational goal other than the defeat of the enemy, as if it had become a kind of ultimate and lethally competitive sport. It was not at first an ideological war, although the propaganda of the various sides attempted to redefine it as an affair of good versus evil. It was turned into an ideological war when Woodrow Wilson arrived on the scene, redefining it as the war to end wars and to install everlasting peace—an American contribution to the disasters of the twentieth century. Today it is evident that stopping the world war, or even surrendering, would at any point have been a more rational strategy for any of the participating nations than going on. The horrendous political, social, and cultural consequences of the war were caused by its unintended, unanticipated, and seemingly uncontrollable descent into purposelessness.

The sense made of the experience by Ernst Jünger combined romanticism about the chivalric tradition, which permitted an individual's honor to be preserved in the circumstances of a war without purpose, and the stoic judgment that the course of society and history is tragic. Violence is not only inevitable, essential to the functioning of history, but can provide the means to individual fulfillment. He found his personal solution, such as it was, in heroism as a moral and aesthetic achievement, and he tried to affirm this as a strategy for German society.

Ernst Jünger's books, internationally celebrated, never described the First World War in political or historical terms. The personal experience of the soldier was his subject, and the soldier was himself.* He describes war as a natural disposition of man, and the moral warrant for combat is the principle that what is essential "is not what we fight for but how we fight," an affirmation expressing egoism and aesthetic sensibility as well as the stoic's view of history. Jünger can be described as a dandy in that his concern was with himself, to assure himself of his own merit according to his own standards, which others were welcome to disregard. These are primarily romantic standards, conceiving of the soldier as an ascetic.

He never stood critically outside this self-conception, as did Lawrence (who eventually hated "Colonel Lawrence of Arabia" and tried to extinguish that creation by becoming Aircraftsman Shaw), or aggrandize the image with cunning allusions or outright falsehoods, as with Malraux. It was necessary for Jünger to *be* the creation. Thus the authenticity of Jünger, which was integral to his being as well as to his egoism.

Wachsmann, like Kageneck, observes that concern for the destiny of Germany had never entered into Jünger's world war books. *In Storms of Steel* ends with the end of his personal war career, his receipt of the decoration *Pour le Mérite*, Germany's then-highest award (created by Frederick the Great at a time when French was the language of courts; abolished by Hitler). That Germany shortly

---

* Nikolaus Wachsmann, a Cambridge historian, says that in his early work Jünger "never instrumentalizes the war for political ends—the main aim for Jünger the writer is the heroisation of Jünger the soldier. He wanted admirers, not followers." Wachsmann's monograph, published in the *Journal of Contemporary History* (London) in October 1998, is a comprehensive examination of Jünger's association with National Socialism.

afterwards called for an armistice is not mentioned. "Hitler, in contrast, in *Mein Kampf*, remembers the day of German defeat as the first time he had cried since his mother's funeral."

Jünger's belief in the inevitability of war as a human activity, a version of historical determinism and historical pessimism, seems at variance with his implicit commitment to vitalism, the notion that life is not the sum of natural processes but in significant part is self-determined. He said (in a 1993 interview in *Le Figaro*) that his initial interest in Adolph Hitler was provoked by the latter's determination to act in order to change Germany's situation.

> The Weimar republic disappointed all of us, and a great many Germans said to themselves at the time that something had to change; there had to be something new. . . . [The philosopher Martin] Heidegger [a friend of Jünger's] quickly saw that nothing good was going to come out of all that. One can always say that one should have seen that even earlier, before the putsch against Roehm in 1934, before the first antisemitic measures. . . .

He goes on:

> God knows, the rise of Hitler didn't please me; I was always repulsed by him, but I also said to myself right at the beginning, here's someone who is going to denounce the diktat of Versailles. It seemed to me then that I was in a situation comparable to that of a young French officer after 1871, after France's defeat [by Bismarck, annexing Alsace and Lorraine to Germany]. Your priority in moments like that is to remedy a bad peace. That's what Heidegger wanted too. In 1934 the assassination of Roehm and the liquidation of the SA [the original Nazi Party militia] was the turning that revealed the true nature of the dictatorship, but it was already too late—another word

could cost you liberty or life, and I could see clearly what was going to arrive.

Jünger's pessimism deepened after he abandoned the disappointments of nationalist politics and his connections with National Socialism. Following his political disillusionment, he assumed a stance, no doubt influenced by his zoological interests, of detachment from party politics and what he regarded as humanity's inevitable struggles. He retreated into private life, literature, and science, assuming a political position, or pose, of detached observer of man as zoological phenomenon, subordinated to natural forces, able to be rescued only by the vitalist energies of the individual.

During the Second World War he used his opportunities and influence to spare individuals from suffering, and prepared an earnest, even grandiose, but politically irrelevant plan for postwar European reconciliation, which was circulated among and taken seriously by the military conspirators who tried to kill Hitler in 1944.

Ernst Jünger, the eldest of three brothers and a sister, was born in 1895 to a prosperous chemist and owner of a successful commercial laboratory, a man of wide interests, whose professional success allowed him to retire in his forties. He encouraged his oldest son's early interest in nature and his fascination with the fauna of the Steinhuder Meer (or moor) a few minutes' walk from their home in Hanover. Jünger later wrote of his father's influence,

> I consider what my father related at table more important than all my scholastic education: my taste for history and my judgements of value came in a sense from him. He was typical of the nineteenth century in that he appreciated great personalities, beginning with Achilles, then Alexander the Great, and going up to the conquistadors and Napoleon. . . . He never had breakfast or dinner without speaking in detail on such subjects.

Despite an evangelical Protestant upbringing, the father did not believe in eternal life. Jünger's mother was another rebel against a religious upbringing, and was responsible for the passion her oldest son developed for literature and the importance he attached to speaking a cultivated German. "Language is virtually the most precious gift which parents can leave to their children. However far the spirit of egalitarianism may go, on the first words someone utters you know with whom you are dealing."

In 1911 he joined a troop of Wandervögel, the scoutlike group that unlike Baden-Powell's original British Scout movement, which was inspired by Boer War military scouting and adventure in the field, had its roots in a particular German romanticism about forests and mountains, condemning urban civilization as embodying unnatural values and an unjust social order.

Jünger's biographers are agreed that the sinking of the *Titanic* in 1912, when he was seventeen, greatly influenced him (as Thomas Nevin writes, in his brilliant biographical study) "as a prophetic emblem of our modern fate, set on its irreversible course." Jünger later described the *Titanic*'s collision with an iceberg on its maiden voyage as a metaphor for modern technological society's hubris, challenging impersonal and imperturbable forces of nature.

An attraction to Africa, born of his reading, led him a year later—six months before his final Gymnasium examinations—to pack his copy of Henry Morton Stanley's account of African travel, purchase a pistol, and take the train to Verdun to enlist in the French Foreign Legion, the most direct way he knew to get to Africa. "I had for months been living a secret rebellion which in my circumstances was difficult to hide. Thus I had already stopped going to my classes, preferring to plunge into my books about African journeys." In his *African Games*, published in 1936, he wrote, "I had acquired the conviction that the lost Eden could be found somewhere in the ramifications of the Upper Nile and the Congo."

Despite the advice of a friendly Legion medical officer in Marseille to go home, he got as far as the Legion depot at Sidi bel-

Abbès in French Algeria, where he found that the doctor's had been sound advice. He later wrote that he was "inclined to regard life above every particular of its circumstances as a journey that you could interrupt at any point where it took your fancy. There seemed to me no sufficient reason at hand for staying on in some oppressive or discomforting situation when the world was so great and resourceful." Therefore he deserted, or tried to do so, being arrested the next morning, dutifully turned in by villagers accustomed to receiving the standing reward for collecting legionnaires absent without leave. He was given ten days' confinement (although charges could have been brought requiring six months' imprisonment). By the time his punishment was served, his father, alerted by the sympathetic military doctor in Marseille, had managed to obtain his discharge, the French lawyer he engaged pleading that the enlistment had been *une folie de jeunesse*. The doctor later sent Jünger a letter in which he said "one experiences everything, including its contrary"; Jünger—writing about the episode in 1936—said he had always remembered this, "because I've often found it confirmed."

◦—◦

Nevin provides a description of the cramming-school studies for the final examinations to which the young ex-legionnaire returned. "The humanist tradition and the cult of the military had their scholastic nexus . . . in Homer. Many senior essay topics were based on readings from the *Iliad:* how does Homer depict Agamemnon in the first seven books? how can the failure of the embassy to Achilles be explained? how, among the epic's heroes, does Hector stir our particular sympathy?" Other senior essay topics were "War is as terrible as plagues from heaven, but it is good, it is a fate like them." Or, "How authentic is the saying of Frederick the Great, 'Life means being a warrior,' " and "A nation is worthless if it doesn't set everything upon its honor." The director of the Gymnasium of Meppen warned in a talk to graduates that "if you must in fact be someone's opponent, do not despise and slight his person but seek rather to learn even from him in ready recognition of his brave striving and will."

In Storms of Steel (1920), Jünger's first book, was made from the journal he kept, or reconstructed, from the time of his enlistment in a Hanoverian regiment in 1914 as a volunteer, departing "under a rain of flowers." "The war," he said, "seized us like a drunkenness," offering "grandeur, strength, gravity . . . the joy of close infantry combat, where blood falls to stain the flowers. . . . No more beautiful death in the world! . . . Above all, no longer at home, but admitted to this fraternity!" The regimental veterans offered him and his contingent of recruits arriving at the training base a dose of reality, mocking them as "crazy volunteers."

Assigned to an active sector, his first experience of bombardment finds him "without fear, strictly speaking; not being visible to the enemy I could not believe that they were firing at me, or that I could be wounded. . . . Thus I could look out into no man's land with grand indifference. It was the courage of inexperience."

Then came his first attack, out of the trench and through a woods,

often going blindly from one tree to the next, harassed by flares and the deafening explosions, turning like a hunted beast around enormous tree-trunks. A shelter many of us were making for took a hit, which caused it to fly apart, sending huge pieces of wood into the air. Panting, I and the sergeant headed towards a huge oak, like squirrels being stoned. Whipped by the rush of air from explosions, I automatically followed him; he turned from time to time looking at me with haggard, shining eyes, bawling what's happening! good God, what's going on? A flash suddenly struck the huge roots of the tree and a blow on my left side threw me to the ground. I thought I had been struck by a piece of flying turf but the warmth of blood quickly made me realize that I was hit. Later I found that a piece of shrapnel like a spearhead had hit me, but my billfold had taken part of the shock. The thin missile, which passed through nine layers of leather before reaching muscle, seemed like a razor. I threw down my pack and made for the trench from which we'd come. Wounded were coming from everywhere, running from the woods under fire. The trench entrance was horrible to see, blocked by the gravely wounded and dying . . . I lost my head completely and brutally pushed past, slipping back three times in haste to free myself from this hellish swarm about the trench. I ran like a bolting horse into the thickest part of the woods, across clearings and paths until I fell into the undergrowth near our main trenches. It was nearly dark when two medics searching the sector found me.

It was the first of his wounds; there were to be fourteen in all. All were recounted with the same matter-of-factness and candor. A French commentator describes Jünger's war writing as of *"une sincérité absolue."*

As Nevin writes, the educated officers of all of the Western European armies in the First World War, most of them brought up on the classics, entered the war as a "Homeric" test, a contest which ruthlessly exalted honor over life. "The Homeric scenario informed Jünger to a fateful degree because his experience of the Great War had an objective correlation in the Greek epic. In Homer, the waging of war overwhelms the purported goal itself. There is no promise of eventual peace or an everlasting domination for the victors. Like the warriors before Troy, Jünger was engaged in fighting for its own sake. This final pointlessness is at the heart of Jünger's war memoirs." The act of writing, when he later set out to "reconcile literature with experience . . . gave him a genie's control over his life. It made experience tolerable by a choreographic recast."

But this Homeric sense of war as a matter of "martial renown, the ruthless exaltation of honor over life" and disdain for death, "would have mattered only to that minute fraction of the soldiers on either side who had the inestimable, elitist benefits of a classical education. . . . [T]hose who entered the [1914–1918] war had in their minds' eyes the epic wars of fathers in the ages of Frederick the Great, Napoleon, and Bismarck. Those who went to war in 1914 had no more the intention of waging a battle mechanized to the proportions of a behemoth than of spawning fascism or national socialism."

In September 1915, Jünger entered officer's school. He took part in the Battle of the Somme (July–November 1916). There, he had the experience of seeing advancing British troops, as he had never seen them before, "hundreds of them [shot down], the officers walking in front of them—I saw one, walking calmly, a cane in his hand . . . we started to fire, and then had nothing to do but reload again and again; it wasn't worth aiming, one simply shot into the mass of them." "The spirit of chivalry," he said, "vanished forever during the battle of the Somme."

An English writer, Mark Girouard, has said the same thing (in *The Return to Camelot: Chivalry and the English Gentleman*). The chivalric idea went sour by 1916, or "at least it had received its death wound. . . . As a dominant code of conduct it never recovered from the Great War partly because the war itself was such a shatterer of illusions, partly because it helped produce a world in which the necessary conditions for chivalry were increasingly absent." Jünger affirmed that chivalry was dead, but perversely spent the rest of his life affirming that for him, personally, it was alive.

He was wounded again in August 1916 and once again in November, followed by the award of the Iron Cross, First Class. In his *In Storms of Steel* he notes his reading during his convalescence: Sterne's *Tristram Shandy*, Huysmans's *A Rebours*. . . .

＊〜〇

In February 1917 he became a company commander. The second Battle of the Somme followed. He was wounded again in July. In the fall he joined the storm troops, who carried out quasi-suicidal assaults on the enemy trenches in order to clear the way for regular infantry. As a storm troop leader he found a "feeling of exalted duty and honor, a sports-like joy in danger, the chivalric push to continue the battle [unknown to ordinary front-line soldiers, those 'patient, iron-laden day laborers of death']." Michael Howard, the military historian and founder of the International Institute for Strategic Studies (himself wearer of Britain's Military Cross), wrote in *The Invention of Peace* that the stalemate of the First World War was eventually broken not by the primitive tank but

> by the precise and flexible use of artillery in support of storm troops capable of providing their own firepower with light machine-guns, flame-throwers, grenades and mortars; groups in which command was devolved down to junior officers and below. . . . The first world war had produced such men, especially in the German army. Their symbol was the grim, purposeful Stahlhelm [steel helmet] that had replaced the faintly comic Pickelhaube [the ornamental prewar helmet crowned by a spike] in 1916. They were classless, efficient, and above all they enjoyed fighting. Peace left them désoeuvrés, as it had the knights of the fourteenth century.

The experience reinforced Jünger's vitalist conviction that matter is subject to the human will and spirit. This belief lay behind his eventual political conclusion that a revolution could be produced by an "emanation of new ideas" finding expression in a body of martyrs and prophetic leaders who would create a dictatorship that could "substitute deed for word, blood for ink, sacrifice for phrase, and sword for pen." It was the line of thought that led him toward National Socialism.

He was grievously wounded in November 1917, and was made a Knight of the Order of Hohenzollern. In 1918, as the German army faltered, he received his final wounds. His appointment to the Order Pour le Mérite, rarely given to a junior officer, and practically never to a twenty-three-year-old lieutenant, was opposed by

Marshal von Hindenburg as a bad precedent. Jünger was in a military hospital when the war ended.

⌗

His self-published (on his father's advice) account of his war experience, *In Storms of Steel*, which came out in 1920, immediately made him famous. He remained in the army (the postwar Reichswehr), working on a redraft of infantry regulations and other military assignments while writing his reflection on the meaning of war, *Battle as Inner Experience*, published in 1922. In it he argued that primeval instinct had ruptured the thin membrane of civilization, and when that happens "the cave dweller [the *urmensch*] breaks forth in the total release of impulse." "Humanity," as Nevin summarizes Jünger, "situated between the divine and the animal, becomes in war . . . divinely animal, something exultantly non-human." Jünger saw this in the transcendental sensations of the war's beginning and in "its will to annihilation . . . in the contest of weapons and in the wanton violence of troops." He also said that "battle is made sacred by its cause, but still more is a cause made sacred by its battle," an attractive paradox which is also an irresponsible argument, philosophically and morally.

⌗

Jünger left the army in 1923 and entered the University of Leipzig to study the natural sciences, but his romanticism was repelled by the scientists' quantification and instrumentalization of reality. However, zoology and marine biology fascinated him, and entomology would become a lifelong passion. He took courses in philosophy and psychology as well, serving during this period as a volunteer Freikorps officer, responsible for the activities in Saxony of the Freikorps Rossbach, formed in East Prussia in late 1918.*

---

* These "free corps," formations of demobilized soldiers, were first organized under official sponsorship in the winter of 1918–1919 to defend the Social Democratic Weimar government of Gustav Noske against the revolutionary left. Their creation

His novella *Sturm* was published as a newspaper serial in Hanover in 1923. It dealt with wartime relationships among a zoology student turned soldier, a professional soldier, and an artist ("all of them pieces of Jünger himself"). In 1925 Jünger transferred to the university's marine biology research station in Naples. During that same year he married Gretha von Jeinsen, from a Hanoverian military family, whom he had met when she was a nineteen-year-old student at the university. With marriage, a military pension, an annuity from his father, and successful books, he was financially independent.

His serious activity in the nationalist cause began the following year. He began writing and editorial work in support of a version of nationalist politics in which he imagined that the courage and solidarity of the battlefield could find expression in a political movement. His first published political article appeared in the new Nazi Party's *Völkischer Beobachter* in 1923. It called for a national dictatorship.*

Jünger's beliefs reflected the Social Darwinian conviction of the late nineteenth and early twentieth centuries that struggle between

---

lent legitimacy to the paramilitary bodies that already had sprung up in the east of Germany to fight the Poles and Bolsheviks, in the Baltic states, and later in the Ruhr to resist the French military occupation. Eventually there were sixty-eight such units of varying but overwhelmingly anti-Weimar political and social views. This militarization of German politics during the Weimar period contributed to the rise of the National Socialists, whose brown-shirt SA (*Sturmabteilung*) was of Freikorps origin. The French historian of the Freikorps, Dominique Venner (*Histoire d'un fascisme allemand*, Paris), writes that while Jünger never took part in the Freikorps' combats, he was the dominant intellectual figure on the national-revolutionary right and was intimately associated with the development of the Freikorps and the phenomenon's political prolongation in the pre-Nazi period.

* A nationalist peroration—"Germany lives and shall never go under!"—was added to the 1926 edition of *In Storms of Steel*, but a decade later was removed from subsequent editions.

the strong and the weak or ill-adapted was the natural mechanism by which the animal kingdom survived and progressed, the human race included. There was a political conclusion to be drawn from this. The military elite thrown up by the war was a body of natural leaders of all nationalities, alone capable, because of their ordeal, to comprehend what civilization had become and to find a resolution to its crisis. They were a new "race" in a metaphorical sense, their "blood" a metaphysical life force. They were in no biological sense a race; Jünger was a scientist and could not take seriously Nazi racism and anti-Semitism, all of which he said "must degenerate into nonsense." "Blood," he said, "legitimates itself more by achievements than by purity."

His *Völkischer Beobachter* article condemned the materialistic Weimar republic and concluded with an endorsement of *völkische*, or "nationalist," dictatorship, "symbolized by the swastika." Jünger said that he believed nationalist revolution more "idealistic" than the materialism of the Communists and Socialists, or of the bourgeois parties. Nikolaus Wachsmann suggests that by 1923, after five years in a peacetime army, under an unstable and frustrated republic, he also wanted the excitement of a revolution. However, the *Völkischer Beobachter* article was in notable contrast to the essentially individualistic, vitalist, and self-regarding outlook of everything he had written until then.

Intellectual elitist though he was, and although he was simultaneously active in Expressionist artistic circles and was a friend of Bertolt Brecht (the playwright who despite a wartime Hollywood exile—as Bert Brecht, the screenwriter—was to become one of the most famous of all Western European Communist literary figures), Ernst von Salomon (film writer and fellow nationalist), and Ernst Toller, the Expressionist poet and dramatist. Jünger in this period employed the vicious and demagogic vocabulary of national socialist polemics, describing some Weimar intellectuals as "pimps" and "filth." His attachment was to a nationalist faction called the National Bolshevist Caucus, of which he was a founder and the ideologist, led by Ernst Niekisch (deported in 1937, murdered by the Gestapo in prison in 1945). It conceived of an alliance of workers with aristocratic warriors.

Jünger's modern apologists argue that in 1923 Hitler was only one of a number of nationalist political figures, and Nazism was not what it was to become by 1932, not to speak of 1939 and 1940, so that Jünger cannot be blamed for what eventually came out of the movement to which he committed himself in the 1920s. However, his employment of the Nazi vocabulary was a concession to that dehumanization of opponents that was an essential characteristic of the Nazi movement and of its proto-totalitarian counterpart of the period, Bolshevism. In the abstract, Jünger demanded the sacrifice of the individual to the nation, led by a charismatic dictator. He was on the left of the nationalist movement but rejected class war in favor of an alliance that could re-create in civilian society the solidarity of combat, and would be led by those who had validated their leadership and already demonstrated the priority of their national commitment by the selfless offer of their lives in combat. He wanted "soldiers as leaders in the battle for power and workers as leaders in the battle for the economy"—an unrealizably romantic notion.

Wachsmann suggests that Jünger may have distanced himself from Hitler and the Nazis because he considered himself a proven leader, in contrast to the former corporal and company runner, Adolph Hitler. However, he also seems never to have sought party or political leadership for himself. This again was the stance of the self-sufficient dandy who considers himself rather better than the rest, even if he chooses not to impose his superiority.

He respected the ruthlessness of the Bolsheviks in Russia and consistently objected to the Nazis' willingness to work through parliamentary institutions and stand for elections, which he considered a compromising collaboration with the discredited bourgeoisie, whereas he wanted revolution. In fact, if the Nazi party had followed his advice it probably would never have taken power. Hitler was successful because he did play the parliamentary game, with a ruthlessness the other parties lacked, turning the parliamentary plurality he won in 1932 into a successful claim to the chancellorship in 1933. The revolutionary Jünger's eventual break with the Nazis was caused in part by his belief that Hitler was merely an opportunist.

It was also the result of an intellectual evolution. Jünger was never a serious politician. He was a literary intellectual with an interest in politics, which is quite a different matter. This would become evident again, in the 1940s, when he drafted his "Word to the Youth of Europe," called *The Peace*, which was completed in the spring of 1944 and envisaged a new universalism incorporating a unified postwar Europe under a strong government, ruling over an organic regionalism, resting culturally on a revivified and reunited Christianity—a proposal not only hopelessly remote from the ideas driving events in Nazi-ravaged Europe in 1944–1945 but indicating no understanding of the uncompromising hatred of Germany that by then existed throughout Europe, or the avowed determination of the western Allies at that point, as well as of the Soviet Union, to impose a Carthaginian peace on Germany—to sow salt in the ashes.*

By the 1930s he had become much more interested in archetypes and metapolitics than in the commonplace and frequently sordid politics of the nationalist movement, with its mediocre members.

---

* *The Peace* imagined a postwar consolidation of Europe to preserve its identity and civilization against Soviet Russia and the United States. This was a theme commonly taken up by conservative Germans opposed to Hitler, but was totally at odds with wartime British and American attitudes and plans, and inconsistent with the apocalyptic and exterminatory character the war itself already had assumed. The first senior commander who read the completed version of this document (on General Speidel's urging) was Erwin Rommel—five weeks before the Normandy landings.

He now was writing in abstract terms about the great issues of technology and mass society. By 1930, when he began work on his book *The Worker* (*Der Arbeiter*) he had become convinced that a society resting on individual humans had been decisively undermined by technology. He describes the arrival of the "newcomer," the source of a new energy, who acts out of nihilism and a Nietzschean will to power to bring about a planetary mobilization of the power of technology and annihilate all forms of transcendence, including leisure, pleasure, and love, reducing man to robot. The influences of the Expressionism of the period, of Nietzsche and Spengler, and of German romantic thought are apparent. Heidegger was fascinated and influenced by the work, although it had little attention outside Germany at the time.* He was a man of his times and his society in his preoccupation with man's cosmic situation, and neither *The Worker* nor *The Peace* works very well for those formed in the realist, positivist, or even the bluff commonsense schools of British and American philosophical and political speculation.

Nevin says:

> His belief that the new world order would induce a succession of wars was more than a concession to . . . [a] hardheaded antiutopianism . . . : because, in his ethic, the new humanity wants commands, not promises, and the deepest joy lies in sacrifice, not convenience, the iteration of conflict is virtual necessity, the indispensable condition for stringent virtues.

❧

By the time Jünger abandoned Hitler, Hitler had himself decided that Jünger was a troublesome dissident and defector from the Na-

---

* The American scholar Walter Struve has said that reading *The Worker*, "one often feels in the midst of a dream—or nightmare. Every image, every scene seems precise, but on reflection becomes obscure. . . . [It] moves gracefully from one point to the next but no point ever seems to be completed," something which could be said of much of Jünger's theoretical writing, at least as it appears in English.

tionalist cause. After Hitler came to power, Jünger suffered the attention and visits of the Gestapo, although he was protected from serious harm by his military prestige. This was to remain the case, narrowly, until just before the war's end. Following the Night of the Long Knives in 1934, when the radical wing of the Nazi Party, led by Ernst Roehm, head of the SA, was destroyed in a series of murders by the SS, which Jünger condemned, Goebbels denounced Jünger as an enemy of the Nazi government.*

Jünger moved his family to the country, resuming his entomological research. He refused election to the German Academy of Literature in 1933. He traveled a great deal and was offered a post abroad by the ministry of foreign affairs, which he refused. In 1939 he bought a former presbytery at Kirchhorst, near Hanover. In September 1939 his allegorical novel, *On the Marble Cliffs*, appeared, a veiled attack on the regime (although the principal villain, "the Head Ranger," a figure of indiscriminate evil, is an immensely rich and "terrifyingly jovial" forest-dwelling warlord—a portrait of Goering, not Hitler). George Steiner called it "the sole major act of resistance, of internal sabotage, in German literature under the Hitler regime."

At the end of August 1939 he was mobilized, and after a brief officers' refresher course was sent to command an infantry company, and to the Sigfried line. There he was again decorated, this time for an act of compassion during the skirmishes along the Rhine in the spring of 1940, recovering under artillery fire the body of a noncommissioned officer.

He took part in the campaign in France that followed. He said to a French interviewer in 1991, who asked about "his" war: "It was not my war. It was Hitler's. I spent the 'phony war' for the most part

---

* An interviewer asked Jünger in 1993 if he had not been afraid of Hitler. He said, "I have often wondered if, fundamentally, it was not he who was afraid of me."

on the Rhine as a company commander. Thank God, I didn't kill or even wound a single man. I feel a certain irony about what followed. Being horse-transported, we never managed to make contact with the enemy, since our tanks were so far ahead of us. . . ."

Stationed in Vincennes, outside Paris, after the armistice, he met the then-colonel Hans Speidel, chief of staff of the German military command in France, who in June 1941 ordered Jünger posted to his own staff in Paris. The military governor at the time was General Otto von Stülpnagel, in Jünger's view an intelligent but weak man, able to see where events were leading but without the strength or will to confront "minds that know no other motive than force."* (Stülpnagel was subsequently responsible for the policy of executing hostages and imposing other brutal reprisals for attacks on German soldiers, which served to provoke rather than deter the developing French Resistance.)

"Speidel knew my books and knew that in Berlin they had been discussing my 'case' because of the publication of *On the Marble Cliffs*, taken as a veiled critique of the regime. He protected me, in short. . . . It was under Speidel's sponsorship that we were able to form in Paris, inside the military machine—at the heart of the beast—a small circle of men faithful to the spirit of chivalry." They were the core of the Paris Wehrmacht's resistance to the power of the SS, and were part of the network eventually responsible for the 1944 attempt to kill Hitler. Speidel in 1944, as the Germans retreated from Paris, countermanded Hitler's order to burn the city.

The group was billeted in the small but elegant Hotel Raphael (still as elegant today) on the Avenue Kléber, next to the German

---

* According to his friend Banine, years later, Jünger said, "The men of 20 July all had very high foreheads and not much chin. Those on the other side had low foreheads (he gestured to his own) and necks like this (new demonstration). Thus you knew in advance how it would finish." She goes on, "Later he based his hopes on Rommel, an energetic character brutal enough to face up to the Nazis," but Rommel was killed before he could act.

military headquarters in the Majestic Hotel (now gone), and referred to themselves as "the Raphaelites."

＊○

Stülpnagel was interested in approaching the literary and intellectual elite among the Parisian French in the expectation of influencing French opinion. Jünger was given light duties of a historical and intelligence nature (later including censorship of civilian letters from Germany, which he found greatly affecting), leaving him considerable time for his own writing and for developing the relationships he already had, from before the war, in French literary and artistic circles. In Paris he also began to draft his project for postwar Europe. Speidel managed to keep him in Paris until 1944, despite the hostility of Field Marshal Wilhelm Keitel, chief of staff of the Supreme Command, who considered Jünger a traitor and wanted him sent to the Russian front.

In Paris, he wrote the journals that three decades later were to make him celebrated in France. He became an habitué of Paris literary and social circles, particularly the salon maintained by the San Francisco–born Florence Lacaze, who had become the mistress, and in 1923 the third and last wife, of Frank Jay Gould, an heir to the fortune of the notorious nineteenth-century American robber baron. A vivid and generous hostess during all her married life (Sybille Bedford, the novelist, said that when Florence Gould "entered a room, people immediately became more vivacious"), war and German occupation posed for her no obstacle to the serious matters of entertainment and conversation. Her salon was frequented by an apolitical, reactionary, or collaborationist part of the Parisian intelligentsia, including Jean Cocteau; the diplomat, poet, and novelist Paul Morand; and the writers Giraudoux, Montherlant, and Drieu La Rochelle, together with several cultivated and handsome German officers. (Jünger and Cocteau discovered a common interest in hallucinogens. Cocteau was an opium addict, and storm troop officers, pilots, and others on the German side in the world war had discovered it to be a useful stimulant. Jünger remained interested in the subject throughout his life.)*

Jünger also met the beautiful and brilliant "Banine," who became for the rest of his stay in Paris his constant yet detached friend and companion (she, like others, attests to his incapacity for emotional intimacy). She provided a notable portrait of him and of their friendship in a book published in 1989.† His connection with the officers active in the anti-Hitler project that eventually resulted in the bungled June 20, 1944, assassination attempt remained largely passive—he was a sympathizer, but again detached.

His new commander as military governor, Karl Heinrich von Stülpnagel (cousin of Otto, his predecessor in the office), sent him to the Caucasus on a three-month assignment in 1943, coincident with the developing German catastrophe at Stalingrad. (He wrote in his journal, "At headquarters the atmosphere is much heavier than with the troops because here one sees the overall situation. The encirclement [at Stalingrad] provokes a state of soul unknown in our previous wars, a sort of numbing as if by cold, corresponding to the approach of absolute zero" (January 7, 1943). He heard the rumors of mass gassing of the Jews. ("I feel an impulse of disgust at the sight of uniforms, epaulettes, decorations, arms; these things

---

* After the war, Florence Gould suffered some difficulties connected with indiscretions of what was called *"collaboration horizontale,"* an activity that as pursued by many less privileged young French women caused them to have their heads shaven and be pilloried in the streets at the Liberation. In Florence's case, with a low profile and high contacts, the matter was managed, and eventually let drop.

† Umm El Banine Assadoulaeff was born to a rich Azerbaijani family. She seized the opportunity of a visit to Constantinople to abandon a husband she had been forced to marry at fifteen, and whom she despised, fleeing to Paris. There, literary acquaintances, including Montherlant, Kazantzakis, and Malraux urged her to publish. Her journals and other works were much later to inspire the post-Communist republic of Azerbaijan to demand her return as "a national glory"—an invitation which she declined. She died in October 1992. Her obituary in the newspaper *Le Figaro* called her "one of those personages of *la vie romanesque* who traverse a century, attracting like a lodestone all the singular figures of their times."

that I once prized—shattered. The old chivalry is finished. Wars now are waged by technicians. Man has become the personage Dostoyevsky described in his character Raskolnikov, who considered his fellows vermin—which is exactly what has to be avoided if one is not to become an insect oneself" [December 31, 1942].) He was ostensibly on the eastern front to evaluate morale, but his colleagues in Paris actually wanted him to assess the readiness of officers there to support an attempt to remove Hitler. The death of Jünger's father cut the assignment short.*

In February 1944, Jünger's seventeen-year-old son, serving with the navy, was imprisoned for criticizing the regime, then sent to disciplinary duty on the Italian front, where within a week he was killed by Italian partisans at Carrara.† After the July plot against Hitler failed, Jünger was transferred from active to auxiliary duty while a case against him alleging high treason was prepared, and in October an order was issued for his dishonorable discharge. In August he had written in his journal: "During recent weeks I have known the bitterness one feels at seeing the best dragged in the slime. In the First World War my friends died at the front—in this one that is the privilege of the happy ones. The rest rot in prisons, are forced to commit suicide or die at the hands of the executioner. The bullet is refused them." In November he wrote: "I am now at a point when the sight of these nihilists becomes physically unsupportable." He also wrote, "while crime spreads on earth like a plague, I abandon myself in the mystery of flowers. Ah!, more than

---

* He returned to Germany for the funeral, then to Paris, where he wrote in his journal that many of his wife's letters describing the mounting Allied heavy bomber offensive against cities in western Germany were "taking on an unholy eschatological quality, like calls from the maelstrom's lowest ring."

† Jünger's second son, a physician, committed suicide in 1993.

ever, glory to their petals. . . ." The war ended before his trial arrived.*

⤙◯

After the war, he declined to fill out the denazification questionnaire issued by the Allied Occupation authorities. They forbade him to publish, because of his nationalist record (the interdiction was lifted in 1949).† He deliberately affirmed a Germany that refused to become Westernized or Americanized.

Jünger never attempted to explain himself other than indirectly, through his novels and journals, the later of which are almost completely apolitical. He said once on German radio, "I am immune to praise." He said of the postwar German Federal Republic in 1982, in a *Spiegel* interview, "My wife and I are loyal citizens, but not enthusiastic ones, of the Federal Republic. For us the reality is the German Reich." His American biographer, Thomas Nevin, wrote (when Jünger was still alive) that as scientist-writer "he affirms an intelligible cosmos of constantly unfolding mystery and beauty, and he affirms the human mind as its worthy celebrant." Nevin describes Jünger's primary themes: "that warfaring is an ineradicable part of our psyche, that technology's gifts to us are sinister, and that

---

* In 1993 he was asked by a *Le Monde* interviewer about his writings on nihilism. He said, "I consider nihilism finished. Action has become so powerful that there is no more time for nihilism. . . . Nihilism is an affair of boredom; it's good for the rich."

† His sometime friend and collaborator in the nationalist cause, Ernst von Salomon, who spent five years in prison as an accomplice in the murder of the liberal statesman Walter Rathenau in 1922, filled out the questionnaire at sardonic and anecdotal length and published the result in 1951 as a book which sold more than a quarter of a million copies in Germany, *Der Fragebogen* ("The Questionnaire" in German, published under that title in the United States and as *The Answers* in Britain in 1954). It is a brilliant and fascinating document in Germany's historical accounting, or dissimulating, as Salomon possessed "the supreme virtue of a writer which is founded on a deep sympathy with some of the most secret and profound instincts of his people," as Goronwy Rees wrote in his introduction to the British edition.

the beauty in nature's order is our stay against confusion and despair."

✦

Jünger's subsequent career was productive and tranquil, even though there was continuing criticism of him in Germany for his nationalist past and glorification of wartime combat. He eventually published more than fifty books, dealing with science and philosophy as well as novels. He tried drama, but said, "Perhaps you have to be more sociable than I am to write good dialogue."

He made adjustments to the biographical record by suppressing some of his political writings of the 1920s, excluding them from his collected works, and several times reediting some of his books of the period. His undoubted apoliticism, or antipoliticism, of later years was often back-projected by those, particularly in France, who wrote about him while unaware of his earlier views. He published, traveled, and continued to pursue his entomological studies, assembling important collections of insects (armored beetles were his special interest; a beetle bears his name, *Trachydora Juengeri*, as does a golden wasp, *Cleptes Juengeri*; he said that "a writer can be forgotten but the name of an insect remains, whatever happens"). He also made an important collection of sandglasses and wrote a book about the measurement of time. In the 1960s he created new scandal by writing a dispassionate account of his experiments with hallucinogenic drugs.

✦

The literary merits of his works were in his time all but universally acknowledged. The French writer Julien Gracq said his was a "Goethean attempt to read and decypher the universe." The late Bruce Chatwin said that "the scale of his erudition is titanic; his singularity of purpose is unswerving; . . . He writes a hard, lucid prose. Much of it leaves the reader with an impression of the author's imperturbable self-regard, of dandyism, of cold-bloodedness, and, finally, of banality. Yet the least promising passages will suddenly light up with flashes of aphoristic brilliance, and the most harrowing descriptions are alleviated by a yearning for human values in a dehumanized world." Ralf Dahrendorf called him "an author who fascinates without informing, who creates a crystal world without color of warmth, a man whose brilliance is untainted by any trace of morality" (which is not true). Gide praised him. He was, without participating himself, at the center of a continuing debate between intellectuals of the Right and Left in Germany. As one writer, André Müller, wrote in the weekly *Die Zeit:*

> After the war when Germany had to find a solution by which "that"—National Socialism—would never come back, it was intolerable to suggest that "that" also was part of the human being. Germany, the Left in particular, did not want to look for evil within itself. It preferred to blame Nazism on external causes: social conditions, evil leaders, so as to pretend that "it" could never happen again. Jünger insisted that everything that occurred under Hitler was durably part of the human being. That for years was terribly difficult to accept in Germany.

By the 1980s Jünger was, in Germany, the most printed of any German author other than Thomas Mann. In 1980 the city of Frankfurt awarded him its Goethe prize, although this was again accompanied by controversy, not so much about his past but because he had become a symbolic figure in the German intellectual wars. He said to a 1993 interviewer, "Everyone writes novels. I did several in connection with my times. But I would say that I prefer the essay, maxims, aphorisms. . . ." Asked if art must be reserved to an elite, he said, "in any case it has to be theological. There has to be a relation to the divine. If not, it is nothing; yet in a short poem this relationship can be more powerful than in the *opera omnia* of a great man. My formation has given me no particular reason to admire Léon Bloy, but he is a singular figure in that he has succeeded in achieving that relationship. . . . Rimbaud did too. Why do you think young people have so much respect for him?"

❧

When his translated wartime journals began to appear in France in the 1960s and after, they found an unexpected popularity.* His international reputation was, in the French expression, "sulfurous," tainted by his political past. However, in September 1984 French president François Mitterrand, who had a lifelong taste for sulfurous personalities, and Germany's Chancellor Helmut Kohl made him part of the official Franco-German observance of the seventieth anniversary of the Battle of Verdun. In November he was Mitterrand's guest at the Élysée Palace in Paris. Chancellor Kohl came to his Wilflingen home for his ninetieth birthday.

In 1986, when he was ninety-one, he went to Malaysia and Sumatra to observe the passage of Halley's Comet. In 1910 his father had gathered the five Jünger children to watch the comet's passage, saying that perhaps the youngest, Wolfgang, would live to see it again. Wolfgang was the first of the children to die, and Ernst, the eldest, the last. In 1988 Chancellor Kohl took him to Paris as part of the of-

---

* In one entry he noted his habit of frequenting a certain bookstore in Paris. In August 1996 a letter appeared in *Le Monde* in which a Jewish physician, Georges Sée, said that in June 1942, wearing the required yellow star, he had just left an Avenue Kléber bookstore at around three o'clock in the afternoon, and encountered a German officer. "Arriving in front of me, he gave a military salute, and passed on. I looked around me. The avenue was deserted! The event upset me. I have wondered ever since at the significance of that gesture. I am now 91 years old. More than 50 years ago I related the episode in a brief story of my life meant for my children, grandchildren, and great-grandchildren. The story was passed about the family until a day, last April, when one of my grandnephews called me to draw my attention to a passage in the *Journal Parisien* of Ernst Jünger [concerning his dismay and sense of shame of his uniform when meeting young girls wearing the yellow star]. I then wrote to Jünger by way of his publisher. . . . I have now received a card from him, written in French, in which he says: 'Cher Monsieur. You saw me entering the bookshop of Madam Cardot, Avenue Kléber, a Jewish friend of mine. . . . I always saluted 'l'Étoile' [the star]."

ficial delegation observing the silver anniversary of the Franco-German Treaty of Reconciliation. In 1993 the chancellor and the French president jointly visited him in Wilflingen. He had become a monument. Two years later, German president Roman Herzog, Chancellor Kohl, and the president of Baden-Wurtemberg called in observance of his hundredth birthday.

✎

Jünger's original interest in religion was cultural. He read the *Spiritual Exercises* of Ignatius Loyola in the early 1920s but, he said, for their interest as a method of self-discipline. He began reading in the Bible during the summer of the phony war. His journal says that in September 1941 he set himself to read it through from beginning to end. He continued this throughout the war, reading it first as literature, later as more. His initial interest in the Catholic church was provoked by its cultural resilience and power, and by its historical place in European civilization, which explains the role he assigned to Christianity in his vain scheme for postwar European reconciliation and reconstruction.

He came under the influence of the work of two Catholic novelists, Georges Bernanos and Léon Bloy. He had reviewed Bernanos's *Soleil de Satan* (*The Star of Satan*) when it came out in Germany in 1928. He saw in it not only its religious content but "a proud, innate hatred of all that's common: rest, peace, and cheap happiness." His review compared its spirit with the commitment of the revolutionary soldier-worker who was his ideal figure at the time. Bernanos had been in the trenches for four years and wrote in "a language made possible only after and through the war." He was also impressed by Bernanos's determined questioning of his church at the same time that he was intensely committed to the reality of its spiritual life and to the struggle of good with the very real powers of evil. The devil figures prominently as a force (and ambiguously as a personage) in *The Star of Satan*, Bernanos's *Diary of a Country Priest*, and *Monsieur Ouine* (*The Open Mind,* in its British publication in 1945).*

Bernanos, a royalist who had been associated with Action Française and was considered a reactionary in the politico-cultural controversies of the 1930s, made himself the most determined and notorious French Catholic enemy of Franco, his position being that crimes committed in the name of religion were more reprehensible than crimes committed against it. He contributed to the Free French radio and press from wartime South American exile, identifying the Nazis as avatars of the Pagan State, whose triumph had been invited by the cowardice and greed of the European bourgeoisie.

➻

Before the war, Jünger's friend, the legal philosopher Carl Schmitt had recommended reading Léon Bloy. Bloy was a controversial failure in his own time (1846–1917), scatological polemicist, visionary, would-be saint, but his eventual influence on twentieth-century Catholicism was very great, by the 1940s extending even to the provincial Catholic colleges of the United States, as well as to the Wehrmacht general staff in Paris. Jünger's initial interest was appreciation for the mechanics and style of Bloy's novels as well as for the personality of this "pilgrim of the absolute," an anachronism in his own time. The neo-Thomist philosopher Jacques Maritain called Bloy "a contemporary of Tertullian and Origen, a Christian of the second century astray in the Third Republic." (Maritain was his godchild, he and his Jewish fiancée, Raïssa, having been turned away from suicide by meeting Bloy in 1905 when they were twenty-year-old students, bearing within them, as Mari-

---

* Malraux later recounted Bernanos's answer to the question of what had changed in Europe since his wartime exile in South America. "In ten seconds he said to me what would have taken me ten minutes. [He said that] with the concentration camps Satan has visibly reappeared over the world."

tain wrote, "that distress which is the only serious product of modern culture.")

Bloy himself said, "I am not a contemporary." A mystic, vituperator of his enemies, impoverished during most of his life, he also said, "My only recourse is the expedient of placing at the service of Truth what has been given me by the Father of Lies." Jünger wrote on March 5, 1943: "Finished Léon Bloy's *Four Years of Captivity at Cochons-sur-Marne*, his journal from 1900 to 1904. What struck me most this time was his complete insensibility to the illusions of technique. Amidst the crowds at the Universal Exhibition of 1900, he lives as a hermit, enemy of the modern. In the automobile he sees a powerful engine of destruction. Generally, he connects technology with approaching catastrophe. . . ."

Nevin says that Jünger was fascinated by Bloy's conviction concerning "private access to the supernatural world." In July 1942 Jünger noted in his journal that "twice [Bloy] mentions that dead people awakened him; they knocked on his door or he heard their names spoken. Then he arose and prayed for their salvation. Thus perhaps our lives are saved not only through prayers said in the past but by prayers to come, to be said after our deaths."

Bloy's great enemy was "the Bourgeois" (an entity to be capitalized). Maritain said Bloy "was the complete opposite of the anarchist who hates the members of the bourgeoisie; he is a Christian who hates the Bourgeois, which is, for those who can understand, one of the modern names of the old Enemy."

Jünger was a self-identified enemy of the bourgeoisie for other reasons, personal rather than moral, notably his commitment to elitism, but also evident in his relations with his parents.*

---

* Nevin remarks that even though Jünger's origins were in the professional bourgeoisie and he had a private income and substantial family of his own, only once in family photographs does Jünger "look even vaguely at home. . . . Perhaps Jünger's anti-middle-class sentiments, which surface repeatedly in his Weimar journalism, conceal a deep yet strongly contained attraction to this way of life that his self-image did not allow him to admit. Who he was and what he had become he had learned from

Nevin writes that it was

substantially thanks to Bloy that Jünger won distance from his own nontheistic fatalism in which the world seems a puppet theater governed by cold and immutable laws, with past and future played out like a senseless card game. "It is humanity's privilege not to know the future," [Jünger] writes. "That is one of the diamonds in the diadem of the will's freedom. Were man to lose it, he would become an automaton in an automatic world." Bloy's *amor fati* engaged Jünger because it had a fervor far deeper than anything humanism could achieve, and a more elevating freedom than mere voluntarism could afford. By the summer of 1943, Jünger was using his own freedom of will in a new way, prayer. It is as though the aristocratic confidence and aloofness has been fissured, the need of something beyond the self at last acknowledged.

The radical belief of Bloy, like that of Bernanos, challenged the detachment that had always characterized Jünger, his remoteness from other human beings and from his subjects. Bloy and Bernanos committed themselves to the identification and confrontation with the force that had manifested itself in Jünger's Germany. In July 1943 Jünger identified his religious sentiments in terms of his obligation to truth. "I can violate moral laws and be treacherous to my

---

war," which is perhaps a reductionist comment. However Jünger's "dogged turning away from intimacy" is expressed in his approving reference in *The Worker* to "the oriental gardens in which no one has memory of father or mother." Friends noted a seeming inability to form, or at least express, deep emotional relationships. His journals mention his wife and sons only incidentally, as if they were supernumeraries. Banine wrote that in the spring of 1944, in fear of the Allied bombings, she decided to leave Paris. She telephoned Jünger to tell him so. "Suddenly, and for the first time in our friendship, he became animated. He seemed a creature of flesh and blood. For a moment I could believe that my going meant something to him. 'It's not possible, it's absurd!' he cried. He seemed bewildered. But my comforting impression that I counted for something for him lasted only a few seconds. His customary coolness returned: perhaps annoyed with himself that he should have displayed a little warmth."

neighbor, but I cannot swerve from what I recognize as genuine and true . . . my approach to theology comes through knowledge. I have to prove God to myself before I can believe in him. That means I have to go back along the same way on which I abandoned Him." In 1987 he renounced the Lutheranism into which he had been born and became a Roman Catholic. In February 1998, he died, on his one hundred and third birthday.

CHAPTER FIVE

━━━━━━━━━

THE HAPPY MAN

Ideological war, which is to say utopian war, in the twentieth century tested human or spiritual possibility, implying a test of our understanding of existence, demanding in nearly every case that "conventional" morality be sacrificed to the demands of a utopian vision.

There were some, however, during the Second World War, and among those taking part in the military sideshows of the cold war, who resisted the categories of ideological warfare. They possessed an intellectual detachment enabling them to keep their view of the Nazi or Marxist-Leninist-Maoist phenomena within an historical framework, rather than the Manichean and apocalyptic one postulated by the enemy ideology. They were prepared to argue that while the wars against these totalitarian movements were well worth waging, they were not really "struggles for the world" (adapting the sometime Trotskyist James Burnham's phrase), which would imply acceptance of the immense and utopian/dystopian ambitions of these movements. History is long; even the most terrible political events are passing ones and eventually self-rectifying (demonstrated by the waning and collapse, because of internal contradictions and their defiance of human nature, of Stalinism and Maoism). It is art and intellectual work that ultimately count, and morality and virtue are the measures of human worth and accomplishment.

These people who held themselves intellectually apart made what might be called a stoic affirmation of solidarity with their society in its crisis, or simply acted in acknowledgment of the historical and human situation they shared with their fellows, and the demands thereby imposed. This is not always an easy position even in a "good" war, such as the Second World War, and is a very difficult one, reflecting an essentially insoluble moral predicament, in such a war as Vietnam, or Iraq (speaking as an American).*

To go to war is not proposed as a choice for most people, but for some it is, and for them it ought to be an existential moral choice, an act of responsible decision contributing to the making of oneself into what one is to be. The issue should be considered a moral one involving discrimination among comparative evils and the perceived consequences, and the inevitable prudential problem of intentions, doing evil in the intention of doing good, an ancient problem.

In practice, escape, the taste for adventure, or a straightforward patriotism are decisive factors. The influence of the twilight of chivalry can be seen among young men who read too much, but that is a superficial rather than deep influence in that chivalry, as an

---

* The Second World War was a popular war for its major participants because populations in Russia, Europe, and Japan considered national survival at stake. (Such is what Americans were encouraged to think when the "war on terrorism" arrived in 2001, a kind of postmodern parody of a world war.) America's national survival was never in question during the Second World War, and from 1941 to 1945 it waged war against Japan out of vengeance reinforced by racial hatred. It made war on Germany as the apparently necessary preliminary to finishing with the Japanese, accomplishing the latter by two unnecessary but cathartic final acts of extermination.

There was virtually no domestic American opposition to the Second World War, after Pearl Harbor. Opposition to the war in Vietnam, and that which developed to the 2003 war in Iraq, came from disillusioned voters, soldiers' mothers, disabused military in the ranks (fraggings in Vietnam, the silent AWOL of the drugged), and by an intellectual and professional opposition to those wars, ignored, naturally, until too late.

individual influence, reflects in considerable measure a notion of how one *should be seen* to conduct oneself.

It was my sense at the time of the Korean War that to take part was an obligation of my cohort (one can scarcely say generation), but I also perceived it, with youthful simplicity, as a defining political event. I believed that I should put myself into the infantry because it was the "manly" thing to do, and because it seemed unacceptable that the gangling black sharecropper boys and the mill-hands and mechanics who made up the rest of my draft of Georgia recruits, arriving at Fort Jackson in January 1951, should all go to the front, where they manifestly were headed, while the middle-class and college-educated stayed behind, working typewriters in headquarters companies.* An unreasonable opinion, I acknowledge, in that there always is need for cannon fodder and there are people whose unhappy role is to provide it, and I was better qualified for typing, or even thinking, than for foot-soldiering. But all this is part of the absurdity of war, as well as the servitude of soldiering.

War is, after all, a moral spectacle of men doing preposterous and sacrificial things for motives they ordinarily do not understand and causes they care nothing about, or only because they are forced to do it—or out of a form of love. After-action interviews reveal that infantry soldiers usually do what they do for the sake of solidarity with their fellow soldiers. It was the self-sacrificial advance of men under fire that is supposed to have led Robert E. Lee to say, "it is well that war is so terrible—we would grow too fond of it." Wars make men physically beautiful. I wrote, in a diary I kept during a period traveling in Vietnam in 1967, of "the undeniable and unmis-

---

* In the Vietnam War, the same privileged young men mostly did not get even that far, as they were pursuing newly planned graduate studies, early marriage, or having their fathers find them places in the Texas Air National Guard.

takable aesthetic self-awareness, the presence, of the combat soldier, blackened face, blackened insignia, rolled sleeves, arms akimbo, charged weapons so potent, death-dealing, life-sparing, transiently and tragically so apart from other men. Military airplanes are beautiful, awesome, stripped, ultimately utilitarian in an activity without inherent utility, that of killing." Scenes of battle cast a spell. No one who has been in one wants it repeated but he or she will recognize the majesty in battle's terrible manifestation of human power. The late American philosopher Glen Gray, who had himself been a combat soldier, called it "an awareness of power that far surpasses [the soldier's] limited imagination [and] transports him into a state of mind unknown to his everyday experiences. Fleeting as these rapt moments may be, they are, for the majority of men, an escape from themselves that is very different from the escape induced either by sexual concourse or alcohol. The raptness is a joining and not a losing, a deprivation of self in exchange for a union with objects that were hitherto foreign."*

War takes people out of the familiar roles of their lives into the exotic. It is outlandish, marvelous, appalling, cathartic. It bores most of the time but offers the most intense excitement. It leaves everyone changed. It haunts the memory. It sets off those who have been part of it from those who have not. Old men do not forget it. The American veterans of the war in Vietnam, even though most loathed that war or felt themselves corrupted by it, afterwards knew, like the men at Crécy, that they were people apart from

---

* Gray, in his book of reflections on battle, *The Warriors*, describes the "enduring appeals" of battle as he experienced them: "the delight in seeing, the delight in comradeship, the delight in destruction . . . the poignancy and intensity of life at risk, the escape from ego's constraints, the pleasure to be taken in destruction and the uses of power." He also writes of the "spirit of evil" on battlefields, "a radical evil which suddenly makes the medieval images of hell and the thousand devils of the imagination believable . . . men who have lived in the combat zone long enough to be veterans are sometimes possessed by a fury that makes them capable of anything. . . . [F]rom the Homeric account of the sacking of Troy to the conquest of Dien Bien Phu, Western literature is filled with descriptions of soldiers as berserkers and mad destroyers."

everyone else in their generation, and that the others could not understand what they understood.

⋅⊙

There has always been a link between the professional military vocation and the monastic vocation; both are ancient and inwardly directed commitments, of ideal and sacrificial character. Both are extreme choices in life, risking total loss—death or lifelong mutilation in one case, and in the other, lifelong sacrifice of the legitimate pleasures and rewards of existence. Each is a gamble with life. Each is linked to a moral order now largely abandoned, to which we cannot return, but which we might have the possibility of reestablishing on new terms (an undertaking which almost certainly will not be attempted).

The soldier and the monk are two cases of exemplary unreasonableness, in which lives are not dictated by evident advantage. I realize that this may seem a rather literary conception of the military vocation, but it is one that historically has been recognized by reflective professional soldiers. It is an ethic that survives even in the American military service, despite all that has been done in recent years to construct barriers between military service and death. The insistence on "force protection" and the objective of "zero casualties," the automation of war to turn it into a rationalized technical process like manufacturing, in which ethical commitments are obstacles to productivity, the bureaucratization of the American services, and the integration of women into the combat arms all represent attempts to recast an ancient military ethic.

This effort to make the military into just another civil service career path is easily comprehensible within the culture of the United States during the final quarter of the twentieth century and the first years of the twenty-first, but is incompatible with the nature of the military institution, whose existence rests upon the individual's offer to sacrifice his life. (In national terms, it might be interpreted as a premonitory abdication, a signal of national decline.)

The traditional military ethic is a direct product of the fact that the indispensable and ultimate function of a military institution is to kill. There is no way by which this can be done without acceptance of the prospect of reciprocal deaths. As a French officer, Général de l'Armée Philippe Morillon, a former commander of the UN Protection Force in the ex-Yugoslavia, remarked in 1995, with respect to the American preoccupation with zero casualties, "how can you have soldiers who are ready to kill, who are not ready to die?"

So chivalric a conception of the military vocation is no doubt rare today even outside the United States, just as the religious conviction which produces a monastic commitment would seem to have suffered drastic diminishment. The decline of these two forms of rejection of contemporary civilization diminishes our culture, in that a capacity for reasoned unreasonableness is capable of redeeming much meretriciousness. The loss opens the way to more barbarian forms of unreasonableness.

While my acquaintance with monasticism has been indirect, and that with soldiering somewhat larger but undramatic and, finally, unsatisfactory, I nonetheless have become convinced by those experiences that the unreasonable life is a reasonable choice, essential to civilization. The monk abandons everything that most people would think makes life worth living for the sake of a God in whom most people do not believe, and whose existence is indemonstrable even to the monk, no matter how intensely he may experience God's existence and presence—or His existence and absence, as in the classic "dark night of the soul."

The monk makes the Pascalian gamble, his life for a salvation which, he acknowledges, might not exist. The soldier is more remarkable because in principle he has nothing to gain except "honor"—the "grandeur" of his "servitude," if we take the words of the nineteenth-century writer and soldier Alfred de Vigny—and this is rather less than the possibility of eternal salvation. What exactly is honor, and what is it worth to a soldier, or to anyone else, when the soldier dies?

The military and monastic communities are committed to something of actual or potentially ultimate weight to the individuals concerned. The military profession prepares an individual to kill on orders, but in doing so must implicitly prepare him (or her, as we must now say) to die, for national goals which he or she is not expected to question, or even necessarily to understand. Civilization has traditionally regarded this as justified, and as bestowing "glory": Vigny's "state of military grace."

To die as a deliberately elected risk in the service of values consciously chosen is one thing. To choose the risk of death in one's country's defense or for national independence or some other political value—for Virginia or the Union, or Israel or Palestine, or to defeat Nazism, or for the revolution, whatever the revolution—may be a rational act. Such is what is done by nearly all those discussed in this book, patriots, nationalists, or revolutionaries.

But the professional soldier dies to liberate the Falkland Islands, which he is justified in assuming will eventually be negotiated away, or to seize a Panamanian president or defeat an Iraqi dictator because they have offended the amour propre of an American president, or install foreign governments congenial to American citizens and investors, or bring democracy and capitalism to countries that do not want them, or to hunt down Islamic illuminati serving another God.

The professional finds honor in the absurdity of the situation. Antigone said to Creon, "There are things which one must not do." Creon replied, "If it becomes necessary that hands be dirtied so that the public order be respected, it is essential that someone do it." It is better that a moral man do it than it be delegated to the sadist or brute. An army, Vigny said, is not only a machine to kill but "is, too, a machine capable of suffering." What it does in the service of the state is at great and potentially fatal cost to its members. Because it is a company of those prepared to die, it possesses the moral authority to set terms and a limit upon the claims of the state. This is military monasticism, where the gamble is that the soldier's state of grace lies within his profession and not in the large and morally indiscriminate world outside.

The monk's gamble is also to give up the external world, but in his case for a narrow and intense contemplative life, where the stakes again are life and death. Either the sacrifice of material consolation will be justified in the love of God or the monk has lost everything—in death, and in the renounced pleasures of life. Again the life is one of ritual and formal aesthetic, ostensibly because these give shape to the act of worship, but also because they inform and give style to the life itself: the discipline of the monastic Hours, chant, ritual movement, the religious habit (the uniform), the observance of hierarchy, the necessary intimacy of common life with those whom one may actually dislike.

The connection of the monk to the soldier is not of much interest to the contemporary world, I admit. The two roles reject contemporary society by transcending its norms. That is exactly the reason I describe them. They are instances of lives lived for virtue, and the only such formal roles in the contemporary world open to anyone who wishes to enlist.

The idea that war includes aesthetic experience, and that this is another reason it permanently attracts men, is scarcely what one wants to think, yet armies have always employed a strategy of rituals, liturgies, myths, chivalries, and vanities to civilize (if that is possible) and limit the essential horror of war. Even peacetime military life is one of *actes gratuits*—whitewashed stones, gravel raked to arbitrary patterns, the uniform worn in one way and not another, the cap at a particular angle, the boots and buttons shined daily in a meticulous ritual that can extend to the preposterous extremes of polished boot-soles.

There is an evident military obsession with artistic effect: the Marine Corps' blue tunics and striped trousers, the Navy's dress whites, Guards' bearskins and Horse Guards' polished breastplates, the Hussars' doubled plum capelet, the Spahis' enormous capes meant to cover the long-abandoned saddle and horse as well as the rider, the Légionnaires' ridiculous epaulettes, the starched trousers into which the West Pointer steps from a tabletop so as not to break the crease, the frivolous feather stuck to the Alpini's steel helmet.

Drill, close-order movement, march, are forms of dance. The goose step is purely ornamental. The Italian Bersagliere run every-where. Even the band runs while it plays. British light infantry, the Rifle Brigade, make a similar boast by marching more rapidly than the rest of the British army. The French Foreign Legion marches more slowly than everyone else, at a deliberate pace inherited from Brandenberger mercenaries of the seventeenth and eighteenth centuries.

All of this is what Alfred de Vigny called "the selection of symbol and imposing of convention, the ritual of the parade ground, [which] is the formal transfiguration of war." It makes tolerable, even normal, the fact that the purpose of war remains to destroy and to kill. The enlisted soldier, Vigny also said, is "executioner and victim."

Consider the case of a particular soldier, an amateur, a man named Vladimir Peniakoff, a Belgian of Russian descent, educated at Cambridge, who during the Second World War came to be called "Popski" and to have his own private army. He found in this an op-portunity to transcend the absurdity of war, resolve a part of its moral complexity, and in the improbable space of the desert and Italian campaigns of the British army in the Second World War, to reestablish chivalric order and compassion among a limited number of people, his own and his enemies. He found harmonies that had eluded Lawrence and Jünger.

He is little known, but has interested me for years because he provides a counterexample to much that is recounted in this book, distant from the intoxications of ideological war and utopian causes, finding moral success in civilizing the conduct of war and in exemplifying what I have spoken of in terms of virtue.

He appropriately concludes Part One of this book because his experience demonstrates that in the Second World War, amidst the ruins of chivalric society, its values survived among certain individuals, affording the possibility for men to engage in the human tragedy of war while affirming humane values. This would seem to offer a hope for the future.

Peniakoff was an engineer by training, from a cultivated, assimilated, partly Jewish Belgian family of Russian origin (his mother was Jewish; his father, a scientist whose brother was a Russian army cavalry officer, apparently was not). The family had emigrated to Belgium in 1894. It employed an English governess and an English drawing mistress, and Vladimir Peniakoff went on to studies at Cambridge. Some years later he remarked of England, "I felt at home there as in no other country." Despite an early infatuation with Paris, his later experience of French expatriates in Egypt produced in him contempt for the French.

He seems to have been very brilliant in his engineering and scientific studies, initially at the Free University of Brussels, where he took up the classics for pleasure, conducting a correspondence with a friend in Greek. He was greatly interested by art and literature, and wrote essays on Greek drama and on the "decadent" Wilde, Beardsley, and Huysmans. Anatole France was a hero, and in 1913 he wrote with excitement in the journal he was keeping about a private meeting with the French author.

In the spring of 1914, in the exhausting preparations for his examinations, he made a motorcycle excursion into the Ardennes. He wrote afterwards,

> Night was falling, it was unusually still, and I was quite alone. All that, with the help of fatigue and hunger, for I was very tired and very hungry, stirred up inside me an old residue of romanticism which I don't usually feel when confronted with the "beauties of nature."
>
> These purely physical impressions brought me to an extraordinarily exalted state. On my way there lay a Trappist monastery. As I passed, a Trappist father was returning from the fields, dressed in the long brown habit. On his shoulders rested a scythe; with his left hand he was telling his beads. He walked with a heavy step, his countenance serene and tired. And suddenly, faced with this rough monk, who to me was no longer a human being, I understood the Christian religion. It had always been a closed book to me; suddenly I could grasp the unexpected conversions, the mystic exaltations. I had faith. . . . I was seized with an irresistible longing to follow this monk, to live in this spiritually charged landscape. . . .

The longing proved ephemeral, but the young Peniakoff concluded his journal entry by saying, "I am very happy to have opened my spirit to a whole new field of feelings and ideas. There is now a whole new literature for me to savour, a whole vast art whose enjoyment will seem deeper and more exquisite."

With the German invasion of Belgium in 1914, the young man and his father took refuge in Holland, and his two sisters and mother, who had Russian citizenship, subsequently went to Switzerland. With the help of relations, Vladimir was found a place at Saint John's College, Cambridge, while his father took on government-sponsored scientific work in Paris, and later went to Russia as part of a Franco-Russian scientific mission.

At Cambridge the young Peniakoff acquired a reputation as an aesthete. He was greatly impressed by Bertrand Russell and by the American-born painter, writer, and pamphleteer Wyndham Lewis, sometime associate of Ezra Pound in the short-lived Vorticist movement, connected to Italian Futurism. With friends, Peniakoff planned a Cambridge version of Lewis's magazine *Blast*, but nothing came of it.

At the age of nineteen he left Cambridge with his degree unfinished and joined his family in France. He was subject to conscription as a Belgian national, and at this point his biographical record becomes unclear. The future Popski's later claims to have enlisted in the French army, served as a gunner, been wounded, spent a year in hospitals and convalescent camps, and been given an 80 percent disability discharge are undocumented. He is known to have done some scientific work assisting his father, and then to have worked as a chemist in a factory in southeastern France, near Grenoble, and later in another factory near Marseille. He and his younger sister fell ill in 1917, apparently from typhoid, complicated in his case by double phlebitis, and the two spent their convalescence in a nursing home in Paris, and then at home. The illness changed him physically from the slim and—as his biographer, John Willett, writes—"Nijinskyish figure of his early photographs," into a balding and rather solidly built young man.

The experience of war and grave illness caused him to abandon the literary personage of his Brussels and Cambridge student years. Everything that precedes 1918, he later wrote, "seems to refer to someone whom I knew in my youth, whom I no longer much care for and who has vanished for good." His sister, Olga, also felt radically changed by the war. The two spent the first postwar university year in Grenoble where they fell into an intellectually lively young group that included refugees from eastern Europe and American officers waiting to be discharged. It was during this year that Peniakoff seems to have made the considered decision to turn to what he and his sister had elaborated as the Task.

He described the Task in an autobiographical novel begun three decades later, near the end of his life. His sister's duties were to deal with intellectual and artistic matters, and to investigate a "New Ethics: based on Common Sense, Humour, Freedom, Friendliness and a Complete Knowledge of Human Behaviour (to be acquired)." On political systems, their shared program said: "Philosophers, Conservatives, Liberals, Socialists, Anarchists, Nihilists: wordy, pompous and boring. To be exposed. Read Karl Marx (learn German)." The narrator in the novel observes that, "Having taken a degree in physics before joining the army, my knowledge of pure science was considered sufficient. I was now to study engineering, then investigate Big Business, Industry, Trade Unions, and the condition of Labour, and turn myself into a working-class leader (public speaking tiresome—seek alternatives). The last item on my agenda was: 'Revolution—practical or not?' "

It was a mocking yet serious undertaking, important enough for Peniakoff to return to its description so many years later, when he was in Vienna, involved in a practical and sometimes controversial way in sorting out the consequences of the Second World War.

The brother and sister returned to undamaged postwar Brussels and a year of rather mondaine life and romance among the regrouped friends of school and prewar, until the spring of 1920 when Vladimir took up his first job as an engineer in his father's factory. A year and a half later his sister wrote of their first postwar years as a time spent in "gaiety, joy and enthusiasm . . . luminous years where I danced in the sun and welcomed insatiably every idea, every emotion that might offer itself, pell-mell, avidly, without care—I feel now that a broad ditch cuts me off from them, a broad ditch across which I can never return. And here I am on the other side . . . a little bruised perhaps but with a profound longing in my heart, my nerves taut and my will alert." This was just before she died, in January 1922, at twenty-three, a victim of the great influenza epidemic.

✦

Peniakoff felt his sister's loss for years. Friends felt that he lost all direction. Two years later he gave up his work in Belgium and negotiated a job in Egypt with the state sugar monopoly, then the biggest industrial undertaking in that country, traditionally run by Belgians. He married an unsuitably young Austrian (and Catholic) girl from a family long installed in Egypt, had two daughters, and became increasingly bored with his life. "I still think," he wrote after two years there, "as I did before coming to Egypt, that sugar technicians are the lowest class of technicians; they are grotesque." He did some desert traveling when he first arrived in Egypt in the 1920s, later took up sailing and canoeing, and learned to fly.

"From 1925 to 1928 I worked in the sugar mill at Nag Hamadi north of Luxor, in Upper Egypt. For eight months in the year, between the sugar seasons, my duties were light and gave me abundant leisure for Palgrave, Burton, Doughty, Lawrence, and Gertrude Bell, writers on Arabian travel; slowly and at second hand I fell under the spell of the Arabs." He began to make excursions into the desert on horseback or camel, and to go on gazelle hunting expeditions. But by the end of the period his interest in traveling dwindled and he said to a friend, "for some time life has lost the delicacy of its savour, and I think I am beginning to feel something that is not far from being like the first stage of boredom." His marriage deteriorated as he endured the vexations of approaching middle age.

He was not political, but on his European journeys in the 1930s he guessed "at a stupid conspiracy behind the pleasant facade" in Germany, but he also, until 1939, felt "provisionally that all was well and that the Germans had found a régime which suited them." His biographer quotes a young friend of Peniakoff's, who saw him in London in 1939, "with black overcoat, rolled umbrella, and bowler hat.... He was scathing about England, but certain that there would be a war, that England would fight and that England would win. I was twenty-six and terribly impressed by Popski. He was lucid and convincing, and made one feel that he knew more than he said."

Willett goes on to say that Peniakoff remained largely isolated from the passions expressed in Europe as the war approached, and as a cosmopolitan with family associations on both sides, "he came to fight the war with no false or artificial passion, and without suppressing the scruples in which he naturally believed."

"I had found little contentment," Peniakoff afterwards wrote, "and I believe that my contemporaries had the same sterile experience." But with the arrival of the Second World War, there began five years during which "every moment was consciously happy." He was intelligent, introspective, and ruthless enough to seize this opportunity. He set aside wife, children, and possessions, and after a year's efforts to find orthodox military use for his knowledge of desert navigation and languages—when according to English friends in Cairo he made himself "a confounded nuisance"—he found a place, at forty-three, in a British-officered unit called the Libyan Arab Force.

This formation, which spent more than a year in frustrating preparations for guerrilla actions that never quite arrived, allowed Peniakoff, in Cyrenaica, to take time off freely to call on Bedouin leaders and visit other military units.

When British forces were compelled to withdraw once again, in the course of the seesaw desert campaign, he stayed at the front, and eventually managed to get himself set up as leader of a small, jeep-mounted intelligence, demolition, and raiding group composed of himself, an Arab officer, a British sergeant, and twenty-two Arab soldiers. They depended on the Long-Range Desert Group for basic transport, and it was fellow officers there who began calling him Popski.

He tried to be taken on by the LRDG, which liked him but was dubious about Europeans in their forties without much military experience. The LRDG commander said, "We liked him very much. He was amiable, a bit slow in thought and speech, but genuinely keen to do as much fighting as he could. His knowledge of things military, other than fighting, was nil, and he seemed to me far too easygoing to have been able to run a Squadron from an administrative point of view."

So it was back to GHQ in Cairo. There he found a senior officer who had been impressed by a report he had written on possible operations in Cyrenaica and who decided to give him a chance to operate on his own. He was given four jeeps, two three-ton trucks, and twenty-two men (nominally; he started with only thirteen). This was designated "No 1 Demolition Squadron (PPA)"—the parenthesis a frivolous but official designation as Popski's Private Army.

❧

The nature of the terrain confined the desert war to a fairly narrow coastal plain of North Africa and the upland plateau of Cyrenaica. To the immediate south were the scarcely traversable Quattara Depression and an inland desert which became the zone of operations away from the main battles for a variety of irregular military units.

Popski and his "army" (Artemis Cooper writes, in her 1989 book on wartime Cairo) "released prisoners of war and did whatever sabotage came their way. They also built up an important intelligence network with the desert tribesmen, who if caught by the Italians would be treated not as prisoners of war, but as collaborators: this meant being strung up with an iron hook through the jaw."

By late 1942, the desert war was nearing its end and by March 1943, as the British pushed Rommel eastward, the possibility of operating on the open desert flanks of the main armies was gone. Popski then astutely moved into the gap between the Eighth Army and the First Army, which included the American forces landed in North Africa in Operation Torch in November 1942.

His was the first Eighth Army unit to switch command to the First Army, under General Dwight Eisenhower. Thus he moved on to the new campaign in southern Europe, accompanying the first wave of troops in the unopposed British airborne landing in the heel of Italy. From there his force took advantage of the mobility of the fighting to go deep into enemy territory during the first twenty days of the campaign, producing much useful intelligence.

After that, opportunities for Popski-style behind-the-lines operations became scarce, and he ended up operating as a lightly encumbered scouting auxiliary of British armored car units. They worked their way up the Apennines, from the boot of Italy, eventually meeting Italian partisans. He worked with a partisan group that impressed him very much, led by a history professor from Pisa. He followed the retreating Germans toward the eastern Italian coast, approaching Ravenna in the company of the Twenty-eighth (Communist-led) Garibaldi Brigade of Italian partisans, ending in Venice.

North of Ravenna, Popski lost his left hand, becoming the unit's sole casualty in a battle with the Germans. It was, "in a sense, . . . the end of Popski's war," Willett writes. During the next four months PPA was commanded by Popski's French second in command, Jean Caneri (a deserter from Vichy French forces). When Popski returned, the war in Italy was practically over, but there was time for a flourish.

> We loaded five jeeps in three RCLs [boats built for inland water operations] and . . . sailed from Chioggia to Venice up the lagoon, entered the Canal San Marco and moored our craft on the quay. I started my jeep and, trembling with excitement for the one and only time during the war, drove into the Piazetta, passed between the

columns, turned left into the Piazza San Marco, and, followed by the others, drove seven times round the square. This was my hour of triumph.

Popski's war after that merged into a kind of private diplomacy, not very successful. PPA operations took him into southern Austria and the join-up with Russian forces. Popski's relations with the Italian Communist guerrillas had left him with the sense that they were purposeful and politically sympathetic, with a view of what the postwar world should become that he respected. As for the Russians, he liked and admired them as fighting men. "Their ruthlessness and lack of democratic principles (in the Western sense)"—Willett writes—"he took for granted; like many White Russians he never imagined that Russia could be otherwise, and he rated her war sacrifices justification enough for her post-war demands."

This led him into freelance as well as official efforts to build up good relations between the British and Russian troops. "The fighting being over, I had to find myself a new job, and I thought it within my powers to bring about a successful transition from a wartime brotherhood in arms to peacetime cooperation between Great Britain and the Soviet Union. Having decided that this was the best use to which my services could be put, I deferred my release from the Army for one year and applied for the appointment of commander-in-chief's liaison with the Soviet Southern Front Headquarters." He received the appointment, but accomplished little, both sides being suspicious and the Russians unwilling to see personal relations develop between the Allies and their own officers and men. Popski lacked serious appreciation of the role of political commissars and secret police on the Russian side, and of the condition of political paranoia in which the Red Army functioned.

❧

He finally gave it up and went to London, married a woman he had met in the British forces in Austria, and set himself up in Cliveden

Place rather luxuriously, as had been his prewar habit. He was talked about for a UN job, but nothing came of it. He tried writing a novel but didn't finish. He continued his efforts to make the British "understand" the Russians, sat on some platforms at meetings of organizations that had been set in motion two decades or more before by Willi Münzenberg, becoming a postwar version of what Münzenberg had called his "innocents" (although the rumor among the Russians was that he was actually a British spy).

He became mildly controversial in public when he criticized British participation in the Korean war. He had never much appreciated Americans (and had never visited the United States), ranking them, among his dislikes, with the French and with the British Guards regiments.

In 1950 he was hospitalized with digestive problems, and then found himself more and more forgetful. He died of an inoperable brain tumor on May 16, 1951.

He had written that "our operations were a kind of game; . . . so to speak, we made our own play and acted the parts ourselves. . . . Our reward and our incentive were not so much our military successes . . . but the pleasure and pride we took in the skilful performance of self-appointed and difficult tasks." The moral standards of his unit were firm, if implicit: no lying, no quarreling, no cowardice, no shirking of responsibility; "The decencies were preserved, prisoners treated humanely, lives laid down 'without making a fuss.' "

Willett says that at the end, "It was no longer the defeat of the Germans or the methods of the British army that primarily interested him, but the men with whom he fought." His signals sergeant, Eric Brooks, said, "his driving force was a kind of humanity."

The happiness Popski and his men found in those years was undoubtedly more significant than anything they accomplished in the field, where their conduct of behind-the-lines reconnaissance and sabotage, and their harassment of Italians and Germans in the

desert, and subsequently in southern Europe, was brave, dangerous, and amusing, but entirely on the margins of the "real" war.
The men he recruited were usually the discards or disciplinary
cases of other units. He was allowed no one who was wanted by a
regular formation. As a result he ended up with prison veterans,
hard men, discards, dreamers. His only means of discipline was to
throw a man out of PPA.

Many of those who served with him did badly in civilian life after
the war, but one corporal in the unit wrote later: "I am deeply
grateful to Popski and to all PPA men for giving me a chance to live
how I have always wanted to live—amongst friends . . . good
friends . . . doing work which for most people is an extreme hard-
ship and is almost impossible." Another enlisted member of the
unit said, "Sometimes, I feel sorry that the war finished." One
wrote "Never . . . do I remember having to do anything that
seemed senseless." An Italian who fought with PPA in its final
months said, "It's my happiest memory."

They were at play in war, a game of arbitrary rules, enforced by
death, providing strenuous tests during which people may find
qualities in themselves that they had not known they possessed. Because the demands of war are intense but narrow, they illuminate
life. A woman who was part of the French Resistance said afterwards, "I do not love war nor want it to return. But at least it made
me feel alive, as I have not felt alive before or since."

Peniakoff and his men were fortunate in the war they fought.
The Second World War in the North African desert was not total
war. Most of the rest of the war was conducted as a genocidal struggle of belief against belief, race against race. As the French novelist
and combat soldier Louis-Ferdinand Céline wrote of 1914–1918, a
struggle of "madmen, all of them heroes, at large and armed to the
teeth . . . sniping, plotting, flying, kneeling, digging, taking cover,
wheeling, detonating, shut in on earth as in an asylum cell; intend-
ing to wreck everything in it, Germans, French, the whole world,
every breathing thing. . . ."

The emptiness of the desert produced something entirely different. The all but complete absence of civilians from the battle-ground, and the premium armored warfare placed on movement, allowed British, Free French, German, and Italian forces to conduct virtually the only campaign of modern times that possessed game-like limits and chivalric qualities. A Free French officer (and later prime minister under de Gaulle, Pierre Messmer) wrote:

Desert warfare is war in an empty country, abandoned by the few nomads who travelled there before operations began, and it is conducted exclusively between professionals, the two armies in the field. That is its first characteristic. As a result, desert war can be fought with a clear conscience, since you know that while you are risking your own life, no one is in danger who is not there to make war. The second characteristic is that desert war resembles war at sea more than conventional land war, since at sea what counts is not how much of the sea you can occupy, but destroying the enemy.

Terrain has no value in the desert. The sole thing that counts is the enemy. As a result, whatever your movements, whether forward or back, you feel an absolute serenity. I don't say this is so for the commanders, because it can't be agreeable for the commanding general to fall back several hundred kilometers, even though this is entirely supportable, as experience in the desert repeatedly demonstrated. But for the troops, fighting at the gates of Alexandria is exactly the same thing as fighting at the gates of Benghazi. It makes no practical difference to them. What counts is the battle itself—whether it is a victory, or whether you manage to escape destruction even if you lose the battle. The desert was a style of war completely different from the style of war we were to know in western Europe, and later in the Far East.

The desert was a place of concentration and liberty. It allowed, even compelled, those who took part in the fighting to focus their lives. The scope was narrow, the stakes the ultimate ones of survival, love, and companionship. It was a distillation of Vigny's "state of military grace," a formalized, deliberate, and limited existence that is also a form of escape from life. This is radically formulated in a Japanese book of instruction for samurai, the *Hagakure* (a favorite of the novelist, rightist political activist, and suicide, Yukio Mishima), which declares that "the way of the samurai is death." Death is freedom from life, and war liberates the possibility of retreating from life while giving death meaning, justification, and a satisfactory form (which Mishima presumably believed he was doing by committing seppuku, at the end of a grotesque and failed attempt at a coup d'état in Tokyo in 1970). Mishima, who had not served in the war, wrote with satisfaction that "during the war, the death impulse was 100% liberated."

To die in war is considered honorable, as well as being easily arranged. To die in ordinary circumstances is frequently miserable and humiliating. Military service, like its monastic counterpart, is a ritualized and professional preparation for honorable death and is therefore extremely attractive to those people who for their own interior reasons want to be free from life. T. E. Lawrence said of the military life, in his celebration of its abnegations, *The Mint*, that it affords "a very real measure of happiness to those who do not look forward or back." Popski wrote, about losing his hand and wrist, "I was pleased to be wounded in this manner—more than pleased; I was filled with a joyful peace, a tranquil certainty of fulfillment. I had been chasing a phantom right through the war and now, at last, I had come on to something solid; my wound was real and nothing could take it from me."

Until modern times, wars were consistently recounted in the primordial literary form of epic, with a hero, a quest and ordeal, tragedy or success, and the acquisition of wisdom. This changed with Stendhal and Tolstoy and their realistic descriptions of battle. It was recognized that the individual's experience of war could as often be absurd or demeaning as cathartic and exemplary. The epic impulse nonetheless remained strong. T. E. Lawrence's over-wrought prose at the start of *Seven Pillars of Wisdom* declares: "Some of the evil of my tale may have been inherent in our circum-stances. For years we lived anyhow with one another in the naked desert, under the indifferent heaven. By day the hot sun fermented us and we were dizzied by the beating wind. At night we were stained by dew and shamed into pettiness by the innumerable si-lences of the stars. We were a self-centered army without parade or gesture, devoted to freedom, the second of man's creeds, a purpose so ravenous that it devoured all our strength, a hope so transcen-dent that our earlier ambitions faded in its glare."

Life ordinarily is experienced as shapeless and unmalleable. We make our ways through days of random incident toward a future that recedes before us, and rarely are we given an opportunity to take determining action that gives meaning to our existence. War provides such an occasion, not necessarily by providing grand causes but in presenting small, crystalline, vital, individual choices. The possibility is provided to impose a significant form upon an in-dividual life through honorable action, if only by taking another's life at the risk of one's own.

But such is the tragedy of existence, which the utopianism and faith in human progress of the century just ended were meant to deny. The moral function of war is to recall humans to the reality at the core of existence: the violence that is part of our nature and is responsible for the fact that human history is a chronicle of tragedies—evoking terror and pity, in which one may, if fortunate, find catharsis.

PART TWO

Utopias

CHAPTER SIX

———

THE MEDITERRANEAN SUPERMAN

Until 1915, Gabriele D'Annunzio, poet, novelist, and playwright, was devoted to the transforming power of art. His chosen personage was that of aesthete, dandy, and lover. After 1915, he became a romantic and flamboyant Italian nationalist and irredentist. Although he was fifty-two when Italy intervened in the world war, he arranged combat service in the army with subsequent attachments to the navy in torpedo boats—even though he was afflicted with terrible seasickness all his life—and to the air service. He carried out spectacularly brave if largely gratuitous acts of warfare that seemed to symbolize and justify the Italian cause, relating it to traditions of honor and chivalry.

One of the most famous writers in Europe at the time of the First World War, he made himself a leader of Italian resistance to the Versailles treaty's settlement of a controversial Dalmatian frontier between Italy and a newly created Yugoslavia. He led a military coup which seized the port of Fiume (now Rijeka), denied to Italy in the Versailles negotiations, and created there a utopian political society which endured sixteen months, drew the attention of the world, and as the historian of the adventure, Michael Ledeen, has written in his indispensable book on the Fiume adventure, produced "a kind of preview of the twentieth century."

Gabriele D'Annunzio was born in Pescara on the Adriatic on March 12, 1863, in a town that one of his Italian biographers, Paolo Alatri, describes as one "for which even 'provincial' is probably too grand a description." His father was a good-natured but licentious man, a prosperous farmer, winemaker, and town notable who ended a bankrupt, having squandered a considerable inheritance "on his relations with women of every condition in the town and in the surrounding countryside." D'Annunzio's British biographer, Anthony Rhodes, notes that in an early novel, *Il trionfo della morte*, D'Annunzio describes a man such as his father: "a person of reason, of thought and feeling, [who] had in his flesh the fatal inheritance of his coarse being. . . . Certain impulses of animalism, gusts of it, moving like storms across cultivated ground, were destroying the spiritual side of his life. They shut off every source of interior light, they opened great voids of misery. . . ."

D'Annunzio was classically educated at a good boarding school, writing poetry on Greek and Roman models from an early age. He said that the discovery at fifteen of the poetry of Giosuè Carducci (awarded the Nobel Prize for Literature in 1906) was "the shock that revealed [to me] what poetry is." He wrote to Carducci, saying "I speak to you from my heart, I feel deep in me a strange and vivid emotion, and my hand trembles in writing this. I want to follow in your steps and also courageously fight for this school of poetry which they call new, and which is destined for a triumph very different from those of the past."

D'Annunzio's first volume of poetry, published at sixteen—publication paid for by his father—was favorably noticed in Rome's literary press, although a derivative note of "decadence" in his work was deplored. The most influential Italian critic of the time, Giuseppe Chiarini, greeted the birth "of a new poet." D'Annunzio assured himself attention by telling the newspapers, anonymously, that the young D'Annunzio had tragically died in a fall from a horse, which prompted new articles on the premature loss of so talented a youth. While the news was eventually corrected, the eulogies remained. It was the first manifestation of a lifelong talent for self-promotion.

❦

He went to Rome at the age of nineteen, when a second volume of poetry and his first of stories had already been published. A decade after Italian troops had ended papal rule in Rome, the city was becoming the political and commercial center of Italy, and replacing Florence as the center of journalism and literature. The Roman middle classes were stirring from the near-feudal torpor of the pre-Risorgimento decades, and the aristocracy was taking up the manners of foreigners. Luigi Barzini says the nobility "for the first time set about acting the part of 'nobles'; they ceased to be patriarchal, with a place in the people's ancient way of life, in order to live a fictitious literary and choreographic existence." Their servants now were silent as they served meals; before, they had intervened in the family conversation. The literary intelligentsia took up French modes of bohemianism.

D'Annunzio wrote to an old friend in Pescara that in Rome he "lived in an absolute whirl of excitement and energy. I have thrown myself into the Roman maelstrom of pleasure and struggle. . . ." He said, "My desire for glory sometimes gives me torment and melancholy." He was respectfully received in literary and intellectual circles on the strength of the three volumes he had published. He enrolled in letters and philosophy at the University of Rome, taking up fencing and riding as well; but he never passed his university examinations. His prose style, Rhodes says, was then "direct, even dry . . . all matter, concrete, with a jealous economy of expression and image." Later it became very ornate, after he acquired "the unfortunate notion that the Italian language possessed 'musical elements, various and powerful enough to compare with the great Wagnerian orchestras.' "

His personal magnetism, particularly for women, was immediately evident, despite his lack of physical distinction (he was short, unhandsome; a school friend described him at the time as "a little bucolic fellow with crinkly hair, and a pair of great, glaucous eyes with almond lids"). Later Isadora Duncan, one of his many lovers, said, possibly sardonically, but feelingly, how she imagined his first encounters in Rome: "The lady he is talking to suddenly feels that her very soul and being are lifted, as it were, into an ethereal region, where she walks in company with the Divine Beatrice. Above ordinary mortals, she goes about with a kind of imaginary halo. But, also, when the caprice is over and he moves on to another lady, the halo dulls, the aureole diminishes, and she feels again of clay. She does not quite understand what has happened, but seems to be back on earth searching desperately for her transfiguration, aware that never in her whole life will she meet this kind of love again."

In the summer of 1882 he broke relations with the young Florentine woman he professed to love; her father objected to their engagement. In the fall, his friend Edoardo Scarfoglio wrote that "he has returned strangely changed. During the summer, because of God knows what unhappy event or psychological phenomenon, a transformation took place. . . . Gabriele left Rome ingenuous, modest, agreeable, and returned tricky, vain, ingratiating. A sudden need to immediately taste all the doubtful and sterile pleasures of popularity has installed itself in him like a cancer of body and spirit. . . . Since the arrival of the winter season opened the doors of the great Roman houses, he has ceded to the flattery of the ladies. . . ." Another friend recalled that D'Annunzio was taken up by a smart crowd "whom his artist's instincts should have kept at a distance."

He became a social and gossip reporter for *La Tribuna*, incorporating foreign words and phrases into his articles—"five o'clock tea," "*parures*," "flirtation"—and alluding to his (wholly imaginary) days of aristocratic pursuits in English country houses. In literary circles it had been (as it remains) fashionable to be unfashionable and negligent in dress, but D'Annunzio now dressed as a dandy. His first novel was peopled with princesses, dukes, and ambassadors.

He encouraged what Rhodes calls the "romantic and morbid fascination" of Roman ladies.

⌒

In 1883 he married into the aristocracy, a child already having been
born to the twenty-year-old Maria Hardouin, dutchess of Gallese,
the sheltered and highly romantic daughter of the second marriage
of a widow of the "black" Roman aristocracy, the papal aristocracy.
Hers was the first great aristocratic house which D'Annunzio entered as a guest and not as a journalist. The daughter was later to
say "I really thought I was marrying poetry."

Her stepfather deplored the forced engagement, refused to at-
tend the wedding, and cut Maria Hardouin off without a dowry.
Her mother, one of the most beautiful women in Rome, to whose
charms D'Annunzio "was not indifferent" (according to another
Italian biographer, Annamaria Andreoli), was later to install herself
with the young couple. She promoted D'Annunzio's career as a society chronicler.

He claimed to love Maria, but eventually left her and the children in an Adriatic fishing village to resume his extravagant Roman
life. He failed to return for the birth of their third child, and eventually she had to sue to obtain support for the children. D'Annunzio displayed respect for Maria all her life, but formally separated
from her in 1891, having met Elvira Natalia Leoni, whom he called
Barbara, who convinced him to stop wasting his talent on journalism. His career as a lover, which was to be spectacular, had resumed.
His first important novel followed.

⌒

The flamboyance of D'Annunzio's writings is of a kind that Anglo-
Americans find unsympathetic. It strikes us as in crucial respects
unserious, unauthentic. Henry James devoted a long essay to the
case in 1902, saying of D'Annunzio's work that the doctrine of
"beauty at any price, beauty appealing alike to the sense and the

157

mind—was never felt to fall into its place as really adopted and efficient. It remained for us a queer high-flavored fruit from overseas,
grown under another sun than ours, passed round and solemnly
partaken of at banquets organized to try it, but not found on the
whole really to agree with us, not proving thoroughly digestible."

D'Annunzio defined himself—James goes on—as

> a rare imagination, a poetic, an artistic intelligence of extraordinary
> range and fineness concentrated almost wholly on the life of the
> senses. For the critic who simplifies a little to state clearly, the only
> ideas he urges upon us are the erotic and the plastic, which have for
> him about an equal intensity, or of which it would be doubtless more
> correct to say that he makes them interchangeable faces of the same
> figure. [His sharpest artistic powers were] first his rare notation of
> states of excited sensibility; second his splendid visual sense, the
> quick generosity of his response to the message, as we nowadays say,
> of aspects and appearances, to the beauty of places and things; third
> his ample and exquisite style, his curious, various, inquisitive, always
> active employment of language as a means of communication and
> representation.

Elsewhere James speaks of D'Annunzio's treatment of "love as a
form of suffering." "The fusion of manner," he says, with "the matter submitted to it . . . is complete and admirable, so that, though
his work is nothing if not 'literary,' we see at no point of it where literature or where life begins or ends. . . ."

❧

This is at the source of D'Annunzio's eventual military and political
engagements. The novelist or playwright conventionally turns experience into fictional art; another kind of artist, such as D'Annunzio, makes art of his life, or tries to do so. Is doing this a form of
confusion? Or a separate art which must be considered on its own
terms: life as a fictional construction, as distinct from art itself? Ital-

ians were eventually to refer to D'Annunzio simply as "the Poet" (Francis Lacassin writes, "without risk of error"; there was no other claimant to the title).

James concludes that D'Annunzio's obsessive concern with sexual passion—"from which he extracts such admirable detached pictures insists on remaining for him *only* the act of a moment, beginning and ending in itself and disowning any representative character." Surely, James says, what makes sexual love interesting is

> its extension and consummation only in the rest of life. Shut out from the rest of life, shut out from all fruition and assimilation, it has no more dignity than—to use a homely image—the boots and shoes that we see, in the corridors of promiscuous hotels, standing, often in double pairs, at the doors of rooms. Detached and unassociated these clusters of objects present, however obtruded, no importance. What the participants do with their agitation, in short, or even what it does with them, *that* is the stuff of poetry, and it is never really interesting save when something finely contributive in themselves makes it so.

Saying that D'Annunzio condemns his creatures to an "almost complete absence of *other* contacts" while engrossed in their passionate adventures, James concludes that: "It may doubtless be conceded that our English-speaking failure of insistence, of inquiry and penetration, in certain directions, springs partly from our deep-rooted habit of dealing with man, dramatically, on his social and gregarious side, as a being the variety of whose intercourse with his fellows, whatever forms his fellows may take, is positively half his interesting motion. We fear to isolate him, for we remember that as we see and know him he scarcely understands himself save in action, action which inevitably mixes him with his kind. To see and know him, like Signor D'Annunzio, almost only in passion is another matter, for passion spends itself quickly in the open and burns hot mainly in nooks and corners."

D'Annunzio became celebrated and rich ("or rather, prodigal," one critic notes), extravagant and indebted, as well as unfaithful to his women, as he remained throughout his life. His liaison with the great actress Eleonora Duse began in 1896, and the income from the plays he wrote for her, which she interpreted in theaters throughout Europe, served to support them both until 1903, when his encounter with a young (and gravely ill) widow, Alessandra di Rudini, provoked their separation. In all there were eight grand love affairs and hundreds of minor ones, Rhodes calculates, all of them—he says—important to D'Annunzio "only in so far as they contributed to D'Annunzio as the Stendhalian hero, nourished on the myth of Roman greatness, determined to repeat it in his own life, to become the superman." (When he later was in Paris, the rich and flamboyant Nathalie Barney—"l'Amazone," Chicago-born dominatrix of the expatriate lesbian community—said, "he was the rage. A woman who had not slept with him made herself ridiculous.")

He was a genius at self-promotion in an age committed to artist as romantic and dramatic creature. In 1909 he took up flying with the American aviation innovator Glenn Curtiss. In 1910 his Italian debts forced him to move to France, which he considered his second country, where he had a large and admiring audience. He returned to Italy after the First World War broke out, and getting himself accepted for active military service at fifty-two, made himself into a spectacular and authentic hero (however, it is reported that the aviators who flew on missions with him looked upon him as undeniably brave but preposterous).

He served as cavalry officer and torpedo-boat commander as well as flyer. The authorities recognized his value as popular hero and dramatist of the Italian cause and let him do more or less as he wanted. The result was a series of exploits: torpedo attacks in Austrian ports, bombing flights, expeditions to drop personal messages by leaflet over Hapsburg palaces in Vienna. These stirred the imagination of Italians and greatly gratified D'Annunzio, who operated from an apartment in the luxurious Danieli Hotel in Venice, and later from a palazzo, the Casetta Rossa, in that city (where his bedroom, according to the French consul in Venice, resembled "an exquisite bonbon box . . . a boudoir rather than a major's sleeping quarters"). From here he also conducted another widely known love affair with the fashionable Countess Morosini, former mistress of the kaiser, and lived with relish the most glorious role in Italy: "with literary genius but also with physical courage, he acted what he sang."

❧

A word about the political background is necessary. Before 1914 Italy had been Austria's ally in the Triple Alliance. When Austria went to war against Serbia in August 1914, Italy remained neutral, as Vienna had neglected to inform Italy before delivering its ultimatum to Belgrade, breaking a promise to consult and agree with Rome on any steps likely to compromise their common interests in the Balkans. The Italians considered the Austrian ultimatum a shocking overreaction to the Hapsburg archduke Francis Ferdinand's murder in Sarajevo.

However, popular pressure built up for intervention on the side of the Allies, against Austria, in order to recover Italian-speaking territories inside Austria-Hungary. Intervention on the Austro-German side might have given Italy Nice and a slice of France (which Mussolini was to seize in 1940), but intervention to support the Allies could give Italy Trieste and the Trentino region in the South Tyrol. The Foreign Ministry negotiated secretly with both sides, looking for the more interesting bargain, thus earning Italy contempt from both Allies and the Central Powers.

A second force pushing Italy toward the war was that larger European sentiment already mentioned, a perverse enthusiasm for war after a long period of peace. There was elite frustration that the new united Italian nation cut a poorer figure than France (in particular) and was treated patronizingly by the other major powers. Italian intellectuals were writing about "ignoble Italy, pacific, the ridiculous Italy, with her pope, her king, and her constitutional democracy" (the poet Giosuè Carducci said that). Italians had been reading D'Annunzio, Marinetti, Georges Sorel, and other theoreticians of violence, and they wanted action. There had been too much peace, too much bourgeois virtue, and the Italians considered that the time had arrived for some thrilling bloodletting.

When D'Annunzio said in one of his interventionist speeches that Italy "is no longer a *'pension de famille,'* a museum, a horizon painted with Prussian blue for international honeymooners, but a *'living nation,'*" the roar of applause would not let him go on. By 1915 the only groups still holding out for neutrality were some Catholics, who admired Catholic Austria and considered France an "atheist nation," and the official Socialists, who said that all war was wicked and imperialistic, and demanded absolute neutrality.

Liberal internationalism's spectacular failure in preventing war had much to do with this surge of nationalism, as well as with Fascism's eventual emergence as nationalism's political vehicle. It was impossible to take democratic Socialist internationalism seriously after the Socialist parties in all the belligerent countries opted for nationalist war over class solidarity and international class interest. Men were willing to die for the Italian nation but not for the international working class.

War itself proved a revelation: Mussolini later wrote, "War alone brings up to their highest tension all human energies and puts the stamp of nobility upon the peoples who have the courage to meet it." Liberal ideas seemed discredited, those of materialistic logic, rationalism, interest-maximizing motivation and action. According to D'Annunzio, the war was a struggle by Latins against Barbarians. War in 1915 was a continuation of Italian civilization's ancient struggle against Barbarian forces descended from German forests.

However, this war was not a success for Italian civilization. The Italian army was badly trained and incompetently led. Its traditions were negative ones. It had never before fought as a national army. The military as well as political leadership in Italy had complacently assumed that the Russian "steamroller" would crush Austria and Prussia within weeks, and Italy could then dart in, to its profit. Instead, the Germans magisterially defeated the Russian army at the battles of Tannenberg and the Masurian Lakes, which then began to disintegrate while revolutionary forces made their appearance in Saint Petersburg. By 1917 Russia was out of the war.

The Italians engaged the Austrians on the Isonzo River, north of Venice, and for two years fought eleven successive battles on a sixty-mile front, failing to advance beyond twelve miles, half the distance to Trieste. In December 1917, the German command reinforced the Austrians with six divisions in order to knock Italy out of the war. Their attack was made on the upper Isonzo, near Caporetto. The Italians broke and fell back more than ten miles to the Piave River, where the Austro-Germans outran their supply lines. (Hemingway describes the retreat from Caporetto in *A Farewell to Arms*.) French and British troops were rapidly moved to Italy to stabilize the line. The Italians had lost some three hundred thousand men taken prisoner, and a still larger number deserted. From then on the Italians fought adequately but ingloriously.

They nonetheless ended the war expecting that their lives would change. D'Annunzio wrote, "Something stronger, more beautiful will be born from all this blood and sacrifice. All forms of art and politics will be overthrown; the new ones will be healthier. I believe that we are entering a new era, whose transformation will surpass that of the Renaissance and the French Revolution." He said,

"Happy are they who shall see this new world; happy too, those, like us, who have announced it, foreseen it, prepared it. . . ." There was also a tradition in Italy of what was called *"reducismo,"* that returning armies remake the state (the word literally means a returning). This was in the air.

By conventional measurements Italy was better off when the war was over than its afflicted or defeated neighbors, France and Austria (the one having had the worst of the war fought on its own territory, and the other defeated and stripped of empire). The social dislocation in Italy nonetheless was great. Still essentially an agricultural society, industrialized war had been a great shock. There had been a million dead and another million wounded. An army had to be demobilized but the civilian economy had insufficient jobs for the ex-soldiers. There was not enough housing. Strikes followed, and devaluation of the lira.

The Italian public became obsessed with what was happening on the northern Adriatic coast, where the Allies, meeting at Versailles, had agreed to put the former south Slavic dependencies of the Austro-Hungarian Empire together with Serbia to create a new Kingdom of the South Slavs, later to become known as Yugoslavia. Woodrow Wilson, Lloyd George, and Clemenceau were handing over to this new Yugoslavia territory that was part of Italy's formal war claims. In the secret negotiations before Italy entered the war, France and Britain had promised Italy part of the Dalmatian coast, including the port of Fiume. However, because Slovenia and Croatia had produced partisan uprisings supporting the Allies and attacking the Austrians, they too expected territorial rewards.

Italian sentiment was influenced by the probably justified suspicion that in 1917 the Allies had attempted to make a separate peace with Austria, at the expense of their promises to Italy. Worse, Woodrow Wilson had committed the United States to the principle of national self-determination for all of the former members of the Hapsburg and Ottoman empires, none of whom was capable of generally agreed territorial definition because of the complex and overlapping ethnic composition of the region.

The new Kingdom of the Serbs, Croats, and Slovenes claimed the whole Dalmatian coast, largely populated by Slavs, including the port of Fiume, which was economically indispensable to the region, a trade outlet for Zagreb, Belgrade, Budapest, and Prague. Italy already had three major Adriatic ports, Trieste, Venice, and Bari. But Fiume was an Italian-speaking city, and Dalmatia itself had once been part of the Venetian Empire. Under the Austro-Hungarian system, it had been governed by Hungary, with the city itself granted a unique juridical status. It had been a *corpus separatum* in many functions. In 1910, of fourteen elementary schools in the city, two were Hungarian and twelve Italian-language. None was Croatian, even though the working class of the city was predominantly Croatian, many commuting from outside Fiume.

∼⦾

Wilson's conclusion that Fiume should be given to the new Yugoslavia was undoubtedly influenced by the fact that the Slavs, who had fought to throw off Austrian rule, appeared in a heroic light to the Allies—certainly to the Americans—while the Italian war record was unimpressive. Italians, as such, were considered by Protestant Americans (and no doubt by a president who was also a Presbyterian clergyman) as expedient, devious, and untrustworthy—that "Mediterranean type" to which Americans and north Europeans of Protestant religion felt superior in "race" as well as in matters of political conduct, civic life, and religious enlightenment.

The leaders of the Italian government, including the Liberal prime minister, Vittorio Emanuele Orlando, were conscious of their difficult position, respectful of Wilson, whose popularity among Europeans at the time of the Versailles conference was overwhelming ("unearthly," as one contemporary American observer said), and diffident about presenting their claims. There were people in the Italian government and political class who recognized that Fiume made sense as a Yugoslav port, and saw that Yugoslavia needed such a port on the Dalmatian coast whereas Italy had Venice and Trieste in the region. The Italian claim was sentimental and historical. But Wilson treated the Italians with arrogance and condescension, insisting on his ideas and his own solution, and rejecting the compromises that were proposed. This provoked in Italy a sentiment which D'Annunzio grandiloquently announced by saying: "Victory, you shall not be mutilated. . . . We fought for a greater Italy. We want a greater Italy. I say that we have prepared the mystic space for her appearance."

Wilson issued an appeal to the Italian people, over the head of their government, setting forth his argument for rejecting the Italian claim. The government considered this an affront, and Prime Minister Orlando dramatically left Versailles to consult parliament. Fiume had been made into a question of national honor.

When Hungarian officials were withdrawn from Fiume just before the armistice, the mayor, an Italian, was left in de facto authority, and the Municipal Council declared that he embodied "the will of the people." When representatives of the new Yugoslavia arrived to raise the flag of Croatia, the Municipal Council declared itself the "Italian National Council of Fiume," and citing the Wilsonian principle of self-determination for all peoples, appealed to Italy for union. At the same time a workers' council with both Croatian and Italian members asked for a plebiscite on the city's future.

When Yugoslav military forces moved toward the city, an Italian warship and four torpedo boats were dispatched with the assignment to protect Italian nationals and Italian interests. A quiet political struggle began over the city's control, which was to last until the following September. France, Britain, and the United States, for different reasons, all opposed Italy's claim. The French, who had sponsored Croatian irregular forces during the war, made themselves patrons of a Croatian Fiume. However, the Versailles conference supposed to settle the matter considered the problem of Fiume one of the lesser issues in sorting out the ex-Austro-Hungarian empire, and in the interim the city, for practical purposes, was run by its Italian community, with a symbolic presence of Allied forces.

Some in Italy wanted simply to seize Fiume. However, the government conscientiously waited on the Versailles conference decision, patiently pressing Italy's claims to Wilson, Clemenceau, Lloyd George, and the other assembled Allied chiefs. It is known that Orlando, the Italian prime minister, was told of various schemes to take Fiume, but the government and the army commander, Pietro Badoglio, were opposed. Among Fiumians, the conviction grew that they had to act themselves, and that is what finally happened.

In the spring of 1919, after Wilson made his maladroit appeal to the Italian public, Italian popular demands had gone beyond anything the government could reasonably expect from the Allies. Increasingly there were calls for force—a coup de main in Fiume. The government became convinced that there could be a popular uprising if Versailles ruled against Italy. Ledeen writes that D'Annunzio, leading the outcry for Fiume, concluded that if "divine Italy" was not safeguarded by Versailles, he would take matters into his own hands. "I am ready today," he told a Dalmatian audience, "to sacrifice every love and friendship, every comfort, to your cause . . . you will have me with you *to the end*. And you know what I mean by this promise. . . ." Ledeen adds: "D'Annunzio was speaking not only for himself and other patriotic veterans of the war but also for a large and potent sector of the Italian political and industrial spheres. Should Orlando and Sonnino [the foreign minister] fail to obtain their goals in France, there were wealthy and powerful men who were prepared to support D'Annunzio, or others like him, who would simply take what they felt was rightfully theirs."

In fact the Allied powers themselves precipitated intervention. In June 1919, they named an Inter-Allied Commission to investigate the situation and make recommendations. By the end of August rumors were circulating that their recommendations would go against Italy. There was supposed to be a new government elected by proportional representation, to include the vote of the predominantly Slavic suburbs.

The Sardinian Grenadiers, the Italian unit that had "liberated" the city the previous November, was ordered withdrawn and replaced, and the commander in chief of Allied forces in Fiume was also replaced, considered by the Allies as too sympathetic to the Italian nationalists.

Early in the morning of September 25, the day the Grenadiers were to leave, the town hall bell was rung to bring people out for the soldiers' departure, and people blocked the streets, shouting "Don't leave us in Croatia's hands!" The soldiers responded with patriotic slogans and cries of "Viva Fiume!" When their replacements, the Regina Brigade, also Italian, arrived, the men were greeted with applause, flowers, and kisses—the latter evidence of what Ledeen calls the "bacchic atmosphere characteristic of Fiume, noted by all who went there."*

The departed Sardinian officers wanted to return to the city and made contact with likely interventionist leaders, including Mussolini and D'Annunzio, but none was yet ready for a march on Fiume. D'Annunzio's Casetta Rossa in Venice was already a center of interventionist planning and conspiracy. He himself re-

---

* One young Sardinian officer had written home that the city "abounded with beautiful girls; the pastry shops were bursting with extraordinary sweets. . . . The Fiumians invited the Italian officers to their homes every night for parties that lasted until the following day. One ate, one danced, one drank; indeed it truly seemed that this city, with its life overflowing with gifts, was the reward for all our exertions during the war." Ledeen remarks, "Fiume was a D'Annunzian city long before the arrival of the poet-warrior."

mained unconvinced that the time was right for a coup, although several Grenadier officers carried a plea to him that said: "And you do nothing for Fiume? You who have all Italy in your hands. . . ."

He ostensibly was preparing another dramatic project, a long-distance airplane flight to the Orient. An anonymous American official in Rome reported to Washington his conviction that the Japan flight was a diversion, adding, however, that the Italian government had already sent two ships to the Pacific in logistical support for the expedition. According to the Italian writer Paolo Alatri, the government was actively encouraging the projected flight to distract D'Annunzio from doing something dangerous and compromising about Fiume. It had already been embarrassed by D'Annunzio's attacks on Wilson in speeches and newspaper articles, and in an interview he gave to the Hearst press in the United States. Prime Minister Francesco Saverio Nitti told his foreign minister that he would himself "see that [D'Annunzio] understands that his silence is essential, but you know all too well that this is not easy." On September 30, D'Annunzio attacked Nitti as someone "without a homeland, neither Slovene, Croat, partisan of Italy, partisan of Austria . . . his motto is 'I do not think except out of fear.' " On October 3, D'Annunzio said, "Those who are not with us are against us." Mussolini later made that his principle, as others have done since.

❧

In mid-August, in a newspaper article declaring that "command passes to the people," D'Annunzio wrote that it was "good and just that an armed poet . . . spokesman of the lyric order [that Italy required], should lead the people by validating what had been suffered and sacrificed in the war with a postwar triumph." When the Inter-Allied Commission recommendations became known, he finally decided to act, settling on the eleventh of September because "the eleventh is a lucky day for me." Nationalist leaders inside Fiume agreed in high excitement.

Near midnight of the tenth, D'Annunzio's convoy set out from Venice, initially with 186 soldiers from the Sardinian Grenadiers who had gone absent without leave, but more troops bivouacked along the route spontaneously joined the march, or set off on their own for Fiume, against orders meant to prevent this. A formation of Arditi was sent to intercept D'Annunzio, with orders to fire on him if necessary, but its commander defected to D'Annunzio and he and his men joined the march. D'Annunzio arrived at Fiume with some two thousand to twenty-five hundred men, four armored cars, and a number of trucks "liberated" from the Italian army. Not a shot was fired.

At the city gate Allied authorities told him he was committing an act of sedition. He brushed them aside and entered the city to cheers. Among the crowd were women who had filled the main square overnight, dressed in finery, some of them armed because they had set out to block a naval vessel from sailing, the *Dante Alighieri*, set to leave Fiume with a contingent of departing Italian troops. The women "sealed the ears" of the sailors "with the wax of their kisses." An enterprising band had even gone aboard and stolen bits of machinery. The *Dante Alighieri* became one of the original vessels in Fiume's independent navy (which eventually was sizable). The former Municipal Council, become the "Italian National Council," had already held a referendum that by an overwhelming majority had given women the vote in civic elections.

Having taken the city, or had it presented to him, D'Annunzio seems to have assumed that his task was over. However, one of the activists who had attached himself to D'Annunzio's movement convinced the National Council that the poet should take command of Fiume. This had not been anticipated. But at six that evening D'Annunzio appeared on a balcony of the Hotel Europa to announce that he had annexed Fiume to Italy. "In the mad and cowardly world Fiume is the symbol of liberty. In the mad and cowardly world there is a single pure element: Fiume! There is a single truth: and it is Fiume! There is a single love: and this is Fiume! Fiume is like a blazing searchlight that radiates in the midst of an ocean of abjection!" He offered the people the flag that had covered the body of a close comrade, killed in the war, saying this "had to be reconsecrated by your faith." He asked the people to swear their allegiance to the city on this flag, demanding, "Do you confirm your commitment?" The crowd shouted, "Yes, yes!" Ledeen goes on:

> There is a traditional theatricality to all Italian politics, and much of it is dictated by the architecture of Italian cities. Built as they are around great public areas, the cities of Italy seem almost to have been created for outdoor celebrations and civic festivals. . . . It is a point that needs to be stressed [that] D'Annunzio's political style was uniquely suited to Italy, where outdoor rallies, whether under the sun or beneath the stars were part of the civic tradition.

He argues that D'Annunzio was creating a new political style which was to have immense effect in Europe as a whole during the years to follow.

> D'Annunzio's innovative genius went far beyond the traditional sphere of politics . . . and his appearance as an actor on the European stage heralded widespread changes in the organization of political celebration. The major elements in the new style were clear in his opening speech to the Fiumians: politics had become something greater, something transcendental. In his dialogue with the crowd, D'Annunzio manipulated the mass of his listeners into a single personality, which spoke to him with a single voice. When he asked for its act of faith, it spoke to him with a single *sì*, and he expected this unanimity. . . . *

* The English author, aesthete, and longtime resident of Italy, Harold Acton, who met D'Annunzio as a child and was deeply impressed, wrote long after that D'Annunzio's "voice was more than metallic; it was intensely human, almost bi-sexual, since its

Flames, Ledeen writes, "are an old religious symbol (an insignia of the Arditi as well) and . . . the concept of Fiume as a city ablaze, consumed by its own passion, had been one of D'Annunzio's theses for some time. It was he who coined the phrase by which the city became widely known: the city of the Holocaust. . . . For him, Fiume was the beginning of a spiritual blaze that would consume all of the rotting and decrepit western world and that would purify the West. . . ."

The coup threw Fiume into a state of excitement approaching the overtly sexual, "a period of madness and baccanale" a witness said. There was drug-taking as celebration, not escape (cocaine, taken by aviators as a stimulant during the war, was associated with heroism and daring enterprises). D'Annunzio's rhetoric of heroism and his dialogue from his balcony with the crowds, which turned into a continuing series of speeches, gave public life constant drama and color.

However, the world beyond Fiume failed to react. D'Annunzio had expected the Italian government either to accept Fiume's adherence to Italy or to fall. In the latter case, he anticipated revolution in Rome. Nothing happened. D'Annunzio's flamboyant gesture failed to produce the expected result. The government initially made known its anger and chagrin, and made an appeal to duty to the people of Fiume. After that, it demonstrated great circumspection. It wanted to remain loyal to the Allies, and while its negotiating position at Versailles was strengthened by what had

---

virility alternated with feminine sweetness. His intonation seemed the fine flower of the Italian Renaissance. Pico della Mirandola must have had such accents, and Cesare Borgia such resonance. That voice made D'Annunzio the idol of Young Italy even when the poet was a shriveled old man with a glass eye. Italian mobs can be the noisiest in the world, yet literally you could have heard a pin drop when D'Annunzio's eloquence took wing in a densely packed public square, and that was before the introduction of loudspeakers."

happened in Fiume, this also was a dangerous factor, since the public generally approved of the Fiume coup, and D'Annunzio's popularity was immense.

The government had believed that it had sidelined officers likely to sympathize with D'Annunzio. It was disconcerted that the army had done nothing effective to stop him. It seemed doubtful that the army would obey new orders to dislodge the poet and the mutinous troops that had joined him. Would the army even defend the government in Rome?

The Allies, for their part, suspected that the Italian government had connived at the Fiume coup. When most were eventually satisfied that this had not been the case, they faced the possibility that the Versailles decision might cause the Italian army and public to overturn the government. Civil war even seemed possible, since if the Rome government were threatened, the Italian Left might rise against what it would see as an attempted military coup d'état. The American diplomatic observers of these events reported in an early version of that form of analysis later known as the domino theory: Peter Jay, at the embassy in Rome, sent a coded telegram to the American delegation at Versailles saying that "disaster . . . may be precipitated at any moment. . . . If civil disruption breaks out in Italy, and law and order go by the board, . . . anarchy will spread within a week to France and later to England."

Woodrow Wilson was not impressed. Characteristically, he interpreted the whole affair as a personal affront. He didn't like Italians anyway. He telegraphed Jay: "Do not allow yourself to be or even seem to be impressed with what is being said to you by members of the Italian government. . . . It is all part of a desperate endeavor to get me to yield to claims which, if allowed, would destroy the peace of Europe. . . . The only course to be pursued *is one of absolute firmness.* . . ." The Italian premier, Francesco Saverio Nitti, was a more intelligent man. He waited to see how D'Annunzio would handle his success.

The poet-warrior waited throughout his first night in Fiume for the response from Rome (and from Paris, since the primary purpose of the coup was to defy the Allied peace negotiators). Hearing nothing, he tried to get the Italian officer who had been the Inter-Allied commander in Fiume to take control of the city he had just personally annexed to Italy. The commander declined, and left for Italy proper. D'Annunzio and his colleagues found themselves with a city to manage and provision.

In practice, the National Council continued to administer the city, but D'Annunzio's entourage persuaded him to assert a power of veto. Rome ordered Fiume embargoed, then relaxed the order to let food and basic supplies enter. The U.S. and British contingents of the Inter-Allied force pulled out on the fourteenth, and the larger French force was gone by the twentieth, all three governments having been told by Rome that order would be restored.

D'Annunzio began to think about a march on Rome itself. On September 16 he met with a group including the Futurist Marinetti to consider that possibility. A logical first step would be to march on nearby Trieste, where there was "a mass of Bolsheviks." An experienced politician, Giovanni Giuriati, sympathetic to the cause, argued that popular sympathy was unsure, that D'Annunzio had no real policy for Italy even if he were to seize power, and that D'Annunzio possessed questionable ability to manage the consequences of seizing power. He thought that a march on Rome would strengthen those who wanted to overthrow the monarchy and install a republic.

Other nationalists were afraid that D'Annunzio would compromise their own ideas of territorial expansion in Dalmatia. The Futurists Marinetti and Ferruccio Vecchi wanted a republican insurrection in Italy, came to Fiume late in September, and soon departed; according to Carabinière reports, D'Annunzio ordered them removed as "agitators." One historian, Emilio Gentile, suggests that it was these disagreements with D'Annunzio that sent the two Futurists off toward the embryonic fascist movement in Milan.*

Nonetheless, the mutinous troops joining D'Annunzio steadily augmented, reaching some nine thousand, at which point he started sending them back as he had no facilities for them. War heros and distinguished generals arrived, indication, as Ledeen says, of "the extent to which D'Annunzio's ideas had penetrated the Italian 'Establishment.' "

In Fiume itself, a kind of permanent festival had been installed, a form of political theater animated by D'Annunzio with a speech nearly every day, eliciting from the public the spontaneous response, the emotional public dialogue, which was his key political invention, and his legacy to Mussolini.

However, this theater required a counterpart in reality: the Fiume adventure had to go somewhere. The government's toleration of what was happening and its willingness to outwait D'Annunzio were a serious threat. Mussolini wrote to D'Annunzio proposing that he demand overthrow of the monarchy and a new government with D'Annunzio at its head.

On the same day Mussolini's letter was sent, the king called a royal council including past prime ministers, the presidents of the chamber and the senate, the military high command, and the principal party leaders. Three days later, after a long parliamentary debate, the Nitti government called for and received a vote of confidence by a large majority. It then called national elections.

On the eve of those elections, D'Annunzio took six hundred of his followers aboard a troop transport, escorted by torpedo boats, to

* Years later, in enforced retirement on Lake Garda, waiting for the call to national power which never came, D'Annunzio ominously said that if it turned out that he was summoned to "save" Italy, "I will need unlimited authority." His drift toward authoritarian conduct in Fiume suggests what this would have meant.

the Dalmatian port of Zara (now Zadar), where he spoke from the city hall balcony, saying that the great question had become that of an Italian Adriatic, which "we will resolve!" He had no sense of the negative effect this peremptory defiance had on his followers in Italy. The elections proved a disaster for D'Annunzio and the nationalists. Another of his biographers, Eurialo de Michelis, said of him that "his ability to make long-term political calculations was limited—it's the least one can say—by the impulsiveness of his character; he could never see more than one thing at a time." Giuseppe Antonio Borgese, himself a D'Annunzian, wrote a sketch of him which acknowledged his very wide range of cultural reference but also the superficiality of it all. He noted D'Annunzio's lack of "disinterestedness. . . . The brain of D'Annunzio was more or less innocent of the laws of philosophical or critical thought. . . . Those intimately acquainted with him know that his conversation, sparkling with images and intoxicated sensibility as it was, cut off the thread of his thoughts with aphorisms before they could be completed. Full of a certain genius, he lacked that more common virtue which, for simplicity's sake, we call intelligence."

The situation in Fiume grew more restless, although there had been further military defections to the cause. The crews of four Italian naval vessels in the harbor defied Rome's orders to set sail. Two companies of Chasseurs Alpins, mountain troops, arrived in December, on a hijacked train. A group of nationalist officers boarded a destroyer in Trieste, locked up the captain and chief engineer, and sailed to Fiume. Young officers in Italy proper supported D'Annunzio or even tried to reach the rebel city. Ledeen quotes an observer in Romagna: "They are avid readers of [Mussolini's] *Popolo d'Italia*. In Faenza it appears that the [officers of the] entire regiment take D'Annunzio's side. . . . In Verona and surrounding region. . . . there is a committee that gathers funds and volunteers for Fiume. . . . [In Italian-occupied] Libya the king is greatly beloved by the army, and the name of Fiume is equally dear to the troops. . . ." The National Council in Fiume was interested chiefly in finding a peaceful and businesslike settlement. Its members were in contact with the Nitti government, but Rome's overtures were rejected by D'Annunzio, whose vision and ambitions were enlarging. He called new municipal elections in late October, to solidify his support among the workers, but there was a slow worsening of the economic situation in the city.

At the end of October, D'Annunzio dramatically enlarged the stakes. He made a speech on the meaning of the war and the expectations it had justified, and declared that his ambition to unite the Italians of Fiume with those of the rest of Dalmatia should serve as the model for the struggle of the oppressed everywhere.

> All the rebels of all the races will be gathered under our sign, and the feeble will be armed. Force will be used against force. And the new crusade of all poor and impoverished nations, the new crusade of all poor and free men, against the usurping nations, the accumulators of all wealth, against the predatory races and against the caste of usurers who yesterday exploited the war in order to exploit peace today—the new crusade will reestablish that true justice that has been crucified by an icy maniac with fourteen dull nails and with a hammer borrowed from the German Chancellor. . . . Our cause . . . directed against the evil of the world . . . extends from Ireland to Egypt, from Russia to the United States, from Rumania to India. It gathers the white races and the colored peoples, reconciles the Gospel with the Koran. . . .

This pushed him into what no one could have imagined at the start of the episode: the declaration of Fiume's independence.

That declaration had an unanticipated effect. Conventional Italian nationalists, and soldiers who had gone absent without leave (or, legally, had deserted) to join D'Annunzio's "Legion," began to drift away, uncomfortable with their position and the failure of the Italian government to take over the city, which would have given them retroactive justification. A radicalization of the Fiume revolution began, toward what might be described as an idealistic anarchism, existing within the framework of what actually had become D'Annunzio's dictatorship. The city continued to be administered by its old Municipal Council, but everything serious was referred to D'Annunzio and the circle around him.

His style of rule in Fiume during the weeks that followed was deeply to influence the style and what may be called the liturgy of Fascism, with real effect upon Fascism's success in Italy, while as Ledeen has noted, inadvertently anticipating another significant phenomenon, the 1968 revolt of the young and their proclamation of an "alternative" politics, which itself has lingering influence among a still later generation of Western intellectuals and critics of capitalism and globalization.

D'Annunzio found adventurous ways to survive. With the old sources of supply for the city cut off, his Legionnaires supported the economy with raids over the border into Italy and Yugoslavia and piracy in the Adriatic (during which the crews of raided ships were often talked into joining the adventure). These bloodless audacities, which seized the imagination and admiration of the Italian public, were carried off with ingenuity and style. D'Annunzio's Legionnaires stole forty-six military horses and rode them to Fiume. The Italian army threatened to blockade Fiume in retaliation. D'Annunzio agreed to return the horses, but at the border of the city handed over the forty-six most emaciated nags the city could find. An Italian general who criticized D'Annunzio was kidnapped in Trieste and held in elaborately courteous imprisonment for a month. D'Annunzio vetoed one project by declaring that "it is too D'Annunzian."

His rankless Legion, losing its regular soldiers, became more and more an exotic collection of former Arditi, military intellectuals, idealists, and adventurers. The English writer Oswald Sitwell saw them in 1920 and said: "We gazed and listened in amazement. Every man here seemed to wear a uniform designed by himself: some had beards, and shaved their heads completely, so as to resemble the Commander himself . . . others had cultivated huge tufts of hair, half a foot long, waving out of their foreheads, and wore, balanced on the back of their skulls, a black fez. Cloaks, feathers, and flowery black ties were universal, and every man—and few women were to be seen—carried the 'Roman dagger.' "

Public life in the city assumed increasingly fantastic forms, deliberately so. Holidays were invented, a new public liturgy adapted from religious liturgy. At the same time the city seemed increasingly pagan. The apostolic delegate complained that hedonism and aestheticism were given precedence over ethics, "Orpheus over Christ." A group of Capuchin friars rebelled against their superiors and demanded a series of reforms, including the right to marry, although, as Ledeen says, a strong liberalizing current had been at work among the city's clergy even before the war, just as Fiume had been a center of feminist reform sentiment.

D'Annunzio's idea of the city "of the holocaust"—which was to say, representative of those who suffered—was developed into a conception that no longer had to do merely with Italy but with the entire world. All this is forgotten today, blocked out by Mussolini and Fascism, but socialist and anarchist forces rallied to the Fiume adventurers, now that the city was supposed to be an international model. There was an attempt to change how people felt and how they saw. "Cultural revolution" was substituted for the historical model of revolution, or was put forward as the means by which the political revolution would be produced. There is an obvious link in this to later theories of third world revolution, as well as to the ideological Western European terrorism of the second half of the twentieth century, whose "Maoist" practitioners conceded that they had no chance to overthrow the state directly but believed they could change how people felt and how they saw their situations by violent acts "unmasking" the realities about them. They consciously took upon themselves the burden of the "inevitable" failure of the revolutionary program in order to change how people saw their lives.*

In October 1919, D'Annunzio complained that having seized Fiume for Italy, "sailors did not disembark; the liberators did not appear. Where was victory halted?" The struggle of the city, he went on, represented the struggle of exploited people elsewhere, in conflict with established powers—"usurping nations, the accumulators of all wealth." In the spring of 1920 he announced formation of a "league of oppressed peoples," the "League of Fiume," meant to challenge the League of Nations ("that conspiracy of privileged thieves and robbers"). The enemy was the Versailles settlement, taken to stand for the old regimes that had made the war, bourgeois statecraft, traditional diplomacy. D'Annunzio appealed to international colonial populations, outcasts, and oppressed minorities to unite in the League of Fiume to fight the old political and imperialist systems: the Irish (then in rebellion against the British), Egyptians, Arabs, Indians, Flemish, Turks, Austrians and Hungarians, and the Croats, Montenegrins, Albanians, and Macedonians being put under Serbian domination in the new Yugoslavia. He demanded support from Italy's radical socialists and the new Bolshevik government in Russia, but failed to get it.

* Palestinian and Muslim terrorism since 1948 has, in contrast, been a simple nationalist phenomenon, as had been the terrorism of the Zionist "Stern Gang" and Irgun Zvei Leumi before 1948. Al-Qaeda is inspired by cultural as well as political nationalism, meant to expel "Zionists and Crusaders" from the Islamic world and punish the latter's enemies for their depradations.

This idea seems to have come from Leon Kochnitzky, a Belgian poet who came to Fiume soon after the coup, and eventually became one of the heads of the city's foreign office, its "office of external relations" (the title given during the French Revolution to what before had been France's Ministry of Foreign Affairs). It was an experiment with serious political intentions. In June 1920, the Italian Interior Ministry discovered from the maritime authorities that 250,000 rifles had been shipped to Egypt from stocks in Fiume (replenished in turn by *copo di mano*—armed raids—including seizure of a ship loaded with armaments meant for the White forces in the Russian civil war). The Italian authorities were not entirely displeased to see unrest stirred up in the new Yugoslavia, but supporting Arab, Irish, and Indian nationalism against the British Empire was another matter.

In the end, the League of Oppressed Peoples became compromised by its convoluted dealings with Balkan nationalists and international adventurers, and by its lack of the money to carry out its more extravagant plans. Kochnitzky resigned his post and left Fiume that summer.

While the League proved ephemeral, the constitution written for Fiume, the Carta del Carnaro, was a document of great originality and permanent interest. It was a product of the left-wing phase in independent Fiume's short history, after the nationalists and Italian expansionists of the first phase had distanced themselves from D'Annunzio, and he had invited Italian unions, syndicalists, and anarchists to take part in the great experiment. One of the most important was Alceste de Ambris, secretary of the Unione Italiana del Lavoro, internationally known as a nonconformist of the Left and also an old friend of Benito Mussolini. (Like Mussolini he had favored Italian intervention in the world war, and had broken with the official socialists on the issue.) He became head of D'Annunzio's cabinet.

He believed that the Fiume experiment could provoke a new order in Italy, "guaranteeing everyone the fruits of their own labor." Once again a seizure of power in Rome was envisaged, carried out this time by unions, students, Mussolini's Fascists, and the Fiumian Legionnaires, all acting together. The Carta del Carnaro was to provide the ideological base for this enterprise. Such an improbable alliance was never put together, although the effort was made. By the summer of 1920, there was a new Italian prime minister, Giovanni Giolitti, the government in Rome had recovered confidence, and popular enthusiasm for the Fiume revolution was waning.

～

It was the beginning of the end for a constitutional experiment influenced by contemporary ideas of corporatism and revolutionary syndicalism, and also emulating the Renaissance experience of political organization by city republics, and indeed by the memory of the Roman republic itself.

The possession of property was linked to obligation in its use. The Carnaro constitution was a political experiment marked by religion as well, not by piety or belief, but by the cultural influence of Italian Catholicism and Catholic social thought (reflecting the corporatism of Leo XIII's encyclical on social issues, *Rerum Novarum* [1891], which attacked both capitalism and Marxism), and by the artist D'Annunzio's recognition of the power of religious liturgy and symbolism.

The political system was to be classless and corporatist: salaried workers, technical workers, clerks, owners and managers, civil servants; intellectuals, artists and teachers; the free professions—each was given corporate representation in governing the city. There was local autonomy. The constitution provided for no executive except in times of extreme peril, when a "dictator" might be named for a fixed period (as in Republican Rome). This, in Fiume, was the office of Commandante, who would be charged to "gather, excite, and conduct all of the forces of the people to battle and to victory."

Laws were to be administered by seven Rectors, each in charge of a separate aspect of public life. These were named to one-year terms by one of the three legislative institutions, two of them elected and one, the Consiglio dei Provisori, representing the "corporations" composed of the economic and professional groups active in the city.

The Consiglio degli Ottimi, or representative house, would be directly elected by universal suffrage, one member for each thousand citizens. It would be responsible for public order, civil and penal law, schools, and art, while the Provisori dealt with economic and professional questions.

Together, these two bodies formed the Arengo, or Assembly, which legislated foreign policy, finance, higher education, and constitutional matters. These legislative bodies were enjoined to act with "sharply concise brevity" and to conduct their deliberations "using a laconic style."

Under these governing bodies of the city as a whole were the communes, the various communities of the city, who were to find their own forms of government by simple majority votes, and to make their own arrangements among one another. The central government reserved to itself the right to challenge unconstitutional communal laws, or to do so on appeal from communal authorities or from one-third of the voters in a commune. Each corporation was told to invent "its emblems, its music, its chants, its prayers; to institute its ceremonies and rites." Festivals, celebrations, dancing, games, and art all were proclaimed vital to the community.

There would be complete equality of the sexes before the law and equal access to all public and private functions and offices, universal health and accident insurance and pensions, unemployment compensation, a minimum wage, and recourse to referendum. There was obligatory sport and protection of the environment—all of this in August 1920, thirty years before such demands became general in Western Europe.

~o~

The Carnaro Constitution was an effort to reconcile a lyrical anarchism and syndicalism with precedents from the Renaissance and Rome. It was a revolutionary effort conducted within the constraints of political possibility and moral realism, unlike what was to follow during the next twenty years in Western Europe. D'Annunzio later wrote, "I wanted to establish equilibrium between two fundamental human tendencies, the need for liberty, for without that there are only slaves, and the need for association, because without that there is no society."

There was a genuine Republicanism in Fiume, as in the Constitution, a confidence that public life could produce exceptional men capable of governing, as had been the case (although the reference was not made) in Federal America. At the same time the Constitution said that "the sole lawful claim to dominion over any means of production or exchange is Labor."

Fascism was independently developing along another course, but its impulse to combine nationalism with a new form of social justice, the impulse that had moved the Arditi, was a victim of its militarization of politics and ended in resembling what was happening in Germany at the time, among the mercenary Freikorps of discharged soldiers. These initially served the Weimar government and various partisan interests, and later conducted more or less clandestine wars against the Bolsheviks in the Baltic states and left-wing forces in Germany. Bands of Italian "Fascisti" were fighting the Socialists, whose Peasant League had seized villages and municipalities in the mistaken impression that revolution was about to break out in Italy. In Russia a secular messianism was being installed, a simulacrum of religion, which was not true of Fascism.

The Fiume adventure was romantic and poetic, even rather light-hearted. Few died, even in the bombardment by the Italian army which ended the affair. The end came abruptly. The Allies had lost interest. The new Yugoslav government seemed to have found its feet, and established its authority in surrounding Croatia and Bosnia-Herzogovina. The conference at Versailles decided to leave the Fiume problem for the Yugoslav and Italian governments to solve. Direct negotiations between the two produced the Treaty of Rapallo of November 1920, defining the border between the two countries, and making Fiume a free city "of Italian character."

That seemed a satisfactory solution to a substantial part of Fiume's population and their representatives on the old municipal council. It seemed to many Italians, Mussolini among them, a reasonable compromise. The advocates of direct annexation of Fiume were undermined by the treaty, and public interest in the cause waned. It seems that most of D'Annunzio's own supporters believed that the settlement had to be accepted.

D'Annunzio resisted, believing that the Italian authorities would never move against him. He declared general mobilization of Fiume and, paraphrasing Nelson, told the Italian forces outside Fiume that "Italy expects every man this day not to do his duty."

This time he had overestimated the effect of his eloquence. The Italian navy began a bombardment of the city. The council members wanted to capitulate. D'Annunzio (by his own characteristically dramatic account) tossed a coin, then said that the Italian people were not worth the sacrifices required by the city's defense (anticipating, as Rhodes remarks, "events to come, twenty-five years ahead, in a bunker in Berlin"). D'Annunzio said that his "supreme poetic effect was accomplished in Fiume."

Fiume during the regency of Carnaro was a work of political art in which the population of a whole city, together with the soldiers and adventurers who had seized it, the crews of the ships hijacked by D'Annunzio's Legionnaires, and the others who found themselves in Fiume or took themselves there, all assumed roles prepared for them in D'Annunzio's imagination, becoming, for a time, part of a living act of the aesthetic imagination. In this they discovered within themselves unexpected possibilities, unexpected innovation.

It proved in the end to have been a work of narcissism. D'Annunzio's entire life had been an actualization of narcissism. He had been capable of inspiring people to surpass themselves and invent new lives, but his romantic commitment to war and violence as forces that could set people free contributed to the swindle the Italian people subsequently were offered by Mussolini when he told them that conquest and empire would make Italy great again.

D'Annunzio himself was not arrested after leaving Fiume. He went to Venice, then to Lake Garda where he was to spend the rest of his life. He was fifty-six when he arrived there in 1921, and many presumed that he would attempt a further political career. The Fascists tried to appropriate his name and following, but D'Annunzio held himself at a certain distance from them. Eventually, he was left with a few of his old Legionnaires. He spent the rest of his life constructing a fabulous monumental villa and park devoted to his own glory, including even the hull of a torpedo boat he had commanded: a monument of vanity. It now is a tourist attraction.

The Mediterranean superman died in March 1938. With him safely dead, Mussolini spoke at his grave.

CHAPTER SEVEN

─────

THE CONFIDENCE MAN

The violent life is not ordinarily a career choice. D'Annunzio was a famous, profligate, and indebted professional poet and novelist before a war arrived to offer him his new career as romantic nationalist, and then as utopian internationalist. The world war turned Lawrence from his archaeological dig and from Oxford, and Jünger from what would probably have been a harmless academic career, preoccupied with beetles and flowers. Lawrence retreated from his ambition "of hustling into form, while I lived, the new Asia which time was inexorably bringing upon us," when to do this proved a damaging illusion, and Jünger, after triumphing over the storm of steel, formulated a theory that made of it all an ennobling and purifying ordeal from which new men and the ingredients of a new human order had emerged.

Another theorist had already postulated a new order of mankind created through struggle, Karl Marx. As reformulated by Lenin as a doctrine of action, Marx's "scientific" theory about the nature of historical progress resulted in the Bolshevik seizure of power in Russia. The Bolsheviks believed their act the first achievement of an international movement that would revolutionize human society itself. Its objective was not a new mastery by a new elite but liberation of "the laboring masses" everywhere, assisting them to fulfill the evolutionary logic of social and economic progress. Their proposition appealed to the power of generosity, idealism, and altruism—quite the opposite to the warrior appeal. But the altruist activist is also, in his or her way, looking for a revenge on life as it is.

The utopian response to the cultural and political crisis of 1914–1918 and its antecedent years—the crisis that defined the twentieth century, and potentially the twenty-first—thus took rightist form in Italy and Germany and a part of Eastern Europe, and a successful leftist form in Russia (with brief and unsuccessful emulation in Budapest and Berlin).

The idea of total and redemptive transformation of human society through political means, the most influential myth of modern Western political society from 1789 to the present day, remains with us. It has been discredited only in its Marxist and Fascist versions, which far from exhaust its present and future possibilities. Its naïve American version, although rarely recognized as such, survives, consisting in the belief that generalizing American-style political institutions and economic practices to the world at large will bring history (or at least historical progress) to its fulfillment.

The Bolshevik Revolution, actually a coup d'état, was produced by people who were committed both to utopian ideology and to the exercise of absolute political power as the necessary means to achieve their goal.

Their success in Russia was unexpected, even to those who carried it out, who feared that the regime they had created could not survive in isolation. The revolution of the proletariat theoretically required the existence of an industrial proletariat, absent in backward Russia, which possessed only a huge and oppressed peasantry. Thus from the start, Bolshevik government was a matter of improvisations. Bolshevik authoritarianism and ruthlessness were evident from very early on in the newly proclaimed Soviet Union, beginning with the induced famine, killing millions, employed to force serfs into the hitherto lacking urban industrial proletariat.

The notion of human and social transformation through the dictatorship of a special class would seem in principle hard to distinguish from the fascist notion of national transformation through will and heroism. Political domination justified by a theory of racial superiority, as in the National Socialist case, is another matter, but it cannot be ignored that the racist idea's origins are Darwinian, and that eugenicism was a progressive cause in Western Europe and the United States until after the Second World War.*

✦

Its totalitarian consequences in Russia and Germany (and elsewhere) notwithstanding, the myth of secular salvation has generally replaced religion in Western high culture, following God's reported death in the late nineteenth century. A secular utopianism, dissimulated behind a variety of theories of human progress, has been pursued, often with singular devotion and sacrifice. As Stephen Koch has written of Felix Dzerzhinsky, founder of the Soviet secret police,

> He was a man whose passion, self-sacrifice, and faith won to the Revolution the allegiance of people driven by what were surely among the highest moral aspirations of their time. For the young Whittaker Chambers, as for the young Isaac Babel, Felix Dzerzhinsky was a visionary, a being who was bringing real justice to the real world, empowering life's highest ideals. In the glory days of the revolution, when Dzerzhinsky and Lenin were laying the foundations of the totalitarian police state, life in the Cheka seemed invested with the prestige of a righteous elect, both at home and abroad. Abroad, what

---

* A significant role in the provenance of Nazism was played by the son of an English admiral, Houston Stewart Chamberlain, whose initial interest was plant pathology and who was greatly influenced by Darwinism and (as George L. Mosse writes) "yearned for a better, more beautiful racial future" in which humanity would acquire the superior virtues of the German race. He married Richard Wagner's daughter. Hitler visited him on his deathbed, to kiss his hands.

was "secret work" but the business of the ultimate liberation of humanity?*

The essential and disastrous quality of twentieth-century political messianism is evident exactly in this coincidence between work for life's highest ideals and the creation of the totalitarian state. Secular religion required that the resolution of the meaning of existence, the ultimate liberation of mankind, occur inside historical time. In practice, this licensed, indeed demanded, any action necessary to defeat the forces of reaction and speed the arrival of the new age. The crucial difference between this modern millenarianism and the messianic expectations of Western religions, Jewish and Christian (and for that matter Islamic, Muslims being also a People of the Book, descendants of Abraham) is that religion awaits the end of time. There is no hurry. Religion anticipates its fulfillment in a new existence outside time. The secular religions that took its place promised human transcendence under the auspices of Lenin, Stalin, Hitler, Mao Tse-tung, and their emulators.

Since the collapse of the Soviet Union and the (obfuscated) dialectical apostasy of the Chinese Communist Party, the idea of revolution from the left has perhaps been overanalyzed by its enemies. The Bolshevik movement's springtime appeal, before and during the 1920s, is sentimentalized by some, but neglected by others discussing the period, certainly by the hard-eyed parochials of modern American neoconservatism, who have assured their readers that had they been there they would never have been taken in.

The moral appeal which the movement made to the instinct of justice, and the opportunity for moral rehabilitation which it seemed to offer after the social collapse produced by the First

---

* In August 1991, when Soviet power was overturned, an angry mob tore down the statue of Dzerzhinsky that stood in the square in front of the KGB's Lubyanka headquarters (and prison). In Vladimir Putin's Russia, there has been a movement to restore it.

World War, endured for many years, despite the sinister practices of Lenin and other early Bolsheviks, and subsequently of Stalin himself—all willfully concealed or rationalized by the faithful because of their determination to believe.

Included among these were men and women of stature and interest. Willi Münzenberg was one such, and has received less than his deserved attention. He changed the nature of modern political communications, whose possibilities and vulnerabilities he intuitively grasped and exploited. We live uneasily with his legacy, even now.

⤙⟳

The manipulation of information, concealment of facts, and invention of virtual realities, with the source of these distortions dissimulated, characterize the political practice of most contemporary governments, possibly democratic governments more than others, given that democratic governments are more vulnerable to public opinion than authoritarian ones, and have the greater need for manipulation (and thanks to their experience of commercial communication and persuasion, are probably better at it).

The political "front" organization, a mechanism for exercising concealed power, has through the years exercised great influence through clandestine manipulation of international opinion. In its modern form it is a creation of the Communist International or Comintern, an ostensibly independent organization established in 1919 by the new leadership of "Soviet" Russia. It survived until midway into the Second World War, when it was formally disbanded under pressure from the Soviet Union's Western military allies, whose governments its avowed purpose had been (and remained) to subvert and overthrow.

⤙⟳

Münzenberg was a founding member of the Comintern, which was organized by Lenin and the other Bolshevik founders of the Soviet state to control the individual Communist movements of the world. It was presented as a voluntary network of autonomous groups working in a common cause. From the start, it was actually an agency of the Communist Party of the Soviet Union and hence of the Soviet government. A "founding Congress" was held in order to create for it a plausible international façade. Thus the Comintern itself was an invention to dissimulate Soviet state power, a "front."

The formal initiation was inauspicious, a meeting in a small hall in Moscow, the delegates some thirty-five in number. Some were foreign Communists who found themselves in Moscow, and as Stephen Koch, Münzenberg's biographer, has written, few possessed any standing in the radical movements of their own countries. The recognized English delegate, for example, was a Russian who had once worked in England. The Japanese delegate was a man named Rutgers who had spent some months in Japan.

The Comintern was conceived and afterwards controlled by the secret "Department of International Links" of the Soviet government, generally called the OMS, whose mission was to influence socialist and other non-Communist leftist circles outside Russia. It possessed its own propaganda and intelligence sections that worked in collaboration with the other intelligence organizations of the new Soviet state, but was itself, from the start, a victim of the complex combination of fear and impulse to power aggrandizement characteristic of Leninist agencies of control, leading to their multiplication. Two of Münzenberg's principal collaborators in his first major Comintern front organization, "International Red Aid," were probably officers of either the Cheka or the Soviet military intelligence service, the GRU, placed in the Münzenberg organization, as Arthur Koestler later quoted Münzenberg as remarking, "to spy on Willi for the *apparat*."*

* The Cheka was the civilian secret police and intelligence apparatus later known as the GPU, OGPU, NKVD, etc., until eventually, after Stalin's death in 1953 and the fall of the organization's then leader, Lavrenti Beria, it became, with somewhat reduced

The basic propaganda technique Münzenberg invented was to involve unknowing "innocents" (as he called them) in activities useful to the Soviet services, to win public sympathy and active support for ostensibly worthy causes that actually were being manipulated to Soviet state advantage. The phenomenon of what came to be called fellow traveling (by the well-meaning) was exploited in a myriad of ways, and the ultimate and generally successful intention of Münzenberg, his colleagues, and of the publications and organizations they created and controlled was to develop sympathy and support for causes useful to the Party that nonetheless were generally accepted as of independent merit, worthy of high-minded support, with which the Soviet Union was also associated because it shared with the "innocents" sympathy for the values and causes being defended. Münzenberg's singular talent was to invent ways "to blur the distinction between legal and illegal work and, trailing clouds of deniability, install his men in the resulting never-never land."*

The goal was "to create for the right-thinking non-Communist West the . . . belief that any opinion that happened to serve the foreign policy of the Soviet Union was derived from the most essential elements of human decency." To criticize was evidence of bigotry or ignorance.

Arthur Koestler describes Münzenberg as follows:

> When I met him he was forty-four—a shortish, square, squat heavy-boned man with powerful shoulders, who gave the impression that

---

powers, the MGB or Ministry of State Security—of which Vladimir Putin is an alumnus. Genrikh Yagoda, Nikolai Yeshov, and Lavrenti Beria, who headed the Cheka's successor organizations from 1934 to 1953, all ended as victims of the Terror they had themselves conducted, denounced, and liquidated as "poisoners, spies, or traitors."

* While a biography, Stephen Koch's book *Double Lives: Stalin, Willi Münzenberg and the Seduction of the Intellectuals* is also an admirable and instructive account of the Comintern and of the Western intellectual atmosphere of the period, based on original research, to which I am much indebted.

bumping against him would be like colliding with a steamroller. His face had the forceful simplicity of a woodcut, but there was a basic friendliness about it. His broad, cosy Thuringian dialect, and his simple, direct manner further softened the powerful effect of his personality. He was a fiery, demagogical, and irresistible public speaker, and a born leader of men. Though without a trace of pompousness or arrogance, his person emanated such authority that I have seen Socialist cabinet ministers, hard-boiled bankers, and Austrian dukes behave like schoolboys in his presence. His only mannerism was to underline a point in conversation by a sudden flashing of his steel-grey eyes under raised eyebrows; and though this was usually followed by a smile, the effect upon the interlocutor was rather like lightning. His collaborators were devoted to him, the girl comrades worshipped him, and his private secretary—tall, lean, game-legged, self-effacing young Hans Schultz—was known sometimes to work until three or four o'clock in the morning to get the ideas that incessantly spouted from Willi's fertile brain into shape. For Willi only dictated what he called "drafts" or "theses," which all ran something like this:

"Write to Feuchtwanger. Tell him articles received and so on. Ask him to do a pamphlet for us, ten thousand copies to be smuggled into Germany, upholding cultural heritage and so on, tradition of Goethe and so on, leave the rest to him, love and kisses. Next, Hans you buy a book on meteorology, find out about highs and lows and so on, find out how the wind blows over the Rhine, how many quarto handbills you can hang on a toy balloon, in which area of Germany balloons released on the French side are likely to come down and so on. Then, Hans, you contact a few wholesale manufacturers of toy balloons, tell them it's for export for Venezuela, ask them for estimates for ten thousand balloons. Next, Hans. . . ."

Münzenberg was the son of an alcoholic tavern keeper in Thuringia who accidentally killed himself. He became a barber's apprentice, and was to remain in many respects a rough provincial in manners, unable to speak any language except German (with a provincial accent), although at the peak of his influence as a publisher in Berlin in the 1920s he occupied an expensive apartment, traveled in a chauffeur-driven Lincoln automobile, and moved in fashionable as well as influential circles. His "partner" (as it is now correct to say; at the period marriage was considered in radical circles an unacceptable bourgeois institution) was a brilliant, multilingual, and beautiful Prussian intellectual, Babette Gross, whose sister was married to the son of the philosopher Martin Buber. She was part of a set of rich and distinguished German intellectual converts to the Communist cause during the Weimar period, many of whom remained faithful to the Soviet intelligence services well into the cold war.

Koestler notes that in the hierarchy of the Comintern Münzenberg was exceptional, remaining an "operator" rather than a "theorist," who stayed out of the battles of ideological factions and fractions which "every two years or so, produced a devastating earthquake in the Communist universe. He did not maneuver for position, and the wrangles about the dialectically correct interpretation of the [Communist party] line left him cold and contemptuous." As anyone who has worked in a large bureaucracy or business organization will recognize, the failure to maneuver for position and patronage, or to conform intellectually to the company "line" (that is, "be a team player") is likely to prove dangerous if not fatal, and in the Comintern, this could be so literally, as in 1940 it eventually proved for Willi Münzenberg.

~❀

The young Münzenberg, already converted to radical views, went from the shoe factory to which he had moved from the barber's shop to work in a pharmacy in Switzerland. An avid reader, initially interested in anarchism, he entered the circle of would-be revolutionaries, eventually becoming a Leninist. He demonstrated a particular talent for organizing networks and for secret work: laundering money, obtaining false papers, moving people across borders. He had been introduced to the Bolsheviks by Leon Trotsky, who was struck by the young German's talents. Lenin passed him along to Karl Radek, the Polish literary intellectual who was provider of the movement's intellectual rationales, and who was also a protégé of Felix Dzerzhinsky.

The group was at that point unaware of the extraordinary gift about to be bestowed upon them by the German general staff, as by the wand of a fairy godmother. Lenin, the general staff decided, this notorious political agitator in Switzerland, was to be conveyed to Russia on the supposition that as he and his followers opposed Russia's participation in the war, an "imperialist war" in their view, they could make trouble for the Russian government in the confused circumstances that had followed the February revolution. The revolution had provoked the tsar's abdication, followed by the Duma's nomination of a provisional government of moderates, led by Aleksandr Kerensky.*

Lenin and some of his associates were passed through Germany to Sweden in a "sealed train," from which they continued to Petersburg's Finland Station. They began immediately to prepare the coup d'état that the Bolsheviks were soon successfully to carry out against that provisional government.

Münzenberg, as a German, was expelled from Switzerland, and was compelled to return to a Germany that itself was nearing defeat. He

---

* This instance of general-staff thinking "outside the box" was to culminate less than thirty years later with Berlin raped and burned, the red flag flying from the ruined Reichstag. A "tough-minded" German general staff, writing its scenario of a successful Leninist intervention into the Russian revolution, had failed to go on to consider what the possible consequences might be for Germany of restored and radicalized Russian power. This was an error which in its essential respects others, including the Soviet authorities themselves, as well as the United States government in and after the cold war, have not failed to repeat.

became active in the revolutionary Spartakus movement, which in 1919 was to merge with the new German Communist Party, and he made his first journey to Moscow as its youth representative, being made president of a newly created Communist Youth International.

That same year the Third International was created, meant as successor to the social-democratic and antiwar Second International, which had effectively collapsed, and was not in any case under Soviet control. The German Communists, especially Rosa Luxemburg, were against a new organization, but by the time the founding congress of the Third was called, Luxemburg was dead and the German representative was convinced to go along.

As head of the Youth International, Münzenberg understood from the start that international support for the revolution did not depend on the will of the masses, a hypothetical force actually divided and confused in every postwar nation, but on the opinion of elites, who exercised serious influence over governments and were responsible for the general climate of opinion in countries officially opposed to the Bolsheviks.

Soviet orthodoxy regarded the middle classes and their intellectuals as compromised by their class status and "objectively" hostile to Communism. Münzenberg insisted that their good will was indispensable even if, as he once said to the doctrinal purists, "I too, prefer the red hundreds." But "the hundreds" in Germany, France, Austria, Britain, and the United States were not rallying to the Soviet cause, whereas a significant segment of well-known writers and cultural figures were.

They included Lincoln Steffens, the leading American "muckraking" journalist, the novelist Heinrich Mann (older brother of Thomas), and the French writers Romain Rolland (who had won the Nobel Prize for Literature in 1916, after his vain appeal against the war, issued from Switzerland in 1914), and Henri Barbusse (who while calling himself an antimilitarist Socialist, had enlisted in August 1914—at the age of forty-one—and spent eleven months at the front, receiving two citations and subsequently publishing a journal, *Le Feu*, describing the horrors of combat but seeing in the combatants the potential for an international fraternity capable of bringing about universal revolution).

Münzenberg understood that such people could not only be quoted or cited in support of the vision they themselves had conceived of the Soviet Union, but organized, promoted, and induced to act within a framework that encouraged or even enforced their support for the new Russia: in short, that they should be manipulated so that their endorsement of Soviet policies would not compromise their reputations as figures independent of Communism. Babette Gross later wrote that Willi "left nothing to chance, particularly not the manipulation of fellow travelers."

Writing about a later period, when this manipulation had become a major international undertaking for Münzenberg's enterprises, involving artists and public figures nearly everywhere in the West, Koch notes that the public manipulation was simpler than the deeper matter of

> managing what might be called the denial within. Every device of vanity and venality, misused trust and intellectual obfuscation was employed. But there was something more. The fellow travelers needed to believe too that their Stalinism was an indispensable part of their own integrity, a key to the working of their intelligence, and to the practice of their arts. They needed to *believe*. In order for this to happen, the apparatus had to seize upon the most salient moral claims of the adversary culture from which these people emerged, and make it theirs. If Americans in the adversary culture understood that the oppression of blacks was the society's great institutionalized crime, Stalinism would take the highest of high ground on the "Negro question." No matter that Stalin ruled a country where a significant part of the population languished in slave labor camps. If the

English adversary culture saw philistinism and middle-class repression as the enemy, Stalinism would embrace iconoclastic taste and sexual liberty . . . the Bohemianism and flamboyant homosexuality of Guy Burgess were an indispensable part of his slick Stalinism and central to his place in Bloomsbury. . . .

The net effect of these facades was to bind Stalinism to the self-evident truths of a given adversary culture, and make that Stalinism feel indispensable to an enlightened life. The role of this in the "denial within" could be very potent. It could be addictive.

The "direct management" of people's lives that this required was very complex, involving the playing of lifelong roles, with heaven knows what mixtures of authenticity and political calculation or commitment, by the Russian aristocrat Moura Budberg, mistress to both Maxim Gorky and H. G. Wells; the Princess Maria Pavlova Koudachova, mistress, wife, and widow of Roman Rolland and an agent under direct Soviet control; Elsa Triolet, companion of the poet and Stalinist apologist Louis Aragon for thirty years; and even the American Ella Winter, lover and then wife of Lincoln Steffens from 1919 until his death in 1936, and subsequently wife of the Hollywood screenwriter Donald Ogden Stewart. Louis Gibarti, who worked with Münzenberg, called her "one of the most trusted party agents for the West Coast."*

---

* The extraordinary extent and success of the Comintern's manipulation of prominent "innocents" is a fascinating story, told well, with an enormous accumulation of documented detail and personal interviews (if with a certain condescension toward its prominent victims), in Koch's book. He describes a significant aspect of the intellectual history of the period, a politico-intellectual adventure integral to the political struggle, and eventually the terrible war, between the Soviet Union and Nazi Germany, and the liberal democracies of the West. He also offers the best account I know of the involvement of Americans with the Comintern and Soviet intelligence, including the little-understood role of Noel Field both in prewar penetration of the American government and as inadvertent agent of the postwar Soviet purges in Eastern Europe—triggered by the Alger Hiss case.

Münzenberg's international career began with the Volga famine of 1921, which had been produced by a combination of drought, the chaotic conditions provoked by civil war and Western intervention, and agricultural collectivization. He proposed, and was made responsible for, an international appeal for aid from workers and sympathizers around the world. This proved an unexpected success, less for the volume of foreign help it elicited (actually considerable, eventually totaling some fifty shiploads of supplies and equipment), but in demonstrating what Münzenberg immediately grasped as a principle basic to propaganda: when people give to a cause, they become emotionally involved with it.

He returned from Moscow to Germany with instructions to enlarge and extend what now became known as International Workers Aid, "bringing together leading writers, artists, scientists and sympathetic politicians of every hue on a 'non-political' platform of aid to Russia," as Arthur Koestler's biographer writes.

Koestler said of contributors to Münzenberg's International Workers' Aid campaign,

> The greater the sacrifice, the stronger the bond; provided, of course, that the cause for which you are asked to make the sacrifice is brought to life in a vivid and imaginative manner—and that was Willi's specialty. He did not, for instance, ask the workers for charitable alms; he asked them to donate one day's wages "as an act of solidarity with the Russian people." "Solidarity" instead of "charity" became the keyword. . . . Willi had found the pattern which he was to repeat in founding the "World Committee for the Relief of the Victims of German Fascism" and in his various Chinese, Spanish and other relief campaigns: charity as a vehicle for political action.

An urgent objective of the Communist movement in the 1920s and early 1930s was revolution in Germany. It had made no ideological sense for the Bolsheviks to have taken power in Russia, since Communism was supposed to be a movement of the industrial proletariat. Marxist theory had identified these workers without tools, compelled to live by selling their labor, as the progressive force which would seize control of the industries which exploited them, and with that power carry out a transformation of society. Russia was a nation of quasi serfs, an ignorant peasantry submissive to the natural and unchanging agricultural cycle, in the reactionary grip of religion and class order.

Germany in 1918 was a mature industrial society with a developed and organized proletariat. Sheer accident—provoked by the First World War—had given Russia to the Bolsheviks, but Lenin himself feared that his new government could not survive unless revolutions followed in the ideologically more suitable societies of Western Europe, and particularly in Germany. "Our backwardness has thrust us forward," he said of the situation in Russia, "and we shall perish if we are unable to hold out until we meet with the mighty support of other countries."

The Comintern's original purpose was to mobilize that support. Its Manifesto demanded that "proletarians of the whole world" not only support the revolutionary government in Russia but struggle against rival socialist movements. It specifically identified as its enemies the German Social Democratic Party, the French Socialist Party, and the British Independent Labour Party. In practice, Münzenberg gave the Comintern the means for amassing a mass audience for this message.

He proved a phenomenal organizer and promoter. He first issued an International Workers' Aid bulletin in Germany, then a popular journal, and subsequently acquired newspapers, magazines, and a press agency. He eventually created or established control over what became an empire of left-wing publishing firms, including two mass-circulation German dailies, book clubs, an illustrated weekly magazine with a circulation of one million, and other magazines (including periodicals for photographers, radio amateurs, and other hobbyists). While the German Communist Party worked for revolution, his organization sponsored avant-garde drama.

David Caute, in his exhaustive history of the fellow-traveling phenomenon, writes that Münzenberg

> went into the film business in a big way. In this sphere, as in all others, he proved his financial genius. He demonstrated that if Communism could not smash capitalism in an afternoon, it could at least make money while it was trying. His was the directing influence behind the Mezhrabpom-Filmgesellschaft, which employed four hundred people in its main studios in Moscow and sponsored such classics as *The End of St. Petersburg, Mother, The Road to Life,* and *Storm over Asia.* . . . It remained only to get people to see these films, and not merely in the art cinemas. Accordingly he launched the popular Volksverband für Filmkunst, enlisting as sponsors Heinrich Mann, [the eminent theatrical and film directors Erwin] Piscator [and] W. G. Pabst and [the cinematographer] Karl Freund.

His IWA trust financed films by Eisenstein and Pudovkin. His efforts were not confined to Germany or even to Europe. He eventually directly or indirectly controlled nineteen magazines and newspapers in Japan alone. By the time Hitler took power, Münzenberg was a Reichstag member with a safe seat (organized by the Party), an elegant apartment, and a chauffeured automobile. Caute writes:

> Part of [his] secret was his amazing independence of local Party control. In the very years when the party and its main literary organ, *Linkskurve,* were blasting away at the cohorts of "social fascism," Münzenberg was simultaneously building bridges, coaxing, cajoling and generally making allies of the same "social-fascists": This the Party tacitly permitted. Besides, he had powerful patrons in Moscow.

He wore two masks. In his rare appearances as a politician, he rigorously toed the Party line. Thus in February 1932 he wrote in *Rote Aufbau* that Trotsky's proposal for an alliance between the German Communist and Socialist parties was nothing short of criminal. Yet at the same time he was engineering an even broader alliance in the shape of the International League against War and Fascism. He was an alert, sympathetic and immensely likable man, and even his more machiavellian exploits had a charm and audacity which inspired affection.

His exploits included making international scandals out of the "Scottsboro Boys" case in Alabama in 1931 (nine black youths accused, almost certainly falsely, of raping two white girls), lynchings and the race issue generally in the United States, and the Sacco-Vanzetti affair (the case of two Italian anarchists in Boston convicted of murder—rightly, it seems in the case of at least one of them), which Münzenberg promoted as an example of American persecution of foreign immigrants. (Many years later, Babette Gross said to Koch of Sacco-Vanzetti, "it was Münzenberg's idea.") The purpose of these American campaigns was not to instigate discontent in the United States, which never greatly interested Stalin, but rather to discredit the idea that the United States was a rival to Russia as a society where the working man was making a better life.

A pacifism campaign was launched in 1928, reflecting Stalin's fear of another Western military intervention in the Soviet Union. It was directed mainly to Western university and intellectual audiences. With Hitler's arrival in power and the Reichstag fire, the campaign against war effortlessly metamorphosed into a campaign against war and Fascism. There were major gatherings in Brussels and Amsterdam with prominent participants.

The Reichstag fire in 1933 provided Hitler with an opportunity to arrest the German Communist leadership and break up the party. Under threat, Münzenberg moved his operation to Paris (he and his wife narrowly escaping the police, still in the chauffeured

Lincoln). There, he received a not unsympathetic reception from the French intelligence services. He and his colleagues all were quietly given refugee cards allowing residence and work in France.

Caute writes:

> [His] financial genius never deserted him. He went about his work, [his collaborator, the novelist Gustave] Regler recalls, with the calm intensity of a chess master moving from board to board, playing twenty games simultaneously. Equally remarkable, he was almost immune to the self-justifying delusions which plague professional propagandists. While many of his exiled Communist colleagues believed their own rhetoric about the imminent revolution in Germany, Münzenberg had taken stock of Hitler's strength and knew it to be formidable. His whole effort was geared to fighting the menace of war, so that he soon switched his propaganda drive from Germany to the democracies. This shift of emphasis produced in turn a shift of priorities within him; his allegiance was now to anti-fascism first and to Communism only second.

His anti-Nazi activities were useful to France while uncompromising to the French government (which, three years later, itself became one of Socialist-Communist coalition, in the Popular Front).

The Comintern challenged the European political system. European politics, since the Westphalian settlement of 1648 created the modern state system, had been a matter of relations between governments and dynastic rulers. In the nineteenth century, after the ideological warfare (to "liberate" the people from the old regime) conducted by French revolutionary governments and then by Napoleon, had failed to stave off defeat by a coalition of imperial and monarchical powers, international relations had again become a matter of adjusting or accommodating state relations and their economic, imperial, or dynastic interests. The object of policy was to bend another government's will or decisions, not to overthrow another government in the name of an abstract principle, or instigate another people to rise against its rulers.

That, however, is what the Soviet Union set out to do, acting through the Comintern. It is why Soviet policy was so disturbing to other governments. The Soviet government considered all other governments illegitimate and their subversion ideologically necessary. Karl Marx's "scientific" interpretation of historical processes, which provided the intellectual foundation for the Communist movement, asserted that history was driven by the struggle of classes, and that only workers' states were ultimately legitimate since the industrial worker embodied the economically productive forces of modern industrial society. There was only one workers' state, Bolshevik Russia.

The doctrine said that all other governments usurped power that history had determined should, and would, eventually belong to the proletariat. This argument provided the Communist militant with certainty concerning the victory of the cause and the worth of personal sacrifices made to advance the struggle. Popular power (or in the Bolshevik interpretation, a "vanguard party" that provisionally embodied popular power), would eventually be installed in the place of defeated and outmoded bourgeois governments, and would lead society until the need for government itself withered away in the Eden-like circumstances of Communism achieved.

To the disaffected and romantic of the Western countries this was an intoxicating notion. To those who held power, possessed property, believed in the established institutions of society, defended bourgeois liberal parliamentary government, or simply believed in evil and that history was tragedy, it was a profoundly subversive claim. In the 1920s, and even more in the 1930s, after the Great

Depression had begun, the number of those who defended the established system on philosophical or moral grounds dwindled, leaving its defense largely to those it materially benefited.

The Comintern thus was a radically new force in international politics. It purported to be an independent international movement of like-minded parties, of which the Bolshevik government in Russia was merely a single member, although the most successful and therefore exemplary one. In reality it was an agency of the ruling Soviet party and hence of the Soviet government, which provided it with money to amplify its appeal, and with instructions. Its magnetism was largely provided and promoted by what eventually became known (initially to insiders) as the Münzenberg Trust.

The 1930s were the years of the Comintern's greatest activity and influence, as well as of its fateful contribution to Hitler's seizure of power in Germany by splitting the German Left (which in the Reichstag election of 1932 had a combined total of deputies larger than that of the Nazis). The Party line imposed on the German Communists, through the Comintern, was that Nazism was merely a phenomenon of capitalism's penultimate crisis, while the Social Democrats—described as "Social Fascists"—provided an obstacle to the success of the workers' revolution, since they distracted a part of the working class and the intelligentsia from supporting the Communist Party, the only valid representative of the working class.

The line was reversed in 1935 when the Communists were instructed "to enter into negotiations with the [Socialist] Second International" in order to establish a united front against "the offensive of capitalism, Fascism, and the danger of imperialist war." It was a little late. Stalin was subsequently to reverse course again and enter into a nonaggression pact with Nazi Germany in August 1939, agreeing to partition the Baltic states and Poland between Russia and Germany—a partition duly executed one week later, when Germany invaded western Poland and Russia simultaneously invaded the Baltics and eastern Poland. Stalin, as sometimes is forgotten today, remained faithful to this quasi alliance with Hitler for two years, until Germany invaded Russia (to Stalin's incredulity, even though he had been repeatedly warned that this would happen by his own intelligence services and by Western informants).

Opposition to the Comintern had meanwhile become the formal basis for the alliance of Nazi Germany with Japan—the Anti-Comintern Pact of 1936 was intended to counter the Communist "world conspiracy" (to quote the language of the treaty). Later adherents were the other wartime allies of Germany, as well as Denmark and Spain.

Opposition to the Comintern, as Alan Bullock wrote in his early biography, *Hitler: A Study in Tyranny,* gave the alliance of Germany and Japan "a universal character which a straightforward agreement aimed against Russia could not have had." He wrote, "People in England as well as in France, who would have looked askance at a blatant German nationalism, were impressed by Hitler's anti-Communism; it served the same purpose as Russia's own peace campaign and similar moves after the Second World War." The Comintern never held another congress after 1935. The war unexpectedly created an alliance of Russia with Britain and the United States, and the Comintern became an awkward reminder of their essential ideological hostility. It was dissolved in 1943 and its postwar successor, the Cominform or "information bureau," met a new kind of Western challenge, and never became more than the shadow of its formidable predecessor.

⟡

Formidable, yes, but what a futile enterprise it had been! The Comintern spent the 1920s and 1930s mainly in attempts to destroy its rivals on the Left. The rise of Fascism was welcomed, as evidence of capitalism's crisis. Events were relentlessly misjudged out of unfounded ideological presumptions, and confidently predicted revolutionary developments never arrived. Hitler's dictatorship "will hasten Germany's progress toward the proletarian revolution," the Comintern presidium resolved in Moscow in 1933. (One supposes that, objectively speaking, it did so for East Germany, if occupation and domination by the Soviet Union from 1944 to 1990 is considered a version of proletarian revolution.)

Serious men and women, even noble ones, gave themselves to this enterprise. Notable Comintern leaders and agents included not only Münzenberg, Koestler, Ignazio Silone, and a considerable number of other Western literary and intellectual figures of the period, but Georgi Dimitrov and others who were to become postwar Communism's leaders, dictators, and usually its eventual victims.

These included Jacques Doriot, the Frenchman who ended as a Fascist after having been expelled from the French Communist Party (for having prematurely supported the idea of a popular front with the Socialists!); the reformist Bolshevik Nikolai Bukharin (removed from his post as head of the Comintern in 1929 and tried and executed as a traitor in 1938); Mao Tse-tung, Ho Chi Minh of Vietnam (a founder of the French Communist Party as well as of an independent Vietnam); Maurice Thorez, who spent the Second World War in Moscow but afterwards returned to France to take control of the French Communist Party (suspect to Moscow, since its leading role in the Resistance might have provoked independent thinking among its leaders inside France); Palmiro Togliatti, the postwar Italian Communist Party leader; and even Earl Browder of the United States, where the American Communist Party was amply financed by the Soviet Union but failed to produce much in the way of results. Some of these people ended ruling their countries, some with a bullet in the neck, or in a camp inside the Arctic Circle.

Dimitrov, secretary general of the Comintern from 1934 to 1943, made a world reputation in 1933 by his brilliant and successful defiance of Herman Goering at the Reichstag fire trial. A Prussian court acquitted him and his codefendants of complicity in the arson (which today is generally acknowledged to have been committed, as the police concluded at the time, by a feeble and mentally disturbed Dutch drifter without serious political motivation). Münzenberg organized a vast and highly successful campaign from Paris accusing the Nazis of having set the fire themselves in order to discredit their Communist opponents and justify rounding them up as enemies of the new government.*

The outcome of all these efforts was failure. The Comintern overthrew no governments and did nothing to stop Mussolini or Hitler. It even actively helped them after the Ribbentrop-Molotov Pact of 1939 made Nazi Germany and Russia allies against Britain and France. The only Communist parties outside the Soviet Union that eventually came to power through their own efforts (and not because the Red Army installed them by force) were the Chinese, Vietnamese, and Yugoslav parties. The first two did so by rejecting the advice of the Soviet Union and the Comintern by making themselves into peasant nationalist movements rather than industrial proletarian revolutionary parties (not a difficult decision, since both countries lacked industrial proletariats but had a great many peasants, but nonetheless an ideological affront to Moscow).

The last-named, Yugoslavia, had to threaten to fight Russia in order to prevent Soviet forces from deposing Marshal Tito and his

---

* Koch argues that this was in part sham on both sides, motivated on Berlin's part by Hitler's need to attack the Communists for domestic political purposes; to admit that the fire had been set by an individual without political motivation spoiled that opportunity. But Hitler also needed to avoid antagonizing Moscow, a potentially dangerous military threat, particularly at that early point in German rearmament. He wished to deal with Soviet Russia on his own timetable. Russia and Germany previously had secretly collaborated in military matters when both were pariah states, Russia as a new revolutionary power, and a defeated Germany under Versailles treaty military restrictions. Stalin understood Nazism as his enemy but also wanted the German military threat directed toward the West. He was convinced that Hitler would never risk a two-front war (and refused to believe that Germany would attack Russia until Operation Barbarossa was actually launched). Koch argues that both Hitler's and Stalin's interests were served by the Reichstag fire trial and the publicity surrounding it, and that there was secret contact between the two sides that protected Dimitrov and his two Bulgarian codefendants.

wartime Partisans and installing Russian puppets in their place. And of course in the end the Chinese and Vietnamese Communists also broke with Moscow, as did the Romanian and Polish Communists; and the Hungarians and Czechoslovaks tried to do so. So much for Communist internationalism.

For many years the most influential English-language historian of the Soviet Union was Edward Hallett Carr, who devoted fourteen volumes alone to that country's history between the Revolution and 1929, and in the 1980s turned his attention to the Comintern. His final volume was *The Twilight of the Comintern*, published in 1983 and dealing with the organization during its most influential years. It is a curious book because it constructs the history of the organization from the available internal Comintern documents covering the period (and was of course written before the closely held real archives of the Comintern began to appear after Communism's fall).

This makes it almost totally unreliable but also deeply instructive about the Comintern, and about Soviet reality at the time. It is what today might be called a virtual history of the Comintern: the organization's official history as calculated to advance its reputation, bury its mistakes and crimes, and promote its objectives, all with only the most expedient connection with reality as actually experienced by the organization.

This virtuality, however, was the basis on which operational decisions were taken by the Comintern (and the Soviet government) because any deviation from the official Party description of reality, in order to accommodate what might be called the "real" reality, could be ruinous if not fatal to the offender. This in the end caused Münzenberg's defection. He lived the "real" worlds of Berlin and Paris, far from Moscow, and was an intelligent man who eventually made the choice of a "real" reality and was killed for it.

Others acted as if the virtual reality were real, and this led not only to personal tragedies and suicides, as the psychological costs became too great to bear, but to entirely practical consequences in the functioning of the Comintern and the Soviet state. The ultimate irreconcilability of virtual and "real" realities produced grave dysfunctions in Comintern propaganda and far more serious failures of Soviet policy. To take the largest error of all, it was not intelligent for the Soviet government to interpret Hitler as an inconsequential epiphenomenon of late capitalism's crisis and to act accordingly. It also was not intelligent to treat the capitalism of the 1930s and 1940s as "late capitalism" doomed to collapse and base judgments essential to the Soviet Union on that presumption.*

---

* A single unimportant example of the distance between Comintern virtuality and what actually occurred appears in Carr's description of the struggle during the 1930s between the Chinese Communist leadership and the Nationalist (or Kuomintang) movement of Chiang Kai-shek. Carr writes that in the summer of 1933 Chiang had gathered around him in Nanking "hundreds of foreign military advisors, not only Germans but . . . also Americans, including the famous aviator Lindbergh. Arms and munitions reached Nanking from all over the world, being financed by American and British loans; 850 airplanes were said to have been ordered in the United States, of which 150 had been delivered." Thus Carr (page 359).

The United States itself at the time possessed nothing remotely approaching that number of military aircraft (the operational strength of the Royal Air Force at the beginning of the Battle of Britain seven years later was only 467). A consultation of standard biographical sources reveals that in 1933 (the year following the kidnapping and murder of their infant son), Lindbergh and his wife spent the summer making an air crossing of the North Atlantic, traveling via Nova Scotia, Iceland, and Scandinavia, looking into possible air routes for the Pan American company, and continuing to western Europe where their travels were widely reported in the press. What were Carr's sources for Lindbergh's supposed service in Nanking during the identical period, as advisor to the anti-Communist Chiang Kai-shek? The proceedings of the Comintern Executive Committee's Thirteenth Plenum and a book published by a German Communist advisor to the Chinese Red forces.

Koestler tells of working with Münzenberg on a publication describing atrocities committed by Franco's forces in the Spanish civil war. Münzenberg's position was that "as we both knew the allegations to be true, the details did not matter and had sometimes to be 'interpolated.' " Since it was known that conservative Americans and international bankers favored Chiang, plausible interpolations could only add color and verisimilitude to the Comintern's account of what Chiang was up to—and so, with Carr, they passed into history.

With the murder of Sergei Kirov, a member of the Politburo, in December 1934 by an agent of Stalin's, four years of purge of the party leadership began, which brought the destruction of virtually all that remained of the old Bolsheviks of the 1918 revolution. Possibly inspired by Hitler's purge in June 1934 of his own potential rivals in the SA (his storm troops from pre-government days)—Robert Conquest's speculation—Stalin created a movement of violence and morbid mistrust that was to sweep millions to death, including many of the most prominent figures in the party, as alleged participants in a vast conspiracy supposed to have been responsible for the Kirov assassination.

Koestler writes that Kirov's death on December 1 "ushered in a new epoch in the history of Russia, and of the International Communist movement. On December 6, 12, and 18, the Soviet authorities laconically reported the execution without trial of a total of one hundred and four persons. A special decree, issued the day after Kirov's murder, deprived the accused of their right of defense and appeal, and ordered that death sentences should be carried out immediately after pronouncement. [Gregori] Zinoviev, first president of the Comintern, [Lev] Kamenev, President of the Moscow Soviet, and many other leaders of the Bolshevik Revolution were arrested and executed. The Terror had begun." A sterile conformism was henceforth enforced, with routinely issued anonymous denunciations ("police spy," etc.) of those supposed to have deviated.

What was to be the last international congress of the Comintern was called in Moscow for July–August 1935, where Dimitrov announced the dramatic shift of "line" to a policy of united or popular front with Socialists and the European democratic Left. For Münzenberg, even though he had created a huge apparatus of collaboration between Communists and individuals and groups from the non-Communist Left, this proved the political turning point. In Moscow, he discovered that control of the Comintern was being altered so as to shift the organization to the authority of the military intelligence service and the NKVD (the current name for what had begun as the Cheka). It formerly had operated its own intelligence service in collaboration with the two state agencies, and had enjoyed considerable latitude in its foreign operations. Now newly created organizations were taking over former Comintern functions, moving the Comintern away from its old roles.

⋆⌔

A year later the first of the great Moscow show trials took place, with the "confessions" and execution of Zinoviev and Kamenev, and the secret arrest of Karl Radek, the Polish intellectual and intimate of Lenin and Felix Dzerzhinsky, who was Münzenberg's early patron and friend in the Party. (Radek was tried in 1937, accused of being a German spy, unexpectedly given only a ten-year sentence, but never seen in public again. Robert Conquest, in his encyclopedic history of the purges, says that the evidence points to his having been murdered in a labor camp two years later.)

Münzenberg recognized that he was in line for a similar end, since he also belonged to that part of the Communist movement which Stalin now was expediently eliminating. He was recalled to Moscow, together with his wife (an ominous request). He was called before the Comintern's International Control Commission and charged with security laxness. Hoping that the utility to the Party of the vast apparatus of fronts and agents of influence that he directed from Paris gave him a margin of maneuver, he seized on the issue of the Spanish civil war, which had just broken out. Stalin had ordered secret arms support for the Spanish Republic's newly established Popular Front government, but needed these paid for with money that could not be traced to Moscow. (The Soviet services were eventually to take complete control of the Spanish Republican government, in the end betraying it [and stealing Spain's gold reserves], again in the interest of keeping Hitler engaged in the West.)

Münzenberg argued that with his networks and apparatus in

213

Western Europe and elsewhere, he was the only person who could produce those funds. He demanded that the Comintern leadership temporarily set aside the security charges and let him return to Paris to carry out Stalin's urgent new orders and to exploit the vast propaganda opportunities provided by the war in Spain. With luck, and opportune support from the Italian Comintern official Palmiro Togliatti, he and his wife managed to get out of Russia.

Then began his cautious disengagement from the Comintern, painstakingly disarming the bomb that could kill them both. His protection lay in the Spanish campaign, in which he in any case passionately believed. Koestler, who was commissioned to write a book on the time he had spent with the Franco forces (ostensibly as a correspondent, actually as a Münzenberg agent), and on the origins of the war, recalls Münzenberg bursting into his flat, "a thing which he never used to do before," to see how the book was getting on. "The Spanish War had become a personal obsession with him as with the rest of us. He would pick up a few sheets of the typescript, scan through them, and shout at me: 'Too weak. Too objective. Hit them! Hit them hard! Tell the world how they run over their prisoners with tanks, how they pour petrol over them and burn them alive. Make the world gasp with horror. Hammer it into their heads. Make them wake up. . . . '" His propaganda principle was "Don't argue with them. . . . Make them stink in the noses of the world. Make people curse and abominate them, make them shudder with horror."

He was particularly indignant, Koestler says, that Franco, like Hitler at the time of the Reichstag fire, "pretended that he had staged his coup just in time to forestall a revolution of ours. As we were openly advocating revolution, we had no reason to wax indignant, except on the technical grounds that we had not been planning a revolution in that particular country and at that particular time. But a professional burglar would, I imagine, be equally indignant if charged with a burglary he did not happen to commit."

Münzenberg had sponsored André Malraux, then a fellow traveler and Münzenberg collaborator, in organizing a bomber squadron of sympathizers and mercenaries to support the Spanish government, which had lost most of its air force to Franco's military rebellion. He published a book on Franco atrocities emulating the "Brown Book of Hitler Terror" published after the Reichstag fire (with "probably . . . the strongest political impact of any pamphlet since Tom Paine's *Common Sense*," in Koestler's opinion).

He organized the mobilization of intellectuals and others ("innocents" or otherwise) across Europe and America in support of the Spanish Republic's government, contributing to the unwarranted reputation the war enjoys to this day of having been Europe's first conflict between democratic forces and a predatory fascism. The dull and parochial truth is that it was a conflict among purely Spanish social forces, with their own histories in the tragic experience of Spain in the nineteenth and twentieth centuries (including "the Disaster"—which is what defeat and loss of empire to the United States in 1898 was subsequently called in Spain). Franco was a reactionary, not a Fascist, although the Italian Fascists and the Nazis supported him, and the Popular Front government was to become a puppet of the Soviet Union.* However for the next fifty years it was the myth that counted, and Münzenberg contributed crucially to the creation of the myth.

◆◇

For him personally, the war provided an opportunity to protect himself and his wife by cultivating involvement with non-Soviet

---

* After unsuccessfully negotiating with Franco in 1940 to obtain his World War II support, Hitler told Mussolini that he would rather have teeth pulled than try again. Franco and Spain, of course, sat out the war, and by 1953 had an alliance with the United States, and in 1955, membership in the UN.

forces which could be convinced to take an interest in his security. However, the Spanish war did not last long. By mid-1937 the Republic's government was entirely in the hands of NKVD agents. The Comintern's operations in Spain, directed from Moscow, were beyond Münzenberg's control. Moscow again told him to return. There were repeated assurances that he had nothing to fear. The word was put around, though, that he was no longer reliable, then that he was a traitor. One of his associates, in New York, was taken aside by the American Communist leader Earl Browder, who warned him that Münzenberg was a traitor. When this man returned to Paris he talked with Münzenberg, who showed him a letter from Dimitrov urging him to come back. Münzenberg said that if he went back he would be shot like the others, then rehabilitated a decade later; that didn't interest him.

The Comintern demanded money Münzenberg controlled in European banks. He said he would surrender it if a young German associate, being held in Moscow to put pressure on Münzenberg, was released. This was done. (Koch notes that the young man was later killed, once Münzenberg was dead.) Münzenberg possessed an immense amount of information that could be deeply damaging to the Comintern and the Soviet Union; that was a weapon he used in asserting independence from the Comintern.

He kept himself highly visible as a leader of the international Popular Front and among the ostensibly independent groups he had created, increasingly aligning himself with the influential "innocents" active in these groups, the most important of which was, for him, the "Heinrich and Thomas Mann Committee" of German writers in exile. This kept him in close contact with the great novelist and with others in the German exile cultural community.

❧

He next started a new journal dealing with ideas and politics, *Die Zukunft* ("The Future"). Koestler, who had formally resigned from the German Communist Party in 1938, was called back to be its editor. He says:

> The idea was to publish an independent, German-language weekly paper which, apart from anti-Nazi propaganda, would work for the rapprochement of the various groups in exile, and develop a program for the day when the Nazi regime was no more. We had a rather good start, with original contributions from Sigmund Freud, Thomas Mann, Harold Nicolson, Duff Cooper, Norman Angell, E. M. Forster, Aldous Huxley, and others. For the planning of a long-term, post-Hitlerian policy we had assembled an editorial Brains Trust consisting of Manès Sperber (who by now had also left the Party), Paul Sering (the pen-name of Richard Loewenthal . . .), Julius Steinberg the sociologist, Willi and myself. We also had a literary supplement, edited by Ludwig Marcuse. . . . [After I resigned] it continued to appear, edited by Thormann, a member of the Catholic Center Party, until the end of 1939 or the beginning of 1940, when most of the staff were sent to the internment camps.

Koch calls the paper

> a classic Münzenberg-style mix of innocence, intellectual grandeur, and unseen agendas. . . . As the decade now hurried towards its climax in war, almost against its own intentions *Die Zukunft* evolved into something that in retrospect has the look of the first truly antitotalitarian journal for the senior intelligentsia. . . . It was a model for publications to come. The manner and even the personnel of *Die Zukunft* suggest Melvin Lasky's postwar publication *Der Monat*, and through that link, the publications of the Congress for Cultural Freedom. . . .

❧

With the Ribbentrop-Molotov Pact in August 1939, followed by Germany's attack on Poland on September 1, Münzenberg broke openly with the Communists. He attacked Stalin in *Die Zukunft*. In early 1940 he published the names of forty important German Communists killed in Stalin's purge, carrying out one of the threats he had made to Moscow. He began weekly restaurant lunches to which he invited known members of the French, British, and other allied intelligence services in Paris, where he analyzed for their benefit, and that of their governments, the developing Nazi-Soviet collaboration. He had enough knowledge about Soviet penetration of the allied intelligence services (much of it achieved through Comintern channels) to treat them with caution, but these contacts were a form of reinsurance. The British were very interested in him, but he warned a friend that one of his "most dangerous enemies" was in British intelligence.

In the spring of 1940, when Germany attacked France, the game was up for him, as he was an enemy alien in France. He was interned. Beforehand, he consulted two people from British intelligence, who advised him that rather than try to leave the country it would probably be safer to accept internment (accomplished, as it happened, as part of a group including American male residents of France, also being interned).

As the Germans advanced on Paris, he and others were sent to a site in the south, to Chambarran, south of Lyon, where he was put to work gardening for the camp commander. His wife was elsewhere, in a separate group of women internees (and survived the war). He seems to have decided at this point to get to Switzerland, where he and his wife had funds, rather than to Marseille, which offered the possibility of escape to North Africa or America. His particular group now was mainly composed of middle-aged Germans, some of them distinguished figures, including Kurt Wolff, later an important American publisher.

Münzenberg was taken up by a young and belated arrival in the camp who claimed to have been in a Nazi concentration camp, and who supported the project to strike out for Switzerland, as did a German Social Democratic trade unionist whom Münzenberg had known in Paris. As the French capitulation approached, the camp was thrown open. Some internees were loaded on buses to go farther south, others were formed up to walk south, but the camp commander indicated that people also were free to strike out on their own. Münzenberg's group of walkers stopped for the night on the edge of the forest of Caugnet, south of Lyon.

There, Münzenberg, the young man, and the German Social Democrat—and according to some accounts a second young man—decided to start for Switzerland. They had learned that a car could be purchased in a nearby village, and Münzenberg had money to buy it. They set off but none of them returned. They were seen in the village. The trade unionist acquaintance turned up much later, in German-occupied Paris, working with a collaborationist labor organization.

There were contradictory reports at second hand as to what actually happened. Koch thinks suicide a psychological possibility in the circumstances but on balance shares the general consensus that Münzenberg was murdered by the NKVD, or conceivably through a collaborative operation of the NKVD and its then allies in the Nazi services. The death occurred in June 1940, while the Nazi-Soviet pact prevailed. The corpse was found under a tree in October, by hunters. There was a broken cord with a hangman's noose around Münzenberg's neck. There was no money on him, but a valuable watch, and an unmailed postcard addressed to his wife.

CHAPTER EIGHT

L'HOMME ENGAGÉ

Irving Howe wrote in the 1950s, of the changes that had been taking place in political fiction, that while "for Dostoevsky and Conrad the very possibility of revolution meant a catastrophic breakdown of order, a lapse into moral barbarism: for Malraux and Silone the breakdown of society is a long-accomplished and inevitable fact."

In 1926, André Malraux wrote that the duty of his generation was to proclaim "the failure of individualism, and of all those doctrines which justify themselves by the exaltation of self. . . . All the passion of the nineteenth century, concerning man, found expression in the vehement affirmation of the eminence of self. But this man and his self, erected on so many ruins, who still overshadows us whether we like it or not, *no longer interests us.* Moreover, we are resolved no longer to listen to the appeals of our weakness, whether it offers a doctrine or a faith. They say that no one can act without faith. I believe that the absence of all conviction, like conviction itself, drives some men into passivity and others to extreme action."

Malraux was the most self-conscious of those twentieth-century men of action who were also intellectuals and artists. By calculation, he attracted public attention throughout his life. He remains a figure of the international literary canon, but the public personality overshadows the work: Malraux was a phenomenon of the political history of twentieth-century Europe, as of its cultural history, his early novels being intentional political acts.

Those novels created "Malraux"—as the *New Columbia Encyclopedia* says, "man of letters and political figure . . . intellectual with a broad knowledge of archaeology, art history, and anthropology . . . led from early manhood a remarkably adventurous life . . . uprisings in Shanghai . . . Loyalist air force in the Spanish civil war . . . tank commander during World War II . . . resistance leader and hero . . . outstanding novels, reflecting the tumult of his time . . . writings on art and civilization." This public Malraux was actually a conflation of achievement with lies—of what André Malraux did with what he wished he had done, and had convinced others that he had done.

He wanted immortality. In France, where the manifestly nonimmortal are elected to the Académie Française,* those considered to possess a serious claim on immortality are awarded publication of their works in the nobly bound and edited *Bibliothèque de la Pléiade*, the collection of great works of French and international literature published since 1931 by the house of Gallimard. Appositely, in 1989, the bicentennial year of the French Revolution—the occasion of the politically committed intellectual's first furious irruption into modern history—Pléiade issued the first volume of a projected six-volume complete works of André Malraux.†

---

* Whose "immortals," as they are known, not without a conscious irony, appoint a "perpetual secretary"—"a living pleonasm," as a recent occupant of the post, Maurice Druon, has said.

† It included the early Asian novels, *The Temptation of the West* (1926), *The Conquerors* (1928), and *The Royal Way* (1930), the English titles of which are straightforward translations of the French, as well as *Man's Fate* (*La Condition humaine*, 1933), the volume that made Malraux famous. The volume also contains Leon Trotsky's criticism of *The Conquerors*, which was essentially that the author lacked "a solid inoculation of Marxism," together with Malraux's response, which was that he was an artist, not a historian of Asian revolutions—a truer remark than most of his contemporaries would have suspected. The second and third Pléiade volumes have since been issued, with *Espoir* (*Man's Hope*, in English) and the autobiographical *Walnut Trees of Altenburg* and *Anti-*

Régis Debray, the writer and political activist who spent part of his
life in a Bolivian prison because he had chosen the Malrauxian role
of homme engagé, made the case against Malraux in *Le Monde* at
the time of Malraux's death, in 1976. He said that Malraux was a
twentieth-century man of image "who never asked if an idea were
right or not, but whether it made an effect," and went on:

> Malraux was the first to understand that the lie no longer exists in the
> twentieth century, any more than truth. He was the first to sacrifice
> idea and reality to *image*. All serious power rests on the imaginary,
> and Malraux, a man of cinema, of mise en scène and décor, was born
> to power. He understood before any of us that novelistic fiction was
> finished and that no fiction would work that could not pass as wit-
> ness, as testimony. This deliberate and organized ambiguity between
> the life of the writer and his work definitively attached the work of
> art to the emotional context of its presentation, just as it identified
> the rightness of a political act with the theatricality of its manifesta-
> tion. The introduction of publicity techniques into the realm of let-
> ters was the genius of Malraux in the 1920's.

Malraux would have put it differently. He might have said, as the
Catholic writer and editor Emmanuel Mounier said in May 1933,
"The vocation of mankind is to create facts"; but Mounier un-
doubtedly had other things in mind than self-promotion.

Malraux was not the first to articulate the position, so significant in
the mid-twentieth century, of "engaged intellectual"—of politically committed and active, often revolutionary, intellectual and
writer. He was, however, the first one to do so with such a very large

---

Memoirs, and *Felled Oaks*, presented as a series of conversations with de Gaulle. (Olivier
Todd, his most recent biographer, says of the last, "a very beautiful book [*très beau livre*],
if you disregard the idea of truth.")

effect upon the modern European and American intellectual and political sensibility. He made it exceedingly difficult, from the 1920s until the present day, for the life of the mind, or of art, to be pursued for its own sake, in indifference to the political society within which scholars and artists function.

The question of the political engagement of intellectuals was debated mainly in France after the First World War, where the disinterested, apolitical intellectual life was defended by Julien Benda and others. Benda argued that political activism constituted betrayal of the intellectual vocation. He said that because of the work of the intellectual class—"clerks"—"humanity did evil for two thousand years but honored good," and that "this contradiction was an honor to the human species, and formed the rift whereby civilization slipped into the world." On the other hand, by taking up "the game of political passions," intellectuals became part of the "the chorus of hatreds among races and political factions." Benda added, "Still less will it be denied that they adopt national passions." Intellectuals thus renounced the exemplary role previously played by "a race of men whose interests are set outside the practical world."

Benda was born in 1867, and his *Treason of the Intellectuals* (*La Trahison des clercs*) was first published in 1927. His was a position anchored in the late nineteenth century, when France's wars of revolutionary nationalism and Napoleonic expansion had cooled in the memory, and the lethal consequences of modern political ideology were unimagined. It was a period of European political and dynastic stability, and of material and social progress. Even during the French Revolution, Goethe had been able to say of himself and his friends, "In our little circle, we took no notice of news and newspapers; our object was to know Man: as for men, we left them to do as they chose."

"Clerks" served an abstract justice; it was possible for them to despise political men and political engagement as complicity in something mean. Benda said, "We may say beforehand that the 'clerk' who is praised by the laymen is a traitor to his office." It is a position scarcely defended today, except in the furthest reaches of scholarship, but there is more to it than Americans—above all—might like to think. George de Huszar quotes Scripture pertinently: "But I say unto you, that every idle word that men shall speak, they shall give account thereof in the day of judgment. For by thy words thou shalt be justified, and by thy words thou shalt be condemned." (As for Benda himself, when the Popular Front arrived, he became, and remained, a fellow traveler of the Communist Party.)

The debate gained its modern resonance when people like Maxim Gorky began to make such declarations as that the duty of intellectuals and artists lies in becoming "active collaborators of the proletariat, which is working for the freedom and the happiness of the proletariat of all countries." Gorky added that to do so one must emulate "the iron will of Josef Stalin, the helmsman of the Party." Theoretical reflection upon the role of the intellectual in society was left behind by events in the late 1930s and 1940s.

Lives, however, are only indirectly rearranged by theory, and André Malraux made himself into an homme engagé first of all because he admired and wished to emulate T. E. Lawrence—Lawrence of Arabia. In *The Walnut Trees of Altenburg* (1945) Malraux makes his hero a Lawrence-like figure who adventures into Central Asia on essentially the same mission Lawrence had claimed for himself ("of hustling into form, while I lived, the new Asia which time was inexorably bringing upon us"). This hero is also explicitly meant to be understood as Malraux's father. The novel makes this clear in the autobiographical accounts of Malraux's own Second World War experiences, which begin and end the book.

Thus Malraux deliberately identifies himself symbolically as Lawrence's son, and as even more than that, since this hero is named Vincent Berger, a name that (Malraux writes in his autobiography, possibly ingenuously) "later became mine for two years—some friends in the Resistance gave it to me as a pseudonym, and it stuck." He adds, "Are such premonitory creations to be explained by the fact that the virus of daydreaming gives rise to action too, as T. E. Lawrence asserts?"

In his writings Malraux repeatedly made reference to Lawrence, measuring himself, as it were. He claimed to have met Lawrence, a meeting about which his biographers are more than skeptical. Olivier Todd says, "For a long time he repeated that he had met the colonel in a grand hotel in Paris or London—the bar of the Ritz, someplace like that! He had never seen Lawrence, but he had imagined it so often and so vividly that it was neither false nor true but 'lived' in the superior reality of fabulous history." In a conversation with an earlier biographer, Jean Lacouture, Malraux said of Lawrence, "The difference between us is that Lawrence always told me that he was convinced that he would fail in whatever he undertook. While I have always believed that I would succeed in what I did! I act to win." This was at least partly true.

He claimed to have written an entire unpublished book about Lawrence called *Le Démon de l'absolu*, which was subsequently destroyed (by himself or by the Gestapo; he said both). In fact, some two thousand pages of draft survive and are published in the second Pléiade volume. Needless to say, they tell one a great deal (that is familiar) about Malraux, and not much (that is true) about Lawrence.

Malraux was born in 1901, in modest circumstances. His mother was the daughter of a baker in the Jura, her mother a seamstress of Italian origin. However, there were artists and entrepreneurs in the family, a sculptor and a military man. Malraux's father was, by all accounts, a high-spirited, unsuccessful man, variously described as an inventor and a banker and as having employment connected with the Bourse, the stock exchange. Lacouture calls him "a failure who seems to have reached his peak in his role as tank officer in 1917–18, and found his life thereafter so insipid that, finally, in 1930, he put an end to it." Todd says that he was a former noncommissioned officer who had small jobs in Paris banks and as a broker and commission man. He was a man of unsuccessful speculations, inventions that didn't pan out, but was more successful as a ladies' man than as a businessman, which led to the breakup of his marriage. The couple separated four years after André's birth, and later divorced. The young Malraux was brought up by his mother, an aunt, and his Italian grandmother, who ran a wholesale grocery business in a Paris suburb. He failed to take his baccalaureate. He was determined, however, from the beginning, "long before I was sixteen . . . to become a great writer."

He made his first appearance in Paris literary circles in the pose of a dandy (with cape and cane), an admirer of D'Annunzio, signing himself "The Mandarin." His first published work was on "Cubist poetry." He was a follower of the Surrealist poet Max Jacob. He was *farfelu* (a word he himself reintroduced to respectable French; the dictionary says "a bit mad, bizarre"). He first made a living on the margin of the book trade by dealing in manuscripts and rare or unusual books, some of questionable provenance, some pornographic. He had from the start "a touch of the charlatan," Maurice Sachs said; of the "magician," according to another collaborationist writer of the prewar and wartime period, Alfred Fabre-Luce; of "the hustler . . . who depends too much on our stupidity," François Mauriac wrote after a public rally on Spain in 1937.

Malraux once said of Lawrence, "Daydreamers are dangerous men for they can play out their dream . . . and make it possible." Malraux succeeded in turning several dreams into reality, including that of becoming a great writer—a great writer who, as it happened, never wrote a great book. *Man's Fate* was enormously and enduringly influential, and it is a splendid book, but a sentimental one, inferior to the roughly contemporary interwar novels of revolution and revolutionary politics written by the Italian, Ignazio Silone; the Hungarian, Arthur Koestler, sometime Comintern agent; and Ernest Hemingway, among others (not to mention Dostoyevsky and Conrad). *Man's Hope* was a superior version of the propaganda novel, as *Days of Wrath* was an inferior one. Malraux's memoirs, his *Anti-Memoirs* (1967), are, as the title indicates, an interesting further work of fiction. A hostile critic, Thomas Clerc of the University of Paris-Nanterre, wrote in *Le Monde* in 2001 that Malraux was a bad writer "because he did not believe in literature. This lack of faith is a mortal sin for an author. It led him to think that to write comes down to communicating. One understands his popularity because he was par excellence a comprehensible writer. Above all he liked ideas incarnated in history. But in failing to think about the powers of language he held himself apart from the modernity of his times, which had understood that you don't make literature with ideas but with words. . . . True literature is never dated; that of Malraux is covered in dust."

Malraux's international reputation was made by *Man's Fate*, published in 1933, but it is a book not easily reread today. Its impact rested on the political circumstances in which it was written and published. Today its lack of character development and narrative pace make it less readable than a good many of its contemporaries, but in 1933 *Man's Fate* seemed to offer revolutionary truth, written by a revolutionary. It described what was taken at the time to be a crucial event of the twentieth century, after the Russian Revolution—the rise of the revolutionary movement in China.

Seven decades later, when Marxism and Leninism are in ruins and China's Communism is recognized as a history of political reaction and repression, that time and such a sentiment seem remote indeed. But Trotsky's remark, in a commentary on Malraux's earlier China novel, *The Conquerors*, that those "events in China . . .

are incomparably more important, for the destiny and culture of humans, than the vain and pitiful carryings-on of all of Europe's parliaments or the mountains of literature being produced in stagnant civilizations," found wide agreement in the 1930s among politically articulate people in Europe and North America. *The Conquerors*, covering much the same ground as *Man's Fate*, failed to have the impact of the later book, undoubtedly because when it was published, in 1928, the postwar world was intact, and Asian revolution was a curiosity, or was considered irrelevant, while by 1933, when *Man's Fate* came out, a very large portion of the politically aware in Europe and America believed that after the crash and fall into depression, the Western world awaited, or deserved, revolution.

Man's Fate was thus as much a phenomenon of the political culture of the time as of the literary, marking a crucial change in political sensibility. It was a great international success. Eisenstein wanted to make a film of it, with music by Shostakovich. According to Malraux, Meyerhold was to make a play of it, with music by Prokofiev. It is decisively a part of political as well as literary history. It has the laconic, aphoristic style, the brilliant set-piece scenes, and the psychological introspection of all of Malraux's novels, but also their episodic quality and lack of true narrative force, and their failure to create living characters other than those who are surrogates of Malraux himself. Thus the young terrorist, Ch'en, is brilliantly presented—because, one surmises—Malraux recognized in himself the potential for becoming a terrorist. Yet Ch'en is a very literary terrorist. The evidence we have today in terrorists' own writings and in the confessions and reflections of the European terrorist "repenti" of the 1970s and 1980s, and what we know of the anarchist terrorists of the late nineteenth and early twentieth centuries, suggests that real terrorists are more confused, more blundering, more self-deceiving, less intelligent. Malraux's terrorist is a model of lucidity and moral responsibility, fascinated by death, of course, as was Malraux:

A craving for the absolute, a craving for immortality—hence a fear of death: Ch'en should have been a coward; but he felt, like every mystic, that his absolute could be seized only in the moment. Whence no doubt his disdain for everything that did not lead to the moment that would join him to himself in a dizzy embrace. From this human form . . . emanated a blind force which dominated it—the formless matter of which fatality is made. There was something mad about this silent comrade meditating upon his familiar visions of horror, but also something sacred—as there always is about the presence of the inhuman. Perhaps he would kill . . . only to kill himself.

The structure and the characters of the novel are determined largely by its political scheme. Gisors, the father of the central character, Kyo, represents a morally exhausted bourgeoisie. He is a university professor who was capable of inspiring Ch'en but who retreats into aestheticism (Malraux's own temptation, to which he eventually succumbed). He reacts to Kyo's death with the thought, "There is something beautiful in being dead," Malraux writes. "He plunged into it deeper and deeper, as if this terrified contemplation [of suffering] were the only voice that death could hear, as if this suffering of being a man which pervaded him, reaching down into the very depth of his heart, were the only prayer that the body of his dead son could hear."

The corrupt and decadent aristocrat Baron de Clappique and the dynamic, cynical, lucid enemy of the revolution, Ferral, the head of the Franco-Asiatic Consortium, are equally representative of a Marxist scheme. Malraux's Gisors observes that "novels are not serious, but mythomania is." The book lacks the human complexity of Silone's novels about Italian revolutionaries, coping with the Party's idealism and betrayals, and also lacks the disabused knowledgeability of Koestler. " 'What will become of Rocco, outside the Party?' " a character asks in Silone's *A Handful of Blackberries.* " 'What becomes of any man when he's left to his own devices?'

'We must save him,' said Stella with determination. 'At all costs. We can't leave him to himself.' "

Silone's and Koestler's figures exist in a rich social context, amid moral contradictions. Malraux's do not. What are you going to do?, Kyo's wife is asked when the Canton uprising has failed. "Try to serve in one of the sections of women agitators. It's practically arranged, it appears. I shall be in Vladivostok the day after tomorrow, and I shall immediately leave for Moscow." The flat, agitprop language and sentiment reveal the difference between Malraux and Silone and Koestler. The latter had actually been on the run, forced into exile.

⚬

Similarly, Hemingway, writing about revolutionary war in Spain, demonstrates that he had actually experienced war, been wounded, was interested in and cared about military matters and partisan war, and thus could accurately describe weapons, terrain, how to handle weapons and blow up bridges. Malraux is making it up. I suppose that *For Whom the Bell Tolls* is not much read today, even in schools, and is ruined for an older generation of American moviegoers by recollections of Technicolor, the earth moving for Gary Cooper, and the "thee's" and "thou's" and "wert's" with which Hemingway tried to render familiar address in peasant Castilian; and, above all, by the eventual demolition, before our eyes, by the public personality, of Hemingway the artist.

Yet it is a more formidable novel than *Man's Fate*, not to speak of *Man's Hope*, Malraux's own Spanish civil war novel. Despite its romanticism, *For Whom the Bell Tolls* is gripping and moving, even thrilling, with realized characters and a more sophisticated appreciation of the political complexities and treacheries of the Comintern at war than Malraux was capable of (or would permit himself, in view of his concern for his standing with the Party).

⚬

Kyo's father says to Kyo's wife, "Marxism . . . in Kyo's eyes it was a will . . . in mine, it is a fatality, and I found myself in harmony with it because my fear of death was in harmony with fatality." Malraux was not, I think, a novelist. His sensibility was poetic, introspective, autobiographical, ultimately solipsistic, his subjects himself, death, and art as an answer to death. Thus his observation in the late meditation on death, *Lazarus* (1974), that when Malraux felt that he was dying, on the occasion of a collapse, he was penetrated by a feeling of "an inexplicably consoling *irony*."

His books on art, including *The Voices of Silence* (1951) and *The Metamorphosis of the Gods* (1957) are his most interesting achievement. His real quality was as an inventive, original, provocative viewer of paintings, statues, things, and people, a creative manipulator of ideas and insights; in this respect he was perhaps a magician but not an illusionist—he really did see, and think. A priest who was active in the Resistance in Alsace disliked Malraux when he met him. Later, Malraux sought him out, took his arm, and began by saying, "What significance can man's history have if there is no God?" The priest, Pierre Bockel, said afterwards that "extraordinary as it may seem, I have always felt since that night that it was through what Malraux said to me that I felt what my own faith might be." He dazzled people by his brilliance, but it was a real brilliance, which upset and moved them and did not merely seduce them.

The career, however, was his principal creation, and what made possible his mark on the modern sensibility. The cape, the cane, the Surrealist-Cubist gamesmanship of the earliest years in Paris were followed by the Indochina adventure, which was inspired by his transparently sincere passion for art, and by his equally sincere need for money and unwillingness to take a conventional job. He and his young wife, Clara Goldschmidt, went to Cambodia in 1923 with a friend, Louis Chevasson, to rob what they expected to be the neglected secondary Khmer temple ruins in the forest near the great monuments of Angkor. They made preliminary contacts with dealers to sell what they expected to carry off. On arriving in Siem Reap, they organized guides and oxcarts, and went into the forest to spend two days with saws and chisels at a wat called Banteay Srei, twenty-five miles from Siem Reap.

The American scholar who is their apologist in the matter, Walter G. Langlois, writes, in *André Malraux: The Indochina Adventure*, "Many obscure points surround the granting of official permission for Malraux's archaeological expedition. It seems highly unlikely that he revealed to the Colonial Office his plan to go to Banteay Srei: any such interest in the ruin would have called attention to the fact that for one reason or another the appropriate authorities in Indochina had not yet listed it as a 'classified' monument; that is, one which had been taken under the direct control and protection of the state. This classifying would have had important legal consequences, but as Malraux later pointed out, until it had actually been done, the temple remains were no more than abandoned rubble in the jungle to be had for their taking."

Be that as it may, the Malraux party concealed the statuary in the boat that was to take them downriver from Siem Reap, and were arrested. Months later, Malraux and Chevasson were let off with a suspended sentence after appeal of their initial convictions. Meanwhile, Clara Malraux, against whom charges were dropped, had organized publicity for their plight among Paris writers and artists. Malraux returned briefly to France, but within weeks the couple set forth for Indochina again. This time, it was to help put out a newspaper (two newspapers, as it turned out) critical of French colonial policy. This experience resulted in the four Asian novels, including *Man's Fate*. Malraux's career as artist engagé was launched.

❧

The writer of revolutionary novels presented himself to the European and American publics as himself a revolutionary—as "leading member of the Young Annam Party (1924). Kuomintang commissar for Cochin-China, then for Indochina (1924–25). Delegate for propaganda in the leadership of the nationalist movement at Canton under Borodin (1925)," to quote the jacket of the 1928 German translation of *The Conquerors*.

The author's note for the Modern Library edition of *Man's Fate*, published in the United States in 1934, elaborates on this: "Malraux went to Indochina in 1921 and from there made an archaeological expedition to Cambodia and Siam. In the 1925–1927 uprising in China he became Commissioner of Propaganda for the revolutionary government of the South. A member of the Committee of Twelve, he was active in the Canton insurrection and participated in hand-to-hand fighting." His American translator, Haakon Chevalier, says in his introduction, "Here, perhaps for the first time, is a writer in whom the revolutionary and the artist are one. André Malraux has lived through—participated in—the events of which he writes, and has understood them; and he has recorded them with superb mastery. The book is eminently successful both as a revolutionary document and as a work of art. . . . He is a revolutionary today, as one imagines that he would have been a militant Christian in the early centuries of our era, a soldier-poet in Dante's time, an Encyclopedist in the eighteenth century—he is a revolutionary because he sees the Revolution as the most vital force of our time." Malraux wrote to Edmund Wilson in October of 1933 that he had been "Kuomintang commissar first in Indochina, then in Canton."

The facts are that his arrival in Indochina for the Cambodian expedition was in late 1923; he returned to France, after his trial, in November 1924; he and his wife landed in Saigon the second time in February 1925; and they finally left Indochina for France eleven months later, in January 1926, "almost chased out . . . cut off from his friends, his hopes dashed, once again financially ruined, his health impaired" (Lacouture). In Saigon, he had collaborated in founding and editing two French-language newspapers, which lasted, separately, for forty-nine and twenty-three issues. They were sympathetic to the nationalist movement but supported reform and assimilation within the French colonial structure. He briefly visited Hong Kong with his wife during this period, to buy a set of type for the second of the newspapers. It was his first visit to China and lasted less than one week.

In 1931, after the Asian novels had been published, Malraux and his wife returned to Asia in the course of a yearlong world trip, sponsored by Gallimard, to collect material for an exhibition of Greek and Buddhist art and civilization. Together, they visited mainland China and, for the first time, Canton; the Canton uprising had taken place six years earlier. After this trip, Malraux did not see China again until he went there as a cabinet minister of General de Gaulle, in 1965. The story of him as an important figure in the Chinese revolution is total invention.

Man's Fate nonetheless made his reputation as an exemplary revolutionary figure, and he made the most of that status as a committeeman and rally speaker. He became a militant fellow traveler, and prominent opponent of the Nazis. "Up to the beginning of the Second World War, Malraux was the radiant symbol of the free liberal intellectual who had dedicated his life to the Communist Revolution and the struggle against Fascism," the American critic Joseph Frank wrote in *The Widening Gyre*.

He was in fact one of Münzenberg's not-so-innocents. He went to Berlin, on request, in connection with the Dimitrov defense. In Moscow, where he was invited in 1934, he said, "We confront a new fact: one must choose, not between democracy and Communism, but rather between Communism and Fascism . . . I believe in a Soviet humanism to come, a humanism analogous to while not resembling the humanisms of Greece, Rome and the Renaissance." While there he also attacked in public the notion of Socialist Realism in art, to the intense annoyance of those who had invited him.

He said that Socialist Realism risked killing in the egg a new Shakespeare.

In Paris, he played a large role in the various "front" campaigns against Fascism. In 1935, he wrote in his novel *Days of Wrath*, "It is hard being a man. But it is no more difficult to become one by deepening one's communion with others than by cultivating one's difference—and the first nourishes with at least as much force as the second that which makes a man a man, that by which he goes beyond himself, creates, invents or conceives of himself." This equivocal statement was about as close as he came to a public avowal of Communism, but Todd calls him "the most visible of the fellow travelers." At the time of the Spanish war Malraux congratulated Georges Bernanos, the rightist Catholic author, for the "inflexible sincerity" of his attack on the Church's complicity with Franco. Bernanos politely replied that Malraux would have done the same. Malraux replied, "That is not the same thing. You are a Christian and you act like a Christian. You chose to write the truth against your party. I am a Communist and I shall never write a word that might cause the slightest injury to the Party."* (He was also asked by Bernanos in 1945 what was the "capital event of our times." Malraux replied, "the return of Satan.")

He withheld his support from the novelist Victor Serge, who had been a friend and was imprisoned in Russia as a Trotskyist. There was a direct clash with Trotsky: in 1937, Malraux refused to confirm Trotsky's claim that Malraux was witness to the fact that on a given date in 1933, when he, Trotsky, was accused (in the second of the Moscow show trials) of meeting saboteurs in Paris to instruct them on subversive missions to the Soviet Union, he had actually been elsewhere. Trotsky afterwards called Malraux "a Stalinist agent," which at that time, objectively, he undoubtedly was—although always behind a screen of ambiguity.

* Just after the war, still working for the Gallimard publishing house, he was offered Boris Souvarine's hostile biography of Stalin, and is reported to have replied, "Your book is true, but is your side going to win?"—and refused the book.

In 1936 Malraux found in the civil war in Spain a Byronic enterprise more urgent and attractive than anything in which he had yet been engaged. In the beginning, the Republican cause conveyed a spirit of anarcho-syndicalism which Malraux described (to a friend) "as of a revelation." He went to Spain on July 21, four days after the rebel general Franco's *pronunciamiento*. A month later, in Paris, he was organizing military assistance for the Republic, which had lost half of its air force to the insurgent generals. He succeeded (with Münzenberg's help) in finding aircraft from French sources and in persuading the French Popular Front government, whose policy was nonintervention, to allow their transfer to Spain.

He organized air crews and took command, even though he had no qualifications as either an aviator or military leader, and subsequently went on operations (also making a film on the squadron's experiences). He seems to have exercised an effective and powerful leadership, based on force of personality and personal courage, over a group that had in it as many mercenaries as political idealists. The actual usefulness of this bomber force, during the short period in which it functioned, is disputed. It served from August 1936 until the end of February 1937, when, weakened by losses, it yielded place to units of the regular Spanish Air Force, being reconstituted with Soviet help. Malraux published his Spanish war novel, *L'Espoir*, in 1937. It first came out as a serial, running in November and December in the Communist newspaper *Ce Soir*. The film appeared in 1938.

He had made himself the hero he had before pretended to be. Thus does life emulate art, and, as Malraux said—following Lawrence—daydreaming give rise to action.

When war came to France in 1939, he declared, "When you have written what I have written and there is a war in France, you join it." The French would not give him a commission in their air force.

Because he had managed to get himself exempted from the usual national service in 1922, he had no assigned place in France's mobilization. He tried the tanks, where his father had served, and was accepted. (He went to Lanvin, the fashionable Rue du Faubourg-Saint-Honoré tailor, for his uniform.) He served briefly during the phony war, skirmished with the Germans when they came (as an infantryman, his unit's tanks having proved unserviceable), and on June 16, 1940, was taken prisoner.

Six weeks later, having volunteered with other prisoners to help bring in the harvest in the countryside southeast of Paris, he and some others walked away. He got to Hyères, on the Mediterranean near Toulon, the family home of his mistress, Josette Clotis (he was separated from his wife, Clara), and was later given the use of a friend's villa in Roquebrune-Cap-Martin, near Menton, on the Côte d'Azur. He, his mistress, and their infant children remained quietly in the south until 1944, spending the latter part of that period in the Dordogne. Although approached by the Resistance, he did nothing illegal in occupied or unoccupied France until the Allied landings in 1944.

He later explained himself by saying that he was a "serious" man, waiting for the Resistance to acquire the equipment and weapons that would make it a "serious" challenge to the Germans. From a military point of view this was sound judgement, in that organized military resistance was futile until the landings in 1944. When at the end of 1941 or the start of 1942 he was approached by Claude Bourdet, co-founder of the Resistance movement called "Combat," he said, "Have you the money? Have you the arms? Come back when you have money and arms." A Communist Resistance leader reported that when Malraux was asked to lead a force formed from Spanish Republican refugees, he said: "For me there are only two things, aviation and the tanks. I am an aviator and a tankist. If you can give me these, I am with you"—an unhelpful response in 1942, as well as a characteristic lie, since he had never fought in tanks, and only for a week or two as infantry, and as an aviator in Spain his combat experience consisted in going along for the ride on some bombing missions (which strictly speaking he did not have to do, although it was an obvious moral and leadership obligation). The wound he claimed to have received in Spain was a bruised leg during a botched takeoff.

Malraux's half brother, Roland, had been parachuted into southwestern France by the British Special Operations Executive (a rival organization to de Gaulle's networks in Occupied France) and was captured in March 1944. His other half brother, Claude, was executed after involvement with a network blowing up German ships in the Seine estuary. Malraux finally joined the Resistance via Roland's contacts, and while afterwards he greatly inflated his role, he seems to have been useful in bringing together British-sponsored and rival (Communist and Gaullist) French Resistance groups. (He was later rumored to have helped himself to Resistance money, a good deal of which was lying about for the taking, in the confusion of the war's concluding months.)

The principal action in which his unit took part was harassment of the SS Das Reich Division's northward movement to join the battle in Normandy in June 1944. That was one of the few actual military successes of the Resistance (distinct from its moral and political significance): it delayed the German division's arrival at the battle against Allied invasion forces by ten days, and caused it to arrive in Normandy in considerable disorder, with a number of tanks damaged or out of action. (The Resistance attacks also prompted the division to carry out a massacre of the inhabitants of Oradour-sur-Glane, the worst atrocity committed in the West by the German Army.)

On the twenty-second of July, rashly traveling on a main highway in a car flying the tricolor and the cross of Lorraine, Malraux and some companions were attacked. Malraux was wounded and captured. Threats by the Resistance of reprisals against German prisoners, and bribes to French police agents and Gestapo members were apparently responsible for his receiving fairly good treatment in German custody. When the Germans evacuated Toulouse, where he was held, the Resistance prisoners, Malraux included, were left behind.

∿

By the end of August, Malraux was in Paris. Friends from the Dordogne mentioned him to people organizing an irregular force in Alsace. Lacouture quotes a fellow member of the Resistance as saying. "Berger . . . is on good terms with London and has just been freed from Toulouse prison. In fact, Berger is Malraux." An outsider, a celebrity, free from local political and personal involvements, with good contacts and apparent experience, he seemed a useful choice as leader. "I may tell tales," Malraux said, "but life is beginning to resemble my tales." The "Brigade Alsace-Lorraine" went into action at the end of September as an auxiliary to the First French Armored Division. It was engaged for five months. It took part in the defense of Strasbourg (which the French refused to evacuate in December 1944, as part of the shortening of lines Eisenhower had ordered in reaction to the German counteroffensive that month; the city was too symbolic for de Gaulle and de Lattre to obey). The brigade invaded Baden, and in March of 1945 it entered Stuttgart.

Malraux again seems to have imposed himself as a military leader with verve and energy, his competence, intelligence, and personality winning general respect. He had the good sense to let the professionals in his headquarters take the tactical decisions, while he discussed grand strategy. He held himself apart from the political conflicts inside the Resistance, but his relations with his old allies in the Communist Party became increasingly equivocal until, on January 25, 1945, he delivered a speech to a Paris gathering of Resistance organizations that proved decisive in the Resistance's political development. The Communists, who from the time of Hitler's attack on Russia are generally acknowledged to have borne the main burden of French armed internal resistance to the Germans, were pressing for the amalgamation of all Resistance organizations into a single body, which they expected to be able to dominate.

Malraux replied, "I am quite willing to form an alliance, but I have no desire to be burgled." His speech at this meeting, at the Mutualité Hall in Paris, the traditional place for left-wing rallies— "in uniform, forelock disheveled, with his peremptory gestures and his trenchant words, for all the world like some technician irritated by amateurs (Let's be serious, we have no time to lose, those of use who are still fighting at the front, etc.)," as Lacouture describes it— was crucial to defeating the resolution for merger.

It was after that meeting that he met de Gaulle. He wrote, of the first encounter, of "remoteness, all the more curious because it appeared not only between himself and his interlocutor but between what he said and what he was." Malraux's account went on: "He established with the person he was talking to a very powerful contact, which seemed inexplicable when one had left him. A contact above all due to a feeling of having come up against a total personality."

The association between de Gaulle and Malraux that followed benefited them both. Malraux lent his powers of oratory, spectacle, and promotion, and his intelligence, to the Gaullist movement, and de Gaulle found in him, eventually, a minister of state. The *maisons de la culture* that Malraux caused to be set up across France ("to transform a privilege into common property," the civil servant responsible for organizing them said of their purpose), the state support he provided for the arts, and even the law requiring the buildings and monuments of Paris and other French cities to be regularly washed, are not the least of the Gaullist legacies to France.

Malraux and de Gaulle were both romantics. That, it seems clear, is what drew them together—de Gaulle, the austere, moral ironist, and Malraux, the *farfelu*. François Mauriac, though, dryly remarked in 1960, "I hold Malraux superb enough to consider Charles de Gaulle as a card in his own game." De Gaulle was the romantic who possessed "a certain idea of France" to which the French only occasionally conformed, as he himself sardonically observed.

De Gaulle, like Malraux, had invented himself, as the leader of France, claiming its legitimate leadership at a time when he was a refugee brigadier general without troops or resources, a former member of a shamefully superseded government, wholly dependent upon the goodwill of British authorities. The difference between Malraux and de Gaulle, though, was the same one that existed between Malraux and his other hero, Lawrence: they were fundamentally serious men, and Malraux was an illusionist.

Or it would perhaps be fairer to say that while Malraux was serious about art his primary creation was self, and in that respect he believed, as many do, in a phrase often heard in France: *Il n'y a que les apparences qui comptent*—"It's only the appearances that count." De Gaulle and Lawrence were serious about objective matters beyond themselves, about achieving something for others, or for history. The elaboration of personality, the calculated grandeur and distance assumed by de Gaulle, his creation of that historical personage "de Gaulle," about whom the memoirist de Gaulle writes in the third person, served the purpose of a serious political undertaking, a conscious service to the history of his country.

In Malraux's case, the creation of the revolutionary personage took place before the actual heroism in Spain, the Dordogne, and Alsace, when "Malraux" became a reality; and the actual person— the chain-smoking, tic-afflicted, stammering André Malraux— conformed to what he had created.* What would have become of André Malraux had there been no Spanish civil war, no fall of France, and no Resistance?

---

* It is generally accepted that he suffered from Tourette's syndrome.

Brigitte Friang, a Résistante at nineteen, subsequently deported, a professional journalist who worked closely with Malraux in setting up the first postwar Gaullist political movement, and again after de Gaulle had returned to power in 1958, cast a cold if affectionate eye upon him. She compared him to a cat. "He installs himself in your 'me,' without offense but relentlessly. You are conquered, subjugated forever, whatever the growls and disdainful abuses of power or privilege you have to endure. Just as one forgives all before the cat's aristocratic beauty, grace of attitudes and gestures ..., one pardons all before [Malraux's] spellbinding imagination, the cosmic vision, the stunning judgement, accompanied by a fraternal complicity that in the end never fails."

De Gaulle was formidably his own man because his romanticism, like that of his ally, Winston Churchill, was governed by a powerful and prudent political intelligence and by historical consciousness. Romanticism in political affairs has more often been linked to immature or apocalyptic ideas—secular translations of the essentially religious impulse to bring history to a halt in general happiness. The actual accomplishments of revolutionary intellectuals, hommes engagés, since the French Revolution is awash with the blood of others. George Sand observed, "During the Terror, the men who spilt the most blood were those who had the strongest desire to lead their fellow-men to the dreamed-of Golden Age, and who had the greatest sympathy for human misery."

The striking thing about Malraux as a politically committed man is that his engagement was to the act of engagement—to action—and not to an ideology or an articulated political philosophy. His early sympathy for Trotsky, exiled to Kazakhstan by Stalin in 1928, owed much to Trotsky's military achievement as creator of the Red Army, and his own admiration of the military career of his father. Trotsky seemed a more cultivated man than the other Soviet leaders but was also a man of action. As Todd writes, Malraux was not really a political man. He was not really clear on what opposed Stalin to Trotsky. "Squaring the circle, he leaned towards Trotsky without opposing Stalin; denounced the Cheka even though it was the creation of the great figures of Bolshevism. . . ." He contributed to a religious conception by the European Left of Soviet Communism, saying that "the Russian revolution, 'inheritor' of the French revolution, is the assumption of the people. Whatever is done in its name by its leaders and officials, its police or soldiers, the revolution itself remains virginal, pure in its intentions and its proclaimed ends." After his first trip to the Soviet Union he was, in Soviet and Comintern eyes, the most promising of all the foreign pilgrims and tourists of Communism who had come to Moscow. Todd goes on, "[they believed] this man must not be wasted. The most astute agents of influence, like his friend Ilya Ehrenbourg, understood that the small dissents asserted by Malraux made him more credible as a friend of Communism, and that he made little use of the conventional wooden language of most pro-Soviet writers. This was a fellow-traveller with style, outspokenness, talent, but unpredictable character: to be exploited with prudence."

Jules Roy, a fellow writer and a contemporary, said of him, watching him with de Gaulle at one of the latter's press conferences, "The adventurer of genius that he is now serves the king of France. He would have served Stalin as well, if the Stalinists had triumphed. He serves he who can serve him."

He supported "Revolution" and Communism, anti-Fascism, Resistance, and Liberation, then Gaullism, but, as Mauriac had perceived, used each in his own game. It is impossible to imagine him as a Marat or a Robespierre, or as Mao, whom he so admired, or as Ho Chi Minh. He had toyed with Trotskyism, been a fellow traveler with slippery ties to the Party; and ended in Gaullism—always remaining his own man. He was too ambitious to do otherwise.

He was too intelligent for too many of his emulators, who, following him, ended badly. André Malraux created an extraordinarily seductive personage, his conception of what he wished to become—an intellectual and artist who was also a liberator, adventurer, and warrior. He became all these, and by doing so inspired a great many other serious and sensitive people to take up an armed role in revolutionary enterprises with less successful outcomes. Malraux presented the Soviet Union and the Communist political movements of Asia and Europe in the 1920s and 1930s as affairs of human liberation, whereas they actually proved to be hideously retrograde, obscurantist, and murderous. Other intellectuals have done as much for movements or causes equally hideous. The specific accusation to be made against Malraux is that for a time he turned his back on the falsity of what he was saying and doing, including evidence provided by his own half brother, a journalist in Moscow during the 1930s.

The dream of revolution is a dream of power. Malraux understood that intellectual power rarely translates directly into political power, even though a crucial element in the seduction of the role of revolutionary intellectual is that it promises to change that, or seems to do so. Malraux seems never to have looked for or to have expected political power for himself. For a man who made of himself the representative twentieth-century figure of revolutionary intellectual, he seemed remarkably skeptical of revolution. His game was deeper. He said that "the problem that underlies everything I write" is "how to make man aware that he can build his greatness, without religion, on the nothingness that crushes him."

The source of his obsession with painting and sculpture was the belief that "we draw images from ourselves that are powerful enough to negate our nothingness." Malraux writes in *The Walnut Trees of Altenburg*, "We can do nothing against time. . . . When I say that each man experiences deep within him the presence of destiny, I mean that he experiences—and almost always tragically, at least for certain moments—the world's indifference vis-à-vis himself."

He anticipated the existentialism of postwar France, where action was held to be an imperative deliberately opposing itself to the anonymity of the world, in the absence of knowledge of whether action would in the end prove to have been valid, or even intelligible. He said of Lawrence, "In reality he desired nothing at all. *It is prodigiously hard to be a man who wants nothing.*"

The postwar alliance of Malraux with Charles de Gaulle reflected the fact that de Gaulle was able to answer the question that Malraux needed to have answered. For what was Malraux's concern with the world's indifference but an expression of his own uncertainty? He was not an autonomous man, or he would not have reinvented himself as someone else.

De Gaulle was an ethical man and a stoic—a stoicism admixed with Catholicism. His ethic was personal: he was accountable to himself; he was an autonomous man. He was obviously a conservative man as well as a rebel (instigating single-handedly a revolutionary repudiation of what the dominant forces of his nation had produced). He was private. His code was internal, permitting no illusion that it would be accepted or applauded by others, or that it would succeed: he was ultimately indifferent to external judgment. De Gaulle had an exceedingly high view of what people, and his country, might become, but he was entirely without illusion that they would succeed in other than inspired moments. "The man lived up to his myth, but *in what sense?*" Malraux wrote of that first interview with de Gaulle. It was a question to be asked of Malraux himself.*

～○

An unkind tongue said that de Gaulle kept Malraux around "because he amused him." However, in their ways it seems that they

---

* After de Gaulle's resignation from the presidency in 1969, following defeat in a referendum on proposed regional reforms, Malraux asked him, "Why did you go on a question as secondary as the regions? Because of the absurdity? He regarded me fixedly: because of the absurdity."

loved one another. Two months before de Gaulle's death, Malraux wrote to him: "To have had the honor to assist you has been the pride of my life—and more, in the face of the abyss [*en face du néant*]." That was too late to be flattery. An incident reported by Malraux's friend Olivier Germain-Thomas concerns de Gaulle's response in 1965, when it was reported to him that Malraux seemed at the end of his rope, tired of the Ministry of Culture, without a literary project, his two sons dead in an auto crash in 1961, in the course of a divorce, seemingly contemplating suicide. After reflection, and without informing his prime minister, Georges Pompidou or his foreign minister, Maurice Couve de Murville, de Gaulle sent Malraux on a special mission to Mao Tse-tung.

On the voyage out (by sea) Malraux was inspired to start his *Anti-Memoirs*. Arriving in China, he presented to President Lin Shao-shi a regal letter from de Gaulle which said: "I have charged Monsieur André Malraux, Minister of State, to convey to your Excellence and to the Chairman Mao Tse-tung the sentiments of friendship felt by the people of France for the great Chinese people. Monsieur Malraux will willingly exchange with you his version of the great problems which interest France and China, and consequently the future of the world. I will attach great value to the information he will convey to me of your views and those of the leaders of the Popular Republic of China." Just the task for Malraux.

Germain-Thomas concludes, "after this new brush with history and legend, Malraux 'asked death to wait,'" and lived another eleven years. He was to weep in 1969 when he learned that, without telling him, de Gaulle had ordered the manuscript of *La Condition humaine* purchased; it now is in the Bibliothèque Nationale.

∽

The mythmaking went on to the end. While Malraux was in China, he said of Canton to Marshal Chen Yi, minister of foreign affairs, "I spent six months there in 1927," and also told him, "I was in prison in 1923 with Ho Chi Minh." (This is Lacouture's account, from independent sources. In his *Anti-Memoirs* Malraux says there was "a preliminary exchange of courtesies.") His book of reflections on death, *Lazarus*, written after a near-fatal illness in 1974, turns again and again to imagined as well as real scenes of violence—those witnessed and those he had made up for his novels. He starts with the morally exalting account, taken from *The Walnut Trees of Altenburg*, of German troops on the eastern front in 1916 advancing behind a gas attack, who when they reach the Russian lines and discover the terrible suffering of their enemies spontaneously begin to drag the Russians out of the gas, back to German medical stations. He conflates himself with his hero-father Lawrence, Vincent Berger, a "youngish anthropologist who had been an advisor to the 'Red Sultan' and assistant to Enver Pasha, now defending the Dardanelles against the Allies," as he writes about 1916 battles, Central Asian exploration, Indochina, China, Spain, the Resistance, the battles in Alsace, arrest.

His life and his imaginative reconstruction of his life make up a single meditation. He writes about air combat in Spain, "the bitter cold of the Ebro," a German firing squad, his hospitalization and brush with death; "the plaints of the Salpêtrière"—his hospital in Paris—"like those of the prison-yard in Shanghai." What prison yard? He was never in prison in Shanghai.

The conclusion of the book is an observation on mortality: "Agnosticism, when it accepts its own irrationality, when it experiences the unthinkable with the force of faith, discovers in the dread of death the reincarnation of the Dance of Death, both equally impermanent. . . . The revelation is that nothing can be revealed." He was an obscurantist to the end.

∾

It must be said that he was a crucial contributor to that confusion of self-aggrandizing fantasy with reality which distinguished the history of the mid-decades of the twentieth century, having its legitimate descendance in the revolutionary terrorisms of late in that century. Revolutionary ideologues lie about the future, while Malraux lied about himself, both he and they believing themselves truth tellers but knowing that they are not: that at best they are successful gamblers. Hannah Arendt wrote that the most significant quality of totalitarian thinkers was their "extreme contempt for facts as such, for in their opinion fact depends entirely on the power of the man who can fabricate it."

Malraux, of course, would have been appalled to have such a statement cited in judgment upon him. He did not count on power—or, rather, he counted only on the power of imagination. He said at the end of his life that "the only response to death is art." In fact, he was not political at all. He was never seriously interested in power as such, although his constant ambition was to be near "great men."

He was an aesthete. His novels and his career were equally formed out of aesthetic ambition. It is his misfortune that the career is more likely to survive. It is our misfortune that the career contributed to that misapprehension of the relationships of thought to power, and of violence to progress, which afflicts us still. He died on the twenty-third of November 1976. Twenty years later, to the day, his remains were transferred to the Panthéon in Paris.

CHAPTER NINE

━━━━━

THE ANTI-COMMUNIST

Aware of its religious significance, Arthur Koestler introduced the first volume of his memoirs in 1952 with a quotation from the Catholic French poet, playwright, and diplomat Paul Claudel describing a flight—in vain—from "the him in me who is more me than myself." It was a thought to which Koestler would return.

He ended the second volume of his memoirs with the claim that his had been the "typical case-history of a central-European member of the educated middle classes, born in the first years of our century."

This was to claim too much. The typical members of the central European educated middle classes of his time (1905–1983), if they were Jewish, as he was, were murdered by Hitler, or possibly by Stalin. If they were not Jewish, they underwent war and misery, possible uprooting or expatriation, a cumulative experience that left typical central Europeans very distant from the experience, assumptions, and sunny expectations of most of their American contemporaries, but also fairly distant from the more tempered assumptions of their western European counterparts, who found themselves on the victorious side in 1945.

What definitely was not typical was the life summed up by one of Koestler's French editors, Phil Casoar, as follows:

The itinerary of our Hungarian, naturalized British subject, is a hectic steeple-chase through the century, resembling one of those silent films projected at accelerated speed, where the hero leaps from train to auto, from boat to airplane, appears suddenly suspended from a crane over a void, only to disappear into a gaping tunnel to a confusing rhythm of rails and switchyards, mixed with ships' sirens, while all sorts of incongruous obstacles surge up before him. Adolescent in Budapest during the brief Bela Kun commune in Hungary, engineering student in Vienna in the 1920s, member of a Zionist dueling-society, inept agricultural laborer in a Zionist settlement in Palestine, prolific young journalist for the German liberal press and dandy-about-town in Weimar Berlin, science correspondent aboard a Zeppelin expedition to the North Pole, ardent young Communist becoming almost without reflection a Comintern agent, traveler in the U.S.S.R., vagabond exile living in a barn in a suburb of Paris, correspondent in Spain during the civil war, prisoner of Franco, freed after an international campaign on his behalf; Communist defector and denouncer of Stalinism, exile in England become English-language novelist, member of the British army Pioneer Corps, observer and critic of the birth of Israel, successful author in the postwar Paris of existentialism and Cold War intellectual combats. . . .

With more to come. A career exhausting even in summary.

The historian John Lukacs, himself of Hungarian origin, calls Koestler a "period piece. . . . He was a twentieth-century Central European émigré intellectual, not atypical of a group of people now largely, although not entirely, extinct. Twentieth-century: because his migrations, both physical and mental, were largely the consequences of the two world wars. Central European: because the cast of his intellectual inclinations was largely Austrian and German, while his character had a few Hungarian (more precisely Budapestian) traits—but then that was typical of many intellectuals in the Weimar-German period. Emigré: because, in midlife, he found refuge in England, which gave him both security and comfort during the second half of his life. Like other Central European intellectuals, such as Marx and Freud, he died in London, where his ashes remain. [His biographer describes him as] 'this intellectual titan of the twentieth century.' That he was not. He was a brilliant journalist and, like many brilliant journalists, a not inconsiderable thinker."

✒

With the instincts of a good journalist, Arthur Koestler begins the first volume of his autobiography with a "hook," his "secular horoscope." From the beginnings of civilization, he starts off, men have believed that the stars have an influence on an individual's fate. "Astrology is founded on the belief that man is formed by his cosmic environment; Marx held that he is the product of his social environment. I believe both propositions to be true. . . ."

Accordingly, he set off for the offices of *The Times*, located in those better days in Printing House Square, London, and consulted the volume of the newspaper's issues that included the paper published the day of his birth, September 5, 1905. He found many interesting things in the announcements, advertisements, court calendar, and social and news reports, but of greatest interest was an editorial article concerning an event that took place on the day and at the hour of his birth, described as "an event of the greatest moment, not merely in the political history of the world, but in the unending moral and intellectual process which we roughly describe as civilization—a fact of the highest importance."

This event was the signature of the treaty of peace between the tsar of Russia and the emperor of Japan, negotiated by Theodore Roosevelt, bringing to an end the Russo-Japanese war, a war that had intensified those revolutionary currents in Russia that subsequently, in interaction with similar forces in post–World War I Germany, were to produce the totalitarian regimes that dominated the history of the twentieth century.

The Times's leader-writer congratulated the victorious Japanese for their demonstration of "the subordination of the individual to the tribe and the State," a lesson that in his opinion had yet to be learned by the excessively individualistic West.

The conclusion Koestler drew from this examination of the correlation of the secular stars on the day of his birth was once again extravagantly stated, but not wholly untrue: "that I was born at the moment when the sun was setting on the Age of Reason."

Looking about us in the twenty-first century, it would be difficult to argue that reason has been convincingly restored to international society, although we seem for the moment fairly distant from the recurrence of such events as those survived by Arthur Koestler (although not perhaps so far as we think). The testimony of his life, books, and journalism was of the great destructive movements of the twentieth century, directly experienced as a Weimar anti-Nazi in Berlin, a Communist and Comintern agent, a freelance collaborator in some of Willi Münzenberg's fabulous undertakings, a spy in the Spanish civil war, narrowly escaping death; a globally successful author of one of the most important political novels written in modern times, one of the first cold war combatants—and one of what must have been the very few (did *any* others exist?) disillusioned Comintern agents of the 1930s to have actually sent in a letter of resignation. He was also a "typical" central European figure as a man driven by his neuroses and the forces of his subconscience, which he tirelessly analyzed.

His career as a Party member had begun in Berlin, where after reporting from Palestine and Paris for the distinguished Ullstein newspaper (and book) publishing group, he became, in 1930, science editor of Ullstein's mass-circulation *Zeitung am Mittag*. He was subsequently promoted to foreign editor and assistant editor in chief while still in his twenties, as well as becoming scientific adviser to the entire Ullstein group.

He had been educated as an engineer, and science was a lifelong interest, later in Koestler's life to become his principal professional interest, particularly in questioning the unqualified materialism of mainstream scientific assumptions. (Lukacs considers Koestler's book about Johannes Kepler, *The Sleepwalkers: A History of Man's Changing Vision of the Universe*, his most valuable and enduring work.) Koestler later said that it was science that rescued him from Communism "by pitting uncertainty and empiricism against Marxist dogma."

＊○

He became a Communist in Berlin to resolve his sense of "inauthenticity," despite the great success he was enjoying with the Ullstein group. The political circumstances of his decision included the rising presence and pressure of the Nazi movement in Germany, particularly difficult for the Jewish Ullstein brothers, proprietors of the group. The vision of Russia as a genuinely revolutionary society, establishing classless fraternity, was pervasive in the circles frequented by Koestler, and he was himself, as he says, although by then an experienced correspondent and journalist, "in my emotional life . . . still an adolescent," open to the romanticism of revolution, persuaded that he was "living in a disintegrating society [as he was], . . . thirsting for faith."

The psychological rather than political sources for this sensed inauthenticity are analyzed at length in his autobiographical works. He was, as he says, a serial bridge-burner (but then, as he also said, had he not been, and had he pursued his career in a pragmatic fashion, he would probably have ended in a death camp). He admits to a belief that certain constellations of events, in the case of his joining the Communist Party a series of petty calamities in his personal life—a carelessly damaged car, serious poker losses, a stupid liaison with a girl he disliked—"seem to express a symbolic warning, as if some mute power were tugging at your sleeve. It is then up to you to decipher the meaning of the inchoate message. If you ignore it, nothing at all may probably happen, but you may have missed a chance to remake your life."

He also acknowledges that the warning may be self-produced by subconscious arrangement, and the warning issued by "the him in me who is more me than myself." He later found that André Malraux had a similar belief about the messages delivered by coincidental events, which Malraux (characteristically) called "the language of destiny."

Koestler returned home from his night of little disasters, and as if looking down from a height saw himself "with great clarity as a sham and a phony, paying lip-service to the Revolution which was to lift the earth from its axis, and at the same time living the existence of a bourgeois careerist. . . ." He felt "the jubilant exultation of being free, and of . . . seeing the burning bridge behind me." On December 31, 1931, he addressed a letter to the Central Committee of the Communist Party of Germany, enclosing a short curriculum vitae, applying for membership.

He suggested to the Party that he leave immediately for Russia to help build the revolution, but was quickly told to forget such ideas and make himself useful as a secret informant and agent of influence inside the Ullstein organization—then one of Germany's most important institutions. He was not a success as a secret agent (possibly on the orders of his unconscious). He told all to a callow associate he hoped to recruit, who then had a fit of conscience and decided to report it to management. Rather than try to persuade the friend to keep quiet, Koestler told him to go ahead (no doubt another manipulation by his unconscious).* He was invited by the Ullsteins to leave. They did not need harboring a Communist

---

* In his memoirs he wrote that "all the crucial decisions which have ordered the course of my life had in the appearance been contrary to reason and yet in the long run had turned into spiritual blessings. It seems as if on these crucial occasions a type of logic were entering into action entirely different from the reasonings of the 'trivial

agent to add to their existing difficulties in a Germany in which mounting anti-Semitic propaganda was contributing to what was about to become a successful Nazi bid for total power.

Another bridge burned, Koestler was ready to go to Russia, with the expressed aim of becoming a tractor driver. He was, after all, a trained engineer. But the Party preferred that he make the journey as an author with a contract with a Soviet publishing house to write a "western bourgeois's" admiring account of discovering the new Soviet Union. He did so, after months of travel in the country, and the book was published in the USSR, but only in a truncated version in German, for circulation among foreigners, as it was deemed "too frivolous" and lacking in the (by then) required reverence for Stalin to be offered to Russian readers. Koestler was told by his Party superiors to go back to Western Europe, to Paris where, following the Reichstag fire, German Communists were regrouping in exile.

He had been shaken by what he had seen in Russia of Soviet reality. His friend the novelist Manès Sperber said he had the impression that Koestler was launched on a crucial self-appraisal. "After he had given up dramatizing himself for an hour [in a café conversation in Saint-Germain-des-Prés in 1933], his real nature, no longer blocked, became visible, and with it his striving for inner integrity. [He had acquired] an uncommon sensitivity and a fear of deception and disappointment; the fear that a pain one cannot prepare for could destroy one's strength to bear it."

Nonetheless, for the next three years he did freelance work for the Münzenberg organization, as well as nonpolitical hackwork, eventually becoming unpaid editor for a Comintern institute "for

---

plane'; as if one's decisions in these rare moments, however paradoxical or apparently suicidal, followed the commandments of the invisible text, revealed for a split second to the inner self."

the study of fascism" (which was drifting toward ideological deviation and was subsequently closed down), and writing articles for a
press agency also run by the Comintern, probably as an espionage
front.

In 1936 Münzenberg sent him to the part of Spain held by
Franco's insurgents. He used his Hungarian passport and journalism record to obtain credentials from a rightist Hungarian daily,
Pester Lloyd, and from the liberal London *News Chronicle*. However,
shortly after his arrival, he was recognized as a leftist by a journalist
he had known in Berlin (the son of the Swedish dramatist August
Strindberg). He decided that it was the better part of prudence to
quit insurgent territory.

He twice went back to Spain for Münzenberg, later in 1936 and
in 1937, these times to the government side. The first trip was an
intelligence mission to collect documents concerning the political
origins of the Franco uprising. A propaganda book made from
them, *The Nazi Conspiracy in Spain*, subsequently enjoyed considerable success in France, but its timing was unfortunate for Koestler
as it appeared just before his third trip to Spain, for the *News Chronicle* and for a Communist-controlled press agency.

This time he was captured by Franco forces during the battle for
Malaga and was recognized and imprisoned. After three months,
and after threats that he would be executed, following a press campaign abroad led by his estranged wife, Dorothea, and orches-
trated by Münzenberg, he was exchanged through the Red Cross
for the wife of a Nationalist pilot being detained in Republican
territory.

⤙⟡

The experience gave him his first successful book, *Spanish Testa-
ment* (1937). It also set him on a course that was to lead to his break
with the Party. During a subsequent book tour, lecturing in Britain,
he declined to follow the Party line concerning the semi-Trotskyist

POUM (in whose militia George Orwell served).* He did so aware that this was a serious challenge to Party discipline, potentially suicidal in terms of his standing within the Party. The Communists insisted that the POUM militants were traitors to the Republican cause.

The POUM was indeed an obstacle to Communist maneuvers to take control of the entire Spanish Left, and eventually, of the Republican government. In this undertaking it was necessary for the Party to destroy groups on the Left that were not under Communist control, either through calumny and false denunciation, or when necessary by physical elimination.

The Moscow trials, which began in August 1936, had also undermined Koestler's commitment to the cause. However, while his refusal to denounce the POUM produced some private reproaches from fellow Communists, there was nothing more. "Even among the lotus-eaters of the British C.P. there must have been some who wrote reports to higher quarters; yet I was not called to account. [Mine was] an abortive suicide, or series of suicides. At every meeting I pressed a figurative revolver to my head, pulled the trigger, heard a faint click, and found that I was still alive and a valued comrade of the Communist Party."

His final break was after he had returned to Paris and spoke to a meeting of the Exiled German Writers' group, where a Party representative suggested that he insert in his talk remarks denouncing the POUM, and he refused. He ended his talk with three considered statements:

"No movement, party or person can claim the privilege of infallibility."

"It is as foolish to appease an enemy as it is to persecute the friend who pursues the same end as you by a different road."

* Partido Obrero de Unificación Marxista, composed of dissident Marxist groups opposed to Stalin but not strictly aligned with Trotsky. Orwell, not an ideologue, rather haphazardly ended in its ranks when he went to Spain to fight.

And finally, quoting Thomas Mann (a member of the exiled writers' group), "In the long run, a harmful truth is better than a useful lie."

Koestler later wrote that "the effect was about the same as if one had told a Nazi audience the startling news that all men are born equal. When I had finished, the non-Communist part of the audience applauded, the Communist part sat in stony silence, most of them with demonstratively folded arms." It was after this that he sent his letter of resignation.

✦

He began *Darkness at Noon* in 1938, working in a village in the south of France, living with a new English companion, a sculptress, Daphne Hardy. He wrote in German and she translated to English. When war was declared in September 1939, he resolved to go to England to join the army there, but while waiting on a visa that the British seemed reluctant to give him, he was arrested by French police as a politically suspect alien.

He was held at the police prefecture, then in an improvised holding space in the dressing rooms at Roland Garros stadium, where the French Open tennis matches are held, and eventually, for four months, at an internment camp for dubious foreigners in Vernet, in the foothills of the Pyrenees, an extremely unpleasant experience which he subsequently described in *Scum of the Earth* (1941). A British contact, with André Malraux's support, finally got the authorities to release him, but he continued to have to report to the police. *Darkness at Noon* was finished a month before the German invasion.

Arrested again, he managed to slip away in the confusion of the invasion, and when France capitulated he decided that the safest course in trying to escape the Gestapo would be to enlist in the Foreign Legion under a false name. He claimed to be a former Swiss taxi driver, and in the (then) tradition of La Légion, was not pressed for details. He ended in Marseille, where he managed to join a group of English soldiers also in flight, and to obtain papers to travel to Casablanca, not yet under German supervision. From there, the group got to Lisbon by fishing boat.

As he still had no British visa he was refused passage to England. At the end of two months, depressed, he made an unsuccessful suicide attempt.* He afterwards wrote, "I had given in to self-pity, with the same ridiculous result [as before]: but after that, I felt much better." He had used, but vomited up, a morphia compound he had been given in Marseille by the refugee Jewish writer Walter Benjamin, a former neighbor in Paris exile and a Saturday-night poker partner. (Benjamin used the rest of his morphine for a successful suicide at Port Bou on the French-Spanish border, when he found the border closed. It reopened the following morning.)

With the connivance of people inside the British embassy in Lisbon, Koestler finally got aboard a KLM flight to London, where he gave himself up, to be interned again. He was imprisoned in London's Pentonville prison when *Darkness at Noon* was published in England, in December 1940.† With that event he suddenly became and was for many years to remain the most celebrated of the intellectual combatants defending liberal democracy in the struggle with Communism.

When released from prison, he joined the only branch of service in the British army that would take him—the Pioneers, a labor and engineering corps. In March 1942 he was finally rescued from

---

* Actually his fifth attempt, and the second in a year; which as his biographer, David Cesarani, notes, is a suspiciously consistent record of failure, given that other exiles and refugees were succeeding with distressing frequency.

† In Pentonville, despite German bombing of London in late 1940, when prisoners were locked up in totally blacked-out cells from four or five in the afternoon until eight the following morning, "I felt, for the first time since the outbreak of the war, in safety. This must sound like a deliberate paradox to minds not acquainted with the logic of the apocalypse. It becomes less paradoxical when one realizes that every one of my political friends and every member of my race trapped on the occupied Continent would have felt the same, and would gladly have changed place with me. In Pentonville, I was one of the lucky few who had arrived at his destination."

manual labor by influential friends and taken on by the Ministry of Information for propaganda and political warfare work.

⚬

Since the cold war has ended, the importance of *Darkness at Noon* is sometimes discounted, in part because its sensational thesis has proven untrue: that the unbelievable confessions of "anti-party" crimes made by old Bolsheviks at the Moscow trials of the late 1930s were motivated by an ultimate loyalty to the revolutionary idea. The truth was much simpler. They were extorted by torture, false promises, blackmail, and threats to wives and children.

However, *Darkness at Noon* proved at the time an enormous blow to the Party and the Soviet Union because it was written by a former Party member and agent, in the vocabulary and framework of assumptions of the Party itself, offering a psychologically plausible explanation for something that had seemed incomprehensible to outsiders. Why didn't those on trial resist, deny the charges, fight for their lives? Instead, they offered docile and even groveling agreement with their accusers, in some cases pleading guilty to crimes that material circumstances made it impossible for them to have committed, or where the factual record showed they had been nowhere near the scene of the crime.*

The scale and importance of these trials has also tended to be forgotten, part of a history now distant and seemingly irrelevant. During 1936–38, millions were killed or sent to bestial forced labor in Siberian camps. Nearly four percent of the entire populations of Byelorussia and the Caucasus vanished in this purge. A third of the membership of the Soviet Communist Party was purged. The dead included six of thirteen members of the Politburo, 1,109 out of

---

* The novel's protagonist, the old Bolshevik Rubashov, is usually thought to have been modeled on Nikolai Bukharin, condemned by Stalin in 1928 as a "right deviationist," expelled from the Politburo in 1929, tried in 1938 for treasonable conspiracy with Trotsky (then in exile) and seeking to restore capitalism, and then executed. He was posthumously rehabilitated under Mikhail Gorbachev.

1,966 delegates to the 1934 Party Congress, more than a third of the elected deputies in the Supreme Soviet, nearly all provincial Party secretaries, and between twenty thousand and thirty-five thousand army officers, including three out of five marshals and thirteen out of fifteen army commanders.

(Even this was not the end. After World War II another great purge was touched off by Tito's defection from the Soviet bloc, reaching its culmination in the alleged "Doctors' Plot" to murder Stalin. Had Stalin not died when he did, in March 1953, it is thought that this new purge, encompassing the satellite states as well as Russia, would eventually have claimed even more victims than had the Moscow trials and their accompanying murders and assignments to forced labor in the Siberian camps.)

Koestler's fictional old Bolshevik, Rubashov, innocent of the crimes with which he is charged, has nonetheless committed his life to the proposition that "the Party can never be mistaken. . . . The Party is the embodiment of the revolutionary idea in history. . . . History knows her way. She makes no mistakes." He is obedient to what his interrogator identifies as "the principle that the end justifies the means—all means, without exception," and this compels him to assent to the interrogator's argument: that the national bulwark of the revolution had to be held "at any price and with any sacrifice. . . ."

Whoever did not understand this necessity had to be destroyed. Whole sets of our best functionaries in Europe had to be physically liquidated. We did not recoil from crushing our own organizations abroad when the interests of the Bastion required it. We did not recoil from co-operation with the police of reactionary countries in order to suppress revolutionary movements which came at the wrong moment. We did not recoil from betraying our friends and compromising with our enemies, in order to preserve the Bastion. That was the task which history had given us, the representatives of the first victorious revolution. The shortsighted, the aesthetes, the moralists did not understand. But the leader of the Revolution understood that all depended on one thing. . . .

Rubashov submits. He agrees not only to sign a false confession to having committed counterrevolutionary treachery, in the service of an unnamed foreign power, but to incriminate others on trial—"the last service the Party will ask of you," the interrogator tells him. As Cesarani acutely observes, *Darkness at Noon* was actually Koestler's apologia for his own past commitment to the Party, and the book made its most powerful appeal to former Communists, or to Communists and fellow travelers shaken in their faith. Michael Foot, decades later to lead the British Labour Party, wrote, "Who will ever forget the first moment he read *Darkness at Noon*? For socialists especially, the experience was indelible. I can recall reading it right through in one night, horror-struck, over-powered, enthralled. If this was the true revelation of what had happened in the great Stalin show trials, and it was hard to see how a single theoretical dent could be made in it, a terrifying shaft of darkness was cast over the future no less than the past."

While *Darkness at Noon* is a damning account of the cynicism and amorality of the Party, justifying a decision to reject its discipline, it also provides a powerful exposition of the idealism that led so many into the Communist movement. In that respect it reiterated the romantic view of Communist engagement that Müzenberg had promoted, and which millions, in the 1920s and 1930s, had acquired from contemporary depictions of the Bolshevik Revolution and its immediate aftermath in such accounts as John Reed's *Ten Days That Shook the World* (whose film version in the 1990s perpetuated the romanticism), and the great works of Russia's revolutionary cinema and plastic art in the 1920s.

Darkness at Noon provided the defector from Communism with a seemingly irrefutable rationalization for having left the Party, and at the same time absolved him or her from guilt for having initially joined it. To non-Communist readers, it provided a shocking insight into a realm of ruthless expedience and systematic falsification of reality. The novel, and Koestler's subsequent contribution to Richard Crossman's anthology, *The God That Failed*,* were two of the most important and influential anti-Communist texts of the wartime and immediate postwar periods, matched in influence only by George Orwell's *Animal Farm* and *1984*.

❧

In the 1940s the Italian ex-Communist writer Ignazio Silone said that the world's final battle would be fought between the Communists and the ex-Communists. Only they grasped the enormity of the issues, he said. The rest of us were dilettantes. This also was wrong. Communism's best opponents were not always the ex-Communists, who often displayed the same intolerance and even fanaticism as their new opponents/old comrades. Koestler was himself to reject the circumspection and "liberalism" that became the style of the (CIA-financed) Congress for Cultural Freedom, the anti-Communist political warfare institution he was involved in founding in 1950.

The intellectual and political confrontation with Communism was Koestler's principal preoccupation during the decade that followed the war. However, he made a short and difficult return to Palestine in 1945, when as a special correspondent of the British press he interviewed the leaders of the two main Zionist underground terrorist groups (the Irgun Zvei Leumi and the so-called Stern Gang—the former, led by Menachem Begin, close to Koestler's old Zionist attachment, the aggressively expansionist Revisionist Zionist movement inspired by Vladmir Jabotinsky).

He went back again in 1948 as correspondent for the *New York Herald Tribune* and French and British papers, coincident with the

---

* Subtitled "Six Studies in Communism," this collection of essays by disabused ex-Communists become militant anti-Communists, edited by Richard Crossman, made a great stir when published in London in 1950.

start of the War for Independence. He published an essay on Zionism and Israel, *Promise and Fulfillment*, in 1949. His Zionist novel, *Thieves in the Night*, based on his earlier experiences, had come out in 1946. He did not write again on a Jewish theme until 1976, when he argued in *The Thirteenth Tribe*, to universal skepticism from scholars, that most Jews of eastern and central Europe descended from the Caucasian Khazar nation, which had adopted the Jewish religion before the kingdom's decline in the eleventh century but otherwise had no connection with Jerusalem or the original Jewish diaspora. Thus, he argued, most European Jews were not of Semitic origin.

He and Daphne Hardy had parted in 1944 and he had a new mistress, Mamaine Paget, whom he had met at a party at Cyril Connolly's in 1944. In 1945 they took a cottage in Wales. In 1946 he visited Paris for the first time since the war, and introducing himself to Jean-Paul Sartre in the basement bar of the Hotel Pont-Royal, was quickly included in a febrile intellectual (and drinking) set that included Sartre, Simone de Beauvoir*, Albert Camus, and his old friend and veteran of the prewar Comintern, Manès Sperber. Another member—a political step apart—was André Malraux, then engaged in building up the Rassemblement du Peuple Français (the RPF) as a vehicle for General Charles de Gaulle's (unsuccessful)

---

* Koestler later had a one-night affair with Beauvoir, which both regretted. He was to figure in her novel *The Mandarins*, as the character Scriassine, who had a "thin, almost feminine smile." "To him Russia was the enemy nation, and he did not have any great love for the United States. There wasn't any place on earth where he really felt at home." Scriassine also believed that "there's only one sickness that really amounts to anything—being yourself, just you." Beauvoir adds that on saying this, "an almost unbearable sincerity suddenly softened his face. . . ."

Mamaine Paget also had a brief but passionate affair with Camus, who wanted her to "run off" with him. She admitted this to Koestler, who nonetheless remained friends with Camus. Edmund Wilson also fell in love with her while on a European trip in 1945 and proposed marriage. He corresponded with her for many years afterwards.

postwar bid to return to power. (That had to await the Algerian crisis in 1958.)

Sartre and Beauvoir were hostile to the capitalist United States but at the time had an ambiguous relationship with the Communist Party, which Sartre persisted in seeing as a valid (and unique) vehicle of the interests of the laboring proletariat. Their differences with the aggressively anti-Communist Koestler were real but did not become a serious issue between them until later.

Koestler returned to Paris in 1947 and 1948 while continuing to live in Wales. Although he had become a naturalized British subject, he and Paget, who by then was his second wife, moved to France at the end of 1948, taking a house near Fontainebleau and later a place on the Seine. His social life was animated by regular visits to Paris and by continuing intellectual and political battle. Sartre and Simone de Beauvoir ostentatiously broke with him in 1949 after he had published a gratuitous and unfunny description in the press of French intellectuals (the "Existenchiks," with parts for Sartre and "Simona Castorovna"), and he fought with Malraux. (New bridges burned.)

By then he had written his contribution to *The God That Failed* and was working on another political novel (*The Age of Longing*, 1951)* and his two principal volumes of autobiography (*Arrow in the Blue*, 1952, and *The Invisible Writing*, 1954), which enjoyed international success. His wife became ill (she suffered from severe asthma) and was hospitalized first in Paris and then London. He was drinking heavily and on one occasion, stopped for drunk driving, punched a commissaire of police, not an intelligent thing to do in France. It took a friend, director of the then Sûreté, to get him out of jail.

---

* The last but one of his novels. There was a final novel in 1972, "a tragicomedy," *The Call Girls*, a rather silly book about intellectuals at an international congress proposing utopian solutions to the threat to human existence posed by nuclear weapons. (Possibly such a conference actually did take place, with such conclusions reached; sillier things have happened.)

In an apology following his penultimate quarrel with Koestler, Sartre wrote to the latter to say that despite the fondness he felt for him, "there is a certain fairly fundamental difference between us, which guarantees that we will be exasperated by each other. . . ." As Cesarani summarizes it, it was "that Koestler had been a Communist, a movement in which individuality was subordinated and psychology was an irrelevancy, an experience that had marked him. Sartre, by contrast, was a product of bourgeois, individualistic culture and habitually separated a person from his or her beliefs or party. . . . Disagreements were inevitable but should not interfere with friendship."

Certainly Koestler grew increasingly belligerent and pessimistic in his anti-Communism. Beauvoir thought that "his anti-Communism made him irrational." In 1947 he had said that he believed the Communists would come to power in France within eighteen months, and at a dinner in Paris with the visiting Walter Lippmann he defended in principle the idea of a preventive war against Russia, saying that although he was personally convinced that war was inevitable he would not advocate a preemptive attack because there was a chance that he could be wrong.

Some of Münzenberg's Comintern front groups had survived the war, and new versions of other prewar organizations were being created under covert Soviet sponsorship. The Comintern itself, in its new guise as an "information bureau" (the "Cominform"), was reconvened by Stalin in 1947. Münzenberg's leagues against war and Fascism, committees for Red Aid or for victims of this or that, his writers' congresses, feature services, emergency committees, youth or student internationals, and the like, reappeared in spirit and form in the guise of the Stockholm Appeal against nuclear war, the World Peace Council and its congresses, the campaign in the early 1950s against alleged U.S. germ warfare in Korea, and accusations that the United States wanted a new world war and was itself becoming a new fascist state in alliance with resurgent Nazi forces in West Germany.

The World Federation of Trade Unions and the International Union of Students, founded respectively in 1945 and 1946, were successors to the labor and student "internationals" of before the war, their secretariats or executive committees securely controlled by Communists, with their posts of prestige and boards of directors composed of "innocents."

꩜

In the spring of 1949 the French Communists organized a "world peace" conference in Paris with Pablo Picasso, Frédéric Joliot-Curie (Nobel laureate in chemistry and early nuclear physicist), and the Italian Communist leader Pietro Nenni. A counterinitiative, socialist and neutralist, was organized. The Rassemblement Démocratique Révolutionnaire had been created by two Paris intellectuals, David Rousset and Georges Altmann, with the support of Sartre.* Rousset had been a Trotskyist and anticolonial activist before the war. During the war he was sent to Buchenwald as a Résistant, and afterwards worked to establish a Europe-wide commission of inquiry into the continued existence of concentration and forced labor camps in Franco's Spain, the Soviet Union, and in some European colonies.

Speakers at Rousset's countermeeting included Silone, Franz Borkenau (another ex-Communist German refugee from Nazism and the former official historian of the Comintern), the Italian

---

* A French Communist official reported to his Soviet contact that "there are two ideological dangers in France. The first is the militant fascism of Malraux with his false heroism—the ideology of Gaullism—and the second is the philosophy of decadence expounded by Sartre which now acts openly against Communism by talking of a 'Third Force.'"

Carlo Levi (author of *Christ Stopped at Eboli*), and the American novelist James T. Farrell. The meeting was otherwise notable for its poster, which reproduced Picasso's dove of peace (symbol of the Communist meeting), furnished with tank tracks and a cannon in place of the beak, identified as "the dove that goes 'boom.' "

The meeting was followed in June 1950 by a Berlin "Congress for Cultural Freedom," put together mainly by the dynamic Melvin Lasky, a young American Social Democratic intellectual working in Berlin, and Irving Brown of the American Federation of Labor, who was already active in organizing opposition to the Communists in European labor movements.* The Berlin meeting was subsidized by the American and British governments and had support from the West Berlin mayor, Ernst Reuter.

Koestler was invited and proved the star of the occasion, which dramatically coincided with the North Korean invasion of South Korea. His speech was the principal and most effective event of the opening day. In it he attacked Sartre and Thomas Mann for hesitating at the choice between Communism and anti-Communism. This was no time, he said, to refuse to see the world in black and white: there had to be a "yes" or "no" answer to totalitarianism. This denunciation of "neutralism" was to become a recurrent and passionate theme in his political writing and speeches.

Some of his listeners received the speech as itself an invitation to a version of totalitarian thinking. According to Cesarani, the British delegates Hugh Trevor-Roper and A. J. Ayer "bridled at the 'hysterical atmosphere in which the Congress was held,' " for which they held Koestler responsible. Others attacked Koestler's dismissal of center-left politics and accused him of still thinking in the dialectical terms of his Marxist formation.

Sidney Hook later demonstrated that Koestler's speech at the

---

* The AFL was one of the most important early channels for official American financing of overseas anti-Communist organizations; such an agreement was made in 1949 between the AFL's Free Trade Union Committee and the Office of Policy Coordination of the CIA.

Congress was a good deal more moderate than it seemed when delivered, but as Mamaine Paget noted in her diary at the time, Koestler in full oratorical flight "was capable of reciting the truths of the multiplication table in a way to make some people indignant with him." He and Sperber drafted the Manifesto with which the meeting ended, in a mass outdoor rally with fifteen thousand Berliners present.

The Congress for Cultural Freedom was founded there, an organization that for the next twenty years, with the active but secret support of the CIA, was to out-Münzenberg Münzenberg, so to speak, in waging the intellectual cold war in Europe, sponsoring serious literary, intellectual, and scientific congresses, and publishing intelligent and influential magazines.* It was destroyed in the 1970s by revelation of its tie to the CIA.

～◯

What followed the Berlin congress was a great disappointment for Koestler. An international committee of twenty-five persons was named to see that the work was continued, and a temporary executive committee was formed including himself, Irving Brown and Melvin Lasky, both with connections to the American government; David Rousset and Silone, who was inclined toward a form of Christian pacifism; and the social democrat Carlos Schmidt. Koestler unexpectedly found himself in an ideological minority. He wanted

---

* They included *Encounter* in Britain (actually a joint enterprise with British intelligence), *Preuves* in France, *Tempo Presente* in Italy, *Forum* in Austria, *Quest* in India, *Quadrant* in Australia, *Cuadernos*, published in Paris but directed to Latin American intellectuals, *Soviet Survey* (whose research and analytical work was sometimes reprinted by Soviet journals themselves), and *China Quarterly*.

There was a link in this to the views on culture of the poet T. S. Eliot, also editor of the literary journal *Criterion*. In an essay in the *Journal of Contemporary History* (April 2000) on Lasky and the CCF, Giles Scott-Smith draws attention to a German radio broadcast in 1947 where Eliot argued that an international "network of independent reviews, at least one in every capital of Europe, is necessary for the transmission of ideas" and for the reconstruction of Europe's literary culture.

an aggressive propaganda organization with offices in Paris and Berlin, attacking neutralism, "educating" public opinion in the Western democracies, and carrying out covert propaganda inside the Soviet bloc. But when a steering committee was named, it included the Swiss editor François Bondy, the Swiss philosopher Denis de Rougemont (author of *Love in the Western World* and an ardent European unionist), and Irving Brown, but not Koestler. He left in disgust, later referring to the Congress as a "literary society."

He told Sperber, "I did not withdraw. . . . I was made to withdraw in a gentle and effective way." He resigned from the executive committee in August 1950. Cesarani notes that his "active involvement with the Congress . . . lasted just over four months. In every respect this was consistent with the pattern of his association with the Zionist Revisionist movement, the Communist Party, the Münzenberg apparatus. . . ." Within a year he was contemptuously dismissing the Congress as an "effete" arts movement.*

Koestler by then was living in the United States, where, on an impulse, be had bought a house in Pennsylvania, on an island in the Delaware river. However, he soon found that he didn't like the United States very much, and he returned to England within twenty months. American friends reproached him for underestimating the damage Senator Joseph McCarthy was doing with demagogic, undiscriminating, and undocumented attacks on officials and public figures as Communists. Koestler went to Washington in connection with his need for a special congressional exemption from the law banning former Communists from permanent residence in the United States (he had needed a special visa even for a book tour promoting *Darkness at Noon*), and he had lunch with

---

* The tale of the Congress and other CIA-financed political warfare operations during the years that followed is a complicated one, directly or indirectly linked to the careers and influence of Arthur Koestler and Willi Münzenberg. It does not, however, belong here, and I have placed it in an appendix.

McCarthy. However, his experience of Washington merely left him depressed with the insularity and ignorance of American politicians. By the time the congressional exemption came, he and Mamaine were fed up ("the pressure of this godforsaken country is getting him down," she wrote to friends).

His irritated assessment, according to Cesarani, was that the United States was

> inefficient as a society and uncongenial to the individual. The breakages and delays in moving into [the house he had bought] were "staggering." Technology was self-defeating: the cars were fast [but because of congestion the traffic slow]. . . . The only comparison was with Russia. "Both countries have one thing in common: utter frustration of the individual, enslavement there by the state, here by a totally mechanized and stereotyped culture-pattern . . . [shaped by] money, ostentation, the crudest, inhuman, neurotic patterns and snobbery." It was a "civilization in a cul de sac. . . . France was in decay, England 'was a case of complete strangulation and stubborn, suicidal isolation,' but America was 'heading for a dead end.' " Children were raised into a form of autism, unable to make contact with other humans. It was a "contactless society" populated by automatons.

With understandable relief, the Koestlers left New York for London.

✌

Koestler ended his career as political writer in 1955 with a despairing essay, "The Trail of the Dinosaur," on the moral history of man, which he said had been irreversibly changed by the dethronement of God at the beginning of the eighteenth century (when man "enter[ed] upon a spiritual ice age"). The curve of man's destructive technological power had since soared, he said, while the curve of his progress in moral philosophy and spiritual clarity, after modest and indecisive rises and falls, had gone "into a steep decline."

He wrote that he had nothing further to say on the political questions "which had obsessed me, in various ways, for the best part of a quarter-century. Now the errors are atoned for, the bitter passion has burnt itself out; Cassandra has gone hoarse, and is due for a vocational change."

A return to scientific writing and speculation followed, some of it delightfully and usefully iconoclastic, such as his reexamination of the Lamarckian argument (that acquired characteristics can be inherited) in *The Case of the Midwife Toad* (1971), and some of it slightly batty (his later exploration of levitation and extrasensory perception).*

He launched new ethical crusades, a campaign against hanging, and an impassioned effort to put an end to the British racket of forcing dog owners arriving from abroad to put their pets into isolation kennels ("concentration camps for dogs" he said) in order to save the British human population from rabies. Rabies is not exactly rampant in Western Europe or the United States, where it is vaccinated against, and the psychological connection of this British obsession to old British political and cultural anxieties about contamination from Europe is fairly evident.†

⁘

Arthur Koestler died by his own hand in 1983. The final bridge was burned. His last wife, Cynthia Jefferies, chose to commit suicide in his company, although she was only fifty-five years old and in good health. That morning she had conscientiously taken their dog to the veterinarian to be put down.

---

* In his will he established an endowed chair in the study of parapsychology, which eventually was created at Edinburgh University.

† The quarantine law has been changed in recent years but there seems to have been limited practical change.

In the message Koestler left, he wrote, "It is to [Cynthia] that I owe the peace and relative happiness I have enjoyed during the final period of my life—and never before." This might not seem the most generous of tributes; however, its implied priorities were those of a man whose lifelong "sickness," as he had indicated to Beauvoir, was enduring that he was who he was, conducting a life-long search to find "the him in me who is more me than myself."*

The experiences of Willi Münzenberg and Arthur Koestler, to-gether with that of André Malraux, the Byronic fellow traveler, illustrate from beginning to end the essential story of Marxism-Leninism's utopian bid to resolve the European crisis that followed the First World War. Münzenberg was part of the effort from the beginning, Koestler was there at the end, as it foundered. The year Koestler died, Mikhail Gorbachev was two years away from becom-ing general secretary of the Communist Party of the Soviet Union and launching glasnost—the somber quest to lay out the truth about what had happened.

---

* Koestler's reputation in the Anglo-American world has since suffered from Ce-sarani's report that he was an aggressive womanizer (which he readily admitted in his autobiographical works), and according to one account a would-be rapist. Why he should be singled out on these counts from among the hundreds of sexually predatory political activists of the period, or the contemporary academics with an eye for the pretty (or handsome) and ambitious student, or all the other intellectuals and writers whose work remains respected despite disreputable private lives, is, I suppose, simply one of the hazards of biography, political bias, and the politically correct preoccupa-tions of the present day. Koestler seems actually to have remained on remarkably good terms with his ex-wives and lovers. Daphne Hardy (Henrion) said in 1998, "He was amusing and very dominating, but never violent, and it was out of character to rape: he didn't have to. For central Europeans, it's an ancient tradition that you're supposed to sleep with any woman you can." Cynthia Jefferies became his occasional secretary in 1949 and remained so for six subsequent years (during which time she herself married and divorced). She returned to London from New York in 1955 in response to a cabled request from Koestler to become his full-time secretary, lived with him from then on, in 1965 married him, and eventually died with him.

CHAPTER TEN

CODA: THE ROMANT[...]
REVOLUTIONARY

In his autobiography, Koestler concedes that his re[...]
difficult to understand how he, as a recruit to Comn[...]
be "ashamed of having been to a university, to cur[...]
his brain, the articulateness of his language, to regai[...]
tastes and habits as he had acquired as a constant[...]
reproach, and intellectual self-mutilation as a desi[...]
writes of one of his Comintern superiors that "he w[...]
Puritan type of spy, motivated entirely by idealism[...]
like Richard Sorge or Ignatz Reiss." (Like others of h[...]
riod, this man, Alex Rado, was eventually accused c[...]
Moscow, was returned to Russia by force, and vanish[...]

Whittaker Chambers, after six years as a Commu[...]
agent, and having decided to break away, could nc[...]
scribe "the world I was leaving [as looking] like the wc[...]
of the future. The world I was returning to seemed,[...]
graveyard. It was, in fact, the same world I had aband[...]
less when I joined the Communist Party in 1925. Onl[...]
sis, which a few men could diagnose thirteen years[...]
reached the visible brink of catastrophe."

All of the people swept up as Communist Party symp[...]
members during the 1920s and 1930s were gripped by[...]

:cessary revolution and a conviction that life and circumstance ere not as they seemed to be to their contemporaries but hid a di-ectical promise, which was that the unhappiness, oppression, overty, and anxiety in society could be swept away with a single ow—to liberate happiness, satisfaction, and justice.

In Bertolt Brecht's *The Measures Taken* (*Die Massnahme*), written 1 1931, which Koestler described as the "climax" of Brecht's liter-ry accomplishment and "the most revealing work of art in the en-ire Communist literature," three Comintern agents justify to their uperior the murder of a fourth comrade and the disposal of his ody in a lime pit. The three are presented as having effaced their ndividual personalities and consciences in the interests of the Party. The Party official, after hearing their report, congratulates hem because "you are no longer yourselves . . . you are without a 1ame, without a brother, blank sheets on which the Revolution will write its orders.

"He who fights for Communism must be able to fight and to re-nounce fighting, to say the truth and not say the truth, to be helpful and unhelpful, to keep a promise and break a promise, to go into danger and to avoid danger, to be known and to be unknown. He who fights for Communism has of all the virtues only one: that he fights for Communism."

The comrade who had to be killed had failed this code. He was, according to Brecht, guilty of four "crimes": those of pity, loyalty, dignity, and righteous indignation, none of them acceptable senti-ments in a Communist agent. Brecht's chorus in the play, called "Controlchorus," demands: "what vileness would you not commit to exterminate violence. . . . Sink into the mud, embrace the butcher, but change the world: it needs it."

&

What intellectual sentiment could be more romantic? What more distant from the common sentiments of ordinary men and women? But this was the moral atmosphere in which Comintern agents

were recruited and formed, and in which they worked in during the 1920s, 1930s, and 1940s.

One can argue that it never has been hard to find people who thought themselves of civilized mind while demanding the elimination of those mortals whom they considered obstacles to man's higher interests as they saw them, rogue individuals or rogue states. However, this was ordinarily in a context of national or imperial policy in which they were following the orders of a government whose moral legitimacy they did not question and whose views they shared, seeing their victims as enemies to the interests of their own nation or race, obstacles to superior human values, a superior civilization, a political destiny.

American government has functioned on this basis since the start of the war on terrorism. One did not have to be a fanatic or ideologue to torture terrorist suspects, or to take an active part in the Phoenix operation in Vietnam, involving the systematic investigation and assassination of suspected Viet Cong agents in Vietnamese civil society, or to assist the CIA's blundering efforts to kill Fidel Castro, or to suggest to susceptible Vietnamese army officers in 1963 that the war effort in Vietnam would benefit from Ngo Dinh Diem's elimination, or to officers in Chile in 1973 that President Salvador Allende Gossens might advantageously be removed, or to Greek officers in the 1960s that the United States was more comfortable with Greece under military dictatorship, or to send the battleship *Missouri* to shell the Palestinian districts of Beirut in 1982 (all of them, without exception, actions which by the strictest utilitarian measures proved damaging rather than beneficial to the eventual American national interest). All were the products of calm analysis by government professionals and high elected officials, convinced of the justice of their cause, emotionally detached, having in these cases temporarily suspended the operations of that portion of their intellectual apparatus where common sense functions.

It was fundamentally different in the underground Communist

case. The commitment was personal, and the consciousness of be-traying "bourgeois morality" intense, since that morality had usu-ally previously been the Communist militant or agent's own. He or she betrayed friends and expediently compromised with enemies in order to execute a task which history had assigned to them, and which they understood as a moral undertaking.

◆◇

There was a controversy in New York in 1988, following an article by Stephen Schwartz in *The New York Times Book Review* concern-ing the individuals associated with a "special tasks" group directed by the (then) NKVD, responsible for arranging the execution of Trotsky in 1940 and the murder or attempted murder of several of his associates, certain non-Communist leftists involved in the Spanish civil war, certain White Russian exile activists, and some Soviet or Comintern defectors.

The members of this group were also said to have earlier been implicated in the secret dealings between Nazi and Soviet secret services to forge evidence of treachery in the Soviet high command. This was needed to justify the great purge of the Red Army in 1937, advantageous to the Nazis because it all but decapitated that army, and to Stalin because it enabled him to destroy potentially uncon-trollable elements in both Party and army. (The collaboration led eventually to the Nazi-Soviet Pact of 1939, whose secret protocols partitioned Poland, gave Russia the Baltic states, and allowed Hit-ler a free hand in central Europe.)

The controversy arose because the persons accused were not professional revolutionaries or louche figures from a political un-derworld. They included the Mexican painter David Alfaro Siqueiros (who personally made an attempt on Trotsky's life); the poet Pablo Neruda, then a Chilean diplomat; Nadyezhda Plevit-skaya, a prominent singer who was part of the White Russian emi-gration in Western Europe; Mark Zborowski, later head of the Pain Center of Mount Zion Hospital in San Francisco; and Max Eitingon, a Jewish psychoanalyst of Russian origin and a member of Freud's inner circle until 1937.

The allegation against Dr. Eitingon provoked a particular controversy in which the American writer and historian Theodore Draper contended that his inclusion was a case of mistaken identity. The argument was conducted, at least on the part of Mr. Draper, with the ruthless discourtesy and allegations of bad faith that characterize most of the public confrontations of the so-called New York Intellectuals (I have never understood why). Robert Conquest, historian of terror and persecution in the Soviet Union and the ultimate Western authority in these matters, finally intervened to suggest that the evidence was insufficient either to retroactively convict or exonerate Dr. Eitingon, but that the evidence for conviction was sufficiently weighty as to justify a Scottish verdict of "not proven."

In the course of his argument Mr. Draper said that it appeared hardly conceivable that a man who "seemingly devoted his entire life to the advancement of psychoanalysis" could have also been a political conspirator and assassin, and that if this indeed were true, Dr. Eitingon must have been "one of the most remarkable cases on record of a double life or personality."

This was a strange comment from the man who wrote a history of the American Communist Party. The overwhelming evidence is that intellectuals who committed themselves to one or another of the utopian totalitarian movements of the last century often led double lives and repeatedly suppressed the normal values and impulses of Western society in the cause of what they considered political necessity. This frequently was accompanied by an outwardly conventional existence, academic or professional respectability, and an unremarkable social status.

As Koestler's career, among others, attests, intellectuals, scholars, artists or persons of artistic sensibility have been disproportionately numerous in both modern revolutionary movements and state intelligence and clandestine services. In wartime or times of perceived national emergency the latter organizations are by far their most popular choices of service. I obviously include myself in this judgment. To people whose normal occupations are sedentary or remote from the mainstream of affairs, such work can be intellectually challenging and emotionally gratifying. As a kind of holiday from life, as a thrilling avocation, such people become spies, saboteurs, propagandists, political warfare operators—licensed to operate outside the law, holders of double-zero prefixes, outside the conventional morality, flying free in a large cause. This is an expression of that longing for clear-cut and decisive change that is a motive for war itself: the belief in progress, a willingness to believe that violence can make the world better, even though the historical record is that in the long run it only makes it different.

Klaus Fuchs, a refugee theoretical physicist in England for eight years during and after the Second World War, who passed atomic secrets to Moscow, and presumably remained a Communist until his death in East Germany in 1988, told his MI5 interrogator in 1950: "[I] used my Marxist philosophy to establish in my mind two separate compartments. One compartment in which I allowed myself to make friendships, to have personal relations, to help people and to be in all personal ways the kind of man I wanted to be and which, in personal ways I had been before. . . . It appeared to me at the time that I had become a 'free man' because I had succeeded in the other department to establish myself completely independent of the surrounding forces of society. Looking back at it now the best way of expressing it seems to be to call it controlled schizophrenia."

The Yale historian Peter Gay intervened in the 1988 discussion with a letter to the *Times Book Review* accusing the artists and intellectuals who were members of the assassination group of having "betrayed everything the civilized mind stands for." This is exactly what Brecht applauded. The "civilized mind" which prevailed among Western elites was exactly what had to be destroyed.

The romantic revolutionary ideology that moved the left in the twentieth century achieved its final international influence in what proved its culminating failure, that of the Marxist internationalism that influenced Third World revolutionaries and the post-1960s Western movements that described themselves as Maoist or as "urban guerrillas." While Maoism itself and the ideology of the Khmer Rouge in Cambodia were indeed (or became) modern and secular versions of the violent millenarian religious movements of the past, most of the late-twentieth-century revolutionary movements in Latin America, the Middle East, and Asia were fundamentally nationalist affairs dressed in a fashionable ideology, otherwise hard to distinguish from, say, Balkan irredentist movements in the nineteenth century. The symbolic figure of this phenomenon was Ernesto (Che) Guevera, companion of Fidel Castro in the Cuban guerrilla campaign that ended in 1959 with the overthrow of the formerly American-supported dictator, Fulgencio Batista.*

Che believed that the Cuban revolution could and should be replicated in other unhappy countries ("one, two, three, many Vietnams!" as he later was to say). His belief was based on the same conceptual error made by the "domino theorists" in Washington, responsible for the American commitment to war in Vietnam as well as to suppression of Latin American revolutionary movements. Neither Havana nor Washington understood that successful revolution in a country has to rise up from indigenous, and to a greater or lesser degree spontaneous, forces within that society. It is not an import commodity, nor is its defeat by external intervention ordinarily possible, even though such an intervention may prolong and deepen the agony. The American project in 2003–2004 to deliver democracy to the "greater Middle East" through politico-military intervention was founded on the identical fallacy.

---

* "Che" means "hey" (as in "hey, you!") and is frequent in demotic Argentine Spanish.

Guevera made himself famous with two failures, the first an abortive intervention in 1965 with some 160 men to back the remnants of the nationalist movement that had supported the newly independent (ex-Belgian) Congo's first prime minister, Patrice Lumumba, when the United States, Belgium, the UN, and various Congolese factions were engaged in a chaotic struggle to control this nominally independent new state and its immense resources. The other was a year later when he took sixteen veterans of the Cuban or Congo adventures, or of both, to Bolivia, in order to provoke a revolution in that country. He launched his campaign without support from any but the most extreme and heterodox elements of the Bolivian Left, in the most desolate region of Bolivia, a country of only 340,000 inhabitants in a territory with a surface equal to Britain, Belgium, and Cuba combined. He botched the affair from the start. Not a single Bolivian peasant joined his guerrillas. His followers drifted away. He left a careless trail that included a cache of suitcases containing civilian clothing for ten men, some of it with Havana store labels. By October 1967, the surviving guerrillas had been scattered and Che was captured. Following radio discussions with La Paz, his captors shot him.

But failure is a paradoxical recipe for success in many fields of endeavor, or for a reputation for success. By the end of the 1960s Washington was convinced that there really might be "one, two, many Vietnams!" The international Left adopted Che as hero, convinced that this was going to happen. Appearance, rumor, personal magnetism, and the press had made him a romantic figure, and death confirmed him in that role. He was celebrated as a Byron, a Malraux, a Lawrence of the 1960s: Che in his beret, with his cigar, inspiration of the revolution that never arrived. Reality eventually had its restorative way, and more than forty years later Che survives as an Andy Warhol serigraph, like Marilyn Monroe—an ignominious icon of commercial communication.

Inside the Western countries, in Western Europe and the United States, post-1968 "Maoist" or "urban guerrilla" movements usually had naïve or sentimental utopian goals and ended badly, as such things do, progressing from the student demand to forbid all of the forbiddens and allow imagination to take power, to the underground assassination group, motivated by the genuine political corruption of an ostensibly democratic state, in which militants perceive a masked Fascism. Possibly the last of the latter, Greece's November 7th group, was partially dismantled in 2002–2003 following a series of political murders dating back to colonels' junta that ruled Greece between 1967 and 1974.

The French Communist intellectual Paul Nizan said in the 1930s that he understood the Communist Manifesto to be saying that man is love and is prevented from loving. What a mistake that proved to be! But it was a mistake that explains a great deal about what subsequently happened in France and elsewhere in Europe then and in the postwar years. Sergio Romano, the Italian historian and commentator, speaking of Italy's "Red Brigade" terrorists (the remark would apply to West Germany's as well), said their "cultural and political progress [was] often marked by the same stages: The Social Christian groups following in the footsteps of the Vatican Council, the youth organizations of the Communist Party, the Marxist or liberation 'groupuscules' proliferating in the universities after 1968, and finally the clandestine organizations. . . ."

Marx had brought rationalism to revolution, and that is why the orthodox Marxists of Western Europe were rejected by the new Red Brigades, Baader-Meinhof gangs, and Red Army Fractions. It is why the Italian Red Brigades made the Italian Communist Party their enemy. The rational and expedient maneuvers of the Communists, their calculating compromises in the pursuit of power, the old contempt of Lenin for "infantile" adventurism, made them the natural enemy of the new terrorists.

Who were these new and violence-haunted apostles of a revolution that refused to come about? These set-lipped German pastors' daughters and brilliant, pious Catholic youth activists—worker-priests of revolution, as a French journalist has described them? They were not originals, even in fairly recent twentieth-century European (and American) history. Their accomplishments scarcely matched those of a few unorganized anarchist terrorists at the end of the nineteenth century. In the years between 1890 and 1901, those people managed to kill the Empress Elizabeth of Austria, President Carnot of France, King Umberto I of Italy, a Spanish prime minister, and President McKinley of the United States. They bombed theaters and cafés in Lyon, Paris, and Barcelona; the Chamber of Deputies and the stock exchange in Paris; police stations and courts and officials' homes. Koestler has said: "Homicide committed for selfish motives is a statistical rarity in all cultures. Homicide for unselfish motives is the dominant phenomenon of man's history. His tragedy is not an excess of aggression, but an excess of devotion. . . . It is loyalty and devotion which makes the fanatic."

The anarchists at the turn of the twentieth century seem nearly all to have come from social and economic groups that had been undermined by the industrial and political changes of the period. (The resemblance to contemporary Islamic terrorism's recruits is obvious.) Members of anarchist groups (not necessarily terrorists themselves) were very often artisans who worked alone—watchmakers, shoemakers, tailors. There was a significant poor-peasant anarchism, chiefly in Spain and Russia. These people, intelligent but isolated, were often autodidact idealists who had concluded from reading Bakunin, Proudhon, and the anarchist tracts then in circulation that to attack the men and institutions of power and privilege could cause the structure of the state to collapse forthwith and inspire a great popular insurrection. They believed that man's "natural" tendency to peaceful cooperation would then be liberated, bringing into existence a new society, without oppression, exploitation, or authority.

In this respect, the doctrines of the late-twentieth-century Red Brigades demonstrated what the modern totalitarian experience has done to darken utopian thought. The Red Brigades did not expect the state to topple forthwith. They intended by attacking state and party power to force the state to become even more repressive than it already was, thereby making life so unbearable for the masses of people that they eventually would be forced to rise in revolution.

Even this, of course, ignored the fact that the only real popular uprisings seen in Europe since the First World War—the partisan struggles during the Second World War and subsequent Eastern European rebellions—were essentially nationalist, and lacking aid from outside they failed. (For that matter, the Russian Revolution of 1917 was essentially a coup d'état carried out against an ineffectual reform government.) The terrorist is irrationally optimistic about the modern state's vulnerability to popular action, especially when the state is provoked to employ the apparatus of repression available to it.

What we know of the terrorists of the last four decades of the twentieth century does not, however, justify a straightforward socioeconomic explanation for their actions. These terrorists might be considered members of a socially displaced class, to the extent that they came from a lumpen intelligentsia. But even that appears more often true of the Red Brigades' sympathizers than of the activists themselves. Renato Curcio studied sociology at the university and made a brilliant record, but was also the child of a liaison between a servant girl and the Italian husband of a rich American living in Rome. He was brought up by his mother, who made her living as a chambermaid. Andreas Baader was a common criminal, not a student, before being swept up in politics with Ulrike Meinhof, a successful journalist. Such people—the actual killers and bombers—might more accurately be described as distressed or psychopathic or sociopathic personalities for whom political terrorism provided a vehicle for impulses that would otherwise have found another destructive outlet.

❦

Distinctions must be made between terrorists who propose more or less rational and potentially attainable objectives and the terrorists who do not. It is not an irrational act to be an al-Qaeda or Palestinian terrorist, or to have been a member of the Zionist Stern Gang, or of the IRA. What such people want or wanted is plainly identified and, given the right circumstances, could come about. Withdrawal of U.S. troops from the Muslim holy places or from the Islamic world as a whole, British withdrawal from all of Ireland, Israel's establishment, a free Palestinian state: these have not been fantasy goals.* On the other hand, a society of "no more wars, no more quarrels, no more jealousy, no more theft, no more assassination, no more police, no more judges, no more administration" plainly is a fantasy. That is the society the anarchist known as Ravachol sought to bring about by a series of bombings that terrorized Paris in the 1890s.

The three countries in the late twentieth century that produced serious terrorist movements of the kind whose goals were essentially unattainable were Italy, Germany, and, in its own way, Japan—the three defeated countries of the Second World War. In Italy in 1978, between the kidnapping and the murder of the Italian president Aldo Moro, a document was issued by the Red Brigades describing the doctrine and strategy of the Italian movement. It defined the ultimate objective of the Red Brigades as "to liberate man finally from bestial exploitation, from necessary labor, from misery, from fatigues, from social degradation." It also made the following passionate comment on the plight of Italy: "Italy functions as the

---

* Although in the al-Qaeda case an apocalypic note, of "visionary terrorism," enters when the argument is made that final defeat of "the Crusaders and Zionists" will cause the truth of the Prophet to prevail and a heaven on earth created.

last province of the [capitalist] empire, as the garbage pail of Europe. . . . The multinationals' division of labor assigns [to Italians] a function anything but exalting . . . that of serving as imperialism's 'white niggers.' "

That kind of language has been heard before. "The humiliating mediocrity of our nation . . . debased by her acceptance and assimilation of European ideas" was the complaint of the Fascist novelist and polemicist Curzio Malaparte, writing in the 1920s. The Futurist Marinetti wanted "to deliver Italy from its gangrene of professors, archeologists, tourist guides, and antiquaries. Italy has been too long the great secondhand market. We want to get rid of the innumerable museums which cover it with innumerable cemeteries." "Words are beautiful things, but muskets and machines guns are even more beautiful"—that was Mussolini himself. "Our people must suffer, we must suffer; only deep and atrocious suffering, experienced by all, like that caused by famine, plague, or civil war, can transform us"—the Fascist Malaparte again.

The theme of national humiliation and revenge was basic to Italian Fascism. But Italian Fascism was fundamentally a nationalist movement; the Left purports to be internationalist, and a defining assumption of all movements of the modern Left is that international revolution and international fraternity are the ultimate goals of the struggle. The late-twentieth-century Italian terrorists thus opened themselves to questions about their real political ancestry.

The theme of humiliation, in any case, offers something of a paradox in Italy's case, because in crucial respects Italy has in political as well as aesthetic matters been one of the most innovative and original of contemporary Western societies, not the most retarded. To begin with one simple, if unpalatable, fact, Italy originated Fascism, one of the two ideological movements to dominate the first half of the twentieth century. It also produced, in Antonio Gramsci and his circle, the first and most influential attempt to reconcile Bolshevik Communism with the political mainstream of the Western liberal tradition.

❧

Western European terrorism was silenced in the final decade of the twentieth century by its own failure to evoke popular sympathy or produce its predicted political results, and by the collapse of Communism. The radical Left has since retreated to the university, where a current of utopian belief still is strong, its intellectual context usually meager. In this respect the Marxists with their thick books of doctrine and analysis were exceptional. More typical of the modern academic Left is the English man of letters Raymond Williams, who said that revolution "remains necessary in all societies in which there are, for example, subordinate racial groups, landless landworkers, hired hands, the unemployed, and suppressed or discriminate minorities of any kind. Revolution remains necessary, in these circumstances, not only because some men desire it, but because there can be no acceptable human order while the full humanity of any class of men is in practice denied." A critic (Renée Winegarten) replied to him, "What precisely does 'full humanity' mean, and when shall it be known to have arrived on earth?"

Williams's kind of statement is meaningless, other than as sentimental aspiration, yet such ideas have been and continue to be taken by many to justify "revolutionary" action. It is not entirely a finished affair even today. Revolutionary utopianism enjoys a residual half-life on university faculties as well as among sectarian survivors of the 1960s. The argument is made that a "true" Communism, and a true secular redemption, can be regenerated even now in resistance to attempted American world domination, described as having produced a mutation in international society that opens the way to radical political transformation. The American academic Michael Hardt and the imprisoned Italian Red Brigades militant Antonio Negri said (in a book called *Empire*, which acquired a certain influence after its publication in 2000) that globalization and Washington's early-twenty-first-century exercises of power have "created a greater potential for revolution" than anything that has existed in the past. They argue that resistance to this new form of oppressive society can produce the unmediated mobilization "of all the exploited and the subjugated" of the world in a new "[global] citizenship of the multitude."* This kind of thought surely serves as a contemporary secular substitute for religion. Yet religion, a notion of a human transcendence outside of historical time, is regarded in the same intellectual circles as self-evident nonsense, sprung from primitive myth.

In the past, an explanation proposed for the crimes of intellectuals was Dostoyevskian, or Nietzschean (or pseudo-Nietzschean): that the militants are victims of pride, of a willingness to believe that superior intelligence means superior being, a superior claim on the universe, the right to use others as means to an end. The justification for such crimes, ostensibly corporatist, resting on doctrines of national, class, or religious destiny, is related; it holds that certain people by virtue of what they intrinsically are, or by the social group to which they belong, or by their knowledge of "objective" historical process or religious truth, possess the moral warrant to dispose of others in the general interest, as conceived by their doctrine.

---

* They wrote that the militant "who best expresses the life of the multitude: the agent of biopolitical production and resistance against Empire [will act like Saint Francis of Assisi, who while struggling] in opposition to nascent capitalism refused every instrumental discipline, and in opposition to the mortification of the flesh (in poverty and in the constituted order) . . . posed a joyous life, including all of being and nature, the animals, sister moon, brother sun, the birds of the field, the poor and exploited. . . ." *The New York Times* review of *Empire* described it as "the next big idea" and *Time* called its authors "innovators to watch." Mitchell Cohen, in *Dissent*, called the book a "combination of political spirituality and sing-song tiers-mondism. . . . While social democracy stutters, postmodernism chants. But what if the poor do not incarnate World Possibility . . . ? What if the multitude is just suffering human beings? . . . Then perhaps it would be better for the left to speak of human beings as if they were ends in themselves rather than 'desiring machines.' "

The terrorist of the 1970s and 1980s claimed that he or she had a vocation to bear witness to injustice by committing injustices himself (or herself) with the intention of ending injustice. Their crimes were justified because of the larger crime they attacked. Their actions reflected an optimism conceived in circumstances that should logically produce despair.

When it is no longer possible to believe rationally in revolutionary progress and the reign of justice, the terrorist may seek his solution in an irrational commitment to their possibility. Thus the terrorist remains a recognizable moral figure, a personage not so distant from the Communist spies and assassins of the 1930s, or from the early Fascists in the 1920s, who, too, thought they were creating a new age of heroism, popular fulfillment, and individual and national nobility.

The Palestinian or Islamic suicide bomber is a culturally idiosyncratic version of the Western militant committed to one or another of the national or corporatist struggles of the day. While the Islamists make a visionary and millenarian formulation of their purposes, the origin of their conflict is a conventional one: they want to expel the United States (and Israel) from the Islamic regions. That is a simple nationalist motivation, essentially identical to that of the other anticolonial or anti-imperialist movements of the nineteenth and twentieth centuries. It is a campaign in which they are unlikely to succeed, but theirs is a perfectly conventional political objective, and their method, terrorism, is a classical strategy. The novelty of what they did in September 2001 (and subsequently) lay in the scale and sophistication of their action.

Whether the cause is metaphysical revolution, Maoist revolt, nationalist revindication, Palestinian liberation, or the creation of an

Islamic society free from the taint of Western corruption and the influence of Western power, the individual willingness to sacrifice self, as well as others, is and remains an inextinguishable political force. The individual militant gains cause to believe that violence demonstrates his triumph over ordinary life: over common cowardice, common human ambitions—proof of his superiority, and through that of his right to remake the way others live, thereby requiring their gratitude. His or her steely inhumanity is a pursuit of the higher humanism that success eventually will validate.

"I am used to being thought a monster to be struggled against. That doesn't bother me. I am a combatant. When one is a revolutionary, one needs to accept the idea of bestowing death and receiving it. To kill or be killed is the simplest thing in the world." Thus Renato Curcio of the Italian Red Brigades. The same could be said by an Islamic suicide bomber.

Another man speaks of the "sublime effect . . . of destructive power," and adds, "Whatsoever is fitted in any sort to excite the ideas of pain and danger, that is to say whatever is in any sort terrible, is a source of the sublime." But this is not an ideologically intoxicated terrorist speaking; it is the great conservative Edmund Burke, describing a psychological reality—a reality at the core of romanticism, motivating the romantic subordination of thought to feeling. Bakunin, the theorist of anarchism, remarked that "the urge to destroy is also a creative urge."

Life ordinarily is experienced as shapeless and unmalleable. We make our ways through random incident toward a future that recedes before us, and rarely are offered an opportunity to take determining action that would seem to give meaning to our existence. War provides such an occasion, not necessarily by providing grand causes, but small, crystalline, vital individual choices. The possibility is provided to impose a significant form upon an individual life, if only by taking another's life. This is the case with terrorists, who act on the dialectical or religious conviction that murder will clarify the existing situation for those who do not yet understand, and will therefore inspire revolution and, eventually, universal joy. They are also drawn by the appeal of life lived to the limit, the enjoyment of power that comes from a gun, the power to administer the dose of death to an ill society, while acknowledging that it may come in return. It is hard to turn back when you have lived like this.

> O joy of creation
>   To be!
> O rapture, to fly
>   And be free!
> Be the battle lost or won,
> Though its smoke shall hide the sun,
> I shall find my love—the one
>   Born for me!
>
> I shall know him where he stands
>   All alone,
> With the power in his hands
>   Not o'erthrown!
> I shall know him by his face,
> By his godlike front and grace;
> I shall hold him for a space
>   All my own!
>
> It is he—O my love!
>   So bold!
> It is I—all thy love
>   Foretold!
> It is I—O love, what bliss!

> Dost thou answer to my kiss?
> O sweetheart! What is this
> Lieth there so cold?

That is by Bret Harte (1836–1902), and is called "What the Bullet Sang."

Conclusion

CHAPTER ELEVEN

PROGRESS

I have been concerned with a particular historical setting, the twentieth century, and with the choices and experiences of certain individuals whose personal histories perhaps tell us more than we have previously understood about the nature of the century, and its implied consequences for the century following, in which we now live.

They lived in a century dominated by the crisis of 1914–1918, and by the efforts made in its aftermath to remake society. The causes most of them served ended badly: Italian and German nationalism, Fascism, Bolshevik internationalism's vision of a paradisiacal workers' society in which the state would have withered away, and eventually an incoherent series of violent utopian undertakings. One might reasonably conclude that these events should have discredited political utopianism, but that is not the case.

Utopian thought rests upon the belief in progress. The first millennium ended in the year 1000 with the disappointment of Christian popular expectation of the Last Days (and the end of history). The nineteenth and twentieth centuries, leading toward the new millennium in 2000, were driven by a secular conviction that history is in movement toward a future that would make sense of the past. Isaiah Berlin has written of the great Russian writers of the nineteenth century, that "what was common to all . . . was the belief that solutions to the central problems existed, that one could discover them, and, with sufficient selfless effort, realize them on earth." The twentieth century's doctrines of utopian possibility necessarily rested on the conviction that history is a progression toward some conclusion that will provide an answer to the fundamental questions of existence.

But what if there is no serious reason to think that historical time contains a future that will be better than the present? That is to say, what if there is no progress? If that is the case, and it is, the twentieth century has closed an era of profound illusions. The twenty-first century has begun in futile manipulations of the intellectual remnants of progressive thought (epitomized in the proposition that history came to an end in the late twentieth century), but the consequences of the collapse of a rational case for progressive expectation must eventually be dealt with by the Western intelligence and (undoubtedly after further human disasters) by the Western political class.

A gap has opened between what is said about the future in conventional public discourse and what people actually expect. In some Western academic circles the relativity of all beliefs is taken for granted, with wide hostility to the claims of Western civilization itself. The political policy debate and popular discourse at the same time are framed as if progress and rationality remain reliable assumptions, despite the empirical evidence to the contrary provided by the events of the twentieth century, and the collapse of the intellectual foundations for such a belief.

Religious revelation promised salvation. Marxism claimed to provide a scientific analysis demonstrating that the working masses of society would eventually inhabit a just and classless world. Liberal optimism said the application of reason and the findings of science could do away with injustice and misery. Today's elites generally disbelieve religion; Marxism in practice created the Gulag and impoverished the states it ruled; liberalism's forecasts of progress were refuted by the two world wars, totalitarianism, and by the ethnic, communal, racial, and religious warfare and savagery manifested in Western Europe, the Middle East, Africa, and parts of Asia during the last two decades alone.

Naïve or desiccated versions of the theory of historical progress provide a vocabulary in which the declarations of governments are still phrased, editorials written, and a good deal of the routine work of the academy is conducted. The downfall of Communism in 1989 was greeted as having vindicated the liberal version of Western optimism. Little that has happened since would validate that view, even in the rich and lucky societies. In many non-Western parts of the world the human condition is disastrous and declining. The United States itself, since September 2001, has, however improbably, considered itself under constant and terrifying threat from Islamic militants, failed states and contagious anarchy, and by rogue nations armed (or not armed) with mass destruction weapons. Its policies still put forward sentimental confidence in the inevitability and benevolence of global democracy (in ignorance or indifference to Aristotle's observation that democracy is justified only because oligarchy and tyranny are worse).

This secular utopianism is the common belief among Western elites. It is scarcely possible to talk about politics, not to speak of life, outside a progressive conceptual scheme. Yet the intellectually most powerful figures of nineteenth- and twentieth-century European political thought, including Tocqueville, Burke, Burckhardt, Acton, Niebuhr, Aron, Arendt, Kennan—all were hostile to the progressive view of history, aware of the precarious role reason plays in political affairs and of the corruptions of power and vanity. The real American conservatives are those who are most anxious about the country's future.

There is a moral and implicitly theological aspect to this, since the assumption that man is going someplace—which is to say, will become better than he is now—is the implied corollary to the belief in historical progress. Socialist man was to have been a great improvement on his presocialist predecessor; and Aryan man, through scientific breeding, was to have improved even upon himself. The most influential modern political formulation of the theory of historical progress, Marxism, was a secularized version of Western messianic religion, although stripped of Judaism's consciousness of evil, suffering, and tragedy.

Fundamental to the Enlightenment faith in human progress, as to the Western religious faith it largely replaced, was a conviction that the forces shaping historical existence are essentially benign. Reason would improve men and society by driving out the unreasonable. The God of Jews and Christians may have been demanding, his ways hidden, and his representatives often intolerant or obscurantist, but there was no doubt that he desired good for the souls he had created. Christian doctrine said that the humble were closer to God than emperors and kings. Marxism's aim—humanity's liberation—was benevolent, even if the necessary class struggle would be violent. Those who threw themselves into the work of religion, reform, or revolution believed they were cooperating with history's dominant forces, and that eventually there would be a happy ending.

This is a conception of history both Western and recent, contrasting, for example, with a traditional Chinese assumption of cyclical dynastic empires, self-sufficient and self-regarding, in which the round of dynastic experience renews itself without progressing in any direction. It took colonialism, Christian missionaries, and Marxism to convince (some) Chinese that history is purpose and progress.

Many other societies have lacked the conception of history itself (which emerged in the West only in the late Middle Ages), and would seem to have conceived of themselves as static (or failed to conceive of themselves at all, the conception of collective "self" being scarcely possible except from the standpoint of a belief in history). Society simply was there, and events were (are) meaningful within the existing social, dynastic, or tribal experience, without a larger significance in time, not "going" anywhere nor being part of any purposeful "story."

Hinduism seeks the absorption of the individual into an impersonal World Spirit. Buddhism is conventionally described as a search for liberation from becoming: that is, from history. Pope John Paul II was criticized for describing Buddhism as aspiring to "a state of perfect indifference with regard to the world," yet that objection would seem to have been directed against what was taken as criticism of a laudatory attempt to be free of evil "by becoming indifferent to the world, which is the source of evil." The Pope's version of Christianity holds the world necessarily good, as God's creation.

Islam, like the Judeo-Christian West, understands itself as possessing a teleological history. The Islamic religion defends a conception of progressive revelation (the Koran completing and perfecting the Jewish and Christian scriptures), and Shiite Muslims await the return to history of the Twelfth Imam, Mohammed's descendant, who did not die but disappeared, and will eventually return as the earth's sole legitimate authority. Jews and Christians both believe history is the spiritual and moral adventure of responsible people accountable to God for their conduct, with a commission from God that will eventually lead to temporal history's completion.

I realize these are descriptions without nuance of complicated matters, but my purpose is to emphasize that the conception of history is peculiarly Western and undoubtedly related to the dynamism demonstrated by Western civilization from the start. It also is implicated in the violence of the West. Without this idea, there would scarcely be a modern Western politics, not to speak of modern war. I have cited Jünger's description of his state of mind before an attack: "The final combat, the ultimate assault. . . . Here the destiny of entire peoples were thrown in the balance; it was a question of the future of the world. The only idea in my mind was the gravity of the moment, and I believe that in every one of us every personal feeling had vanished, and fear had left us."

Only an eschatological view of history would permit so apocalyptic a view of a small-unit infantry action by a German nationalist who nonetheless (to quote his French translator) "[believed] not a word of those superb Hegelian or Marxist prophesies concerning the arrival of the Absolute." It nonetheless has been the conventional assumption of the twentieth century that the future could hinge on such an episode. If this particular battle is not won, not only the world but time itself is lost. It is the ur-form of the domino theory. It is possible to believe this only if history is understood as the unfolding story of an intelligible human destiny.

The notion of secular progress and an historical destiny unrelated to any divine scheme seems to have originated in Western thought in the seventeenth century. John Lukacs writes that Francis Bacon seems to have been the first to write of progress in terms of time (rather than space: "a royal progress"). The seventeenth was also the century when historical consciousness itself emerged, Lukacs argues: a self-consciousness about where the individual is placed with respect to the existence of society and the passage of time. It was an aspect of the emergence of modern individual self-consciousness. In the seventeenth and eighteenth centuries the conviction also emerged that nature's laws were being explained, the classical past recovered, the middle ages left behind, and civilization being reestablished on the basis of reason and natural science.

John Locke, chiefly responsible for the modern belief in secular progress, drew from his conviction that men are born with "a title to perfect freedom and uncontrolled enjoyment of all the rights and privileges of the law of nature" the conclusion that humanity's progressive liberation from constraints on this freedom is the purpose of history. From this idea came the French and American revolutions, as well as the doctrine of the free marketplace. The economic liberalism celebrated by contemporary neoclassical economists, and the aggressive individualism promoted by libertarians and the Left both advance versions of the Lockean claim that individual happiness and the community's well-being are products of the individual's liberation from constraint. These claims are responsible for what modern Western society has become. (Were he among us, Locke, a Puritan, would undoubtedly find this a disconcerting judgment.)

While John Milton, also a Puritan, was conscious of the peril and tragedy of existence, Locke himself (as the Cambridge scholar Basil Wiley wrote) offered "confidence in the rationality of the universe, in the virtuousness of man, in the stability of society, and in the deliverances of enlightened common sense." He also assumed that "underneath are the everlasting arms" which Scripture had promised would be there, to prevent men from falling—an assumption excluded by his followers today.

Milton was the poet of Satan's defiance and of spiritual risk: "So farewell hope, and with hope farewell fear, / Farewell remorse: all good to me is lost; / Evil be thou my Good." Milton's romantic interest in evil seems better suited to a twentieth century of cataclysmic wars, genocide, the deliberate destruction of civilian societies and of the libraries, museums, and monuments of civilization, than is Locke's confidence in goodness.

The question of man's progress is distinct from that of civilization's progress, or lack of it. Whether man as a species is going someplace has a conventional answer in the proposal that evolution takes us toward a more elaborate or subtle life-form. It is assumed that a more elaborated man will be a more intelligent one who, if he is not morally superior to his ancestors, will at least be less disposed to irrational and self-destructive behavior. However, our present historical period has provided no evidence of species progression or mutation: a more advanced man has yet to appear, whatever the fossil evidence may indicate about the physical characteristics of former man, our prehistoric predecessors.

I would myself propose that not only does no evidence exist of man's moral progress but that none is to be expected. That a moral continuity has existed among men and women since the times of the Magdalenian cave painters and the Attic tragedians seems to me cause for a certain confidence. Our ancestors, the Greeks of the classical age, identified humanity's moral undertakings as Sisyphean, as they remain today, even if in this century, as in the last, we attempt to deny it.

Some certainly may find in this view counsel of despair, since if there is a moral constancy among men and women through time, then the immense sacrifices that have gone into the effort to improve society might seem to have been a waste. I would reply that civilization has obviously progressed, for example by installing and enlarging certain norms of disinterested international and national behavior (such as standards of human rights, law, and a structure of international law), but has done so without man's essential change and without any automaticity in the historical process, or security in what has been accomplished. This is demonstrated by recent popular as well as governmental hostility in the United States toward prevailing Western standards in international cooperation and law, deliberately choosing to become an "outlaw" nation because of a conviction of America's superiority over others. The "retrogression" of the last century to barbaric methods of warfare, such as deliberate attacks on civilian society, and the various practices of totalitarian governments was not in fact retrogression, but a phenomenon that may recur, and in some cases has recurred.

Man has improved in competence, knowledge, and manners. He eats with a fork, uses the computers he has invented to spare him myriad boring tasks, and conducts his wars, when he can, in a way that allows him to avoid the distress of a direct encounter with the pain he inflicts on his victims. This is a form of progress from the axe-wielding and pelt-wearing human past. Western man also today assumes that gadgetry and industry will continue to leap forward in near-geometric progressions. He is beckoned by technology toward a future in which human consciousness is superseded by a more accommodating virtual reality, and invited by economists to a seamless global marketplace that creates ruinous disruptions in the short term allegedly to provide universal happiness in the long term. Where all this will really end, only God would know, should He (She) still exist.

After the collapse of Communism in 1989, the poet Czeslaw Milosz expressed concern about what might take Marxism's place. Communism had been, he said, a revolt against the European nihilism which Dostoyevsky and Nietzsche had perceived and articulated, providing a vision of the future that was an antidote to that nihilism. Marxism proved a fraud, leaving worse than it found, but the unstructured or essentially chauvinistic notions of political process (and of the end of history) that have since replaced Marxism are too sentimental to counter the ambient nihilism of contemporary Western culture, leaving the way open once again to ruthless men without illusions. In this intellectual climate, it is easy to conceive of the future in Hobbesian terms of totally self-interested power struggles, however disguised these may be in the rhetoric of liberalism.

A nihilism with respect to values authorizes, if it does not dictate, a politics of power aggrandizement. It is paradoxical that this conclusion should have been accepted by some as consistent with the philosophy of Leo Strauss—Platonist, defender of the existence of natural law and enemy of modern liberal relativism, an important influence on the intellectuals who acquired influence in the government of George W. Bush. Strauss's position was that the truth about society is too terrible for ordinary people to deal with. The progressive beliefs dominating liberal society are myths, the virtue of classical philosophy is humanly unattainable, and morality does not "pay." Power aggrandizement is the necessary route to national survival, and God, if he exists, is unknowable. All this has to be kept from people if they are to tolerate their lives and accept to be governed. Thus an elite must tell them consoling lies.

✎

Nihilism in Nietzsche's time was an intellectual phenomenon, not a doctrine of action, in a society whose cultural and political structures were intact. The announcement that God was dead was in fact announcement that Western high culture had come to believe that God was dead. Nietzsche suggested that it must act accordingly, affirming human responsibility. Leninism and Nazism redefined what was to be considered virtue and evil, and executed their judgments in the conviction that in this matter no objective truth exists: that power establishes what is true. Those in the academy today who also defend this proposition defend a totalitarian epistemology.

The notion that God is dead coexists today with a substitution of metaphysical, and implicitly theological, conceptions of international struggle for the political conceptions of the past. The enemy is identified as a metaphysical or spiritual reality, "Great Satan," or Evil, or as Terror—the notion of terrorism, a method of action, treated as having a form of existence and a susceptibility to attack that is independent from those who employ it. If the war is with Evil, this takes us well beyond the justifications offered in the past for total war, which held that for ideological or eugenic reasons a regime's enemies deserved defeat or extermination, being a superceded class or an inferior race. If the enemy is Evil (the Evil One?), there can be no quarter given, no negotiation, no compromise, no pity, no mercy. This marks an advance of American political thought toward the darkness of totalitarian conceptions and discourse, translating human conflict into metaphysical combat.

The totalitarian experience we have already been through in the twentieth century, in which the lives of the individuals considered in this book were crucially implicated, gave us what George Steiner has called the diminishment of man himself. The "long carnival of inhumanity" that accompanied the century's various utopian or dystopian undertakings *"lowered the threshold of man,"* and nothing is so terrible as to surprise us now.

Against the liberal view of history as progress there has always been the tragic view, that history is a struggle by humans against their limitations, in which their dignity is found in the struggle, itself without a resolution in historical time. This view insists upon the predicament of history, its insolubility. The believer in original sin and divine providence finds common practical ground here with that stoic atheist and humanist, Freud, who reminded his readers that the aim of life is death, and who denied "that there is an instinct toward perfection at work in human beings, which has brought them to their present high level of intellectual achievement and ethical sublimation and which may be expected to watch over their development into supermen. I have no [such] faith. . . . I cannot see how this benevolent illusion is to be preserved."

History does not pause, and decisions are inevitably taken within some philosophical or ideological framework. If the intellectual framework we had before is discredited, what takes its place? There is at present no evident answer. Until now, Western interpretations of history have assumed that it had a meaning. Divine revelation had supplied it, or science and reason would identify it, but it was there. By finding it, and acting upon it, the ethical and metaphysical questions of human existence would eventually be resolved. This made possible civilizing and mediating codes of conduct in society, of the kind identified with chivalry. Modern nihilism rejects the discipline and limitation that are part of the belief in an objective referent for human action.

The second millennium closed with the intellectual, political, and moral possibilities of a belief in progress explored to the extreme and exhausted. In the new millennium, with God dead and history without purpose, except that which power can impose, we approach the Hobbesian universe. Or we move toward an even worse one, in which the Miltonian moral categories are invalidated: "Evil be thou my Good . . . all good to me is lost."

～○

The problem in history remains moral, the old problem of evil, gratuitous among men, unrewarding and therefore illogical as a long-term evolutionary strategy, and inexistent among animals. One must choose what one thinks about this, and the choice depends on whether man is conceived of as an autonomous moral agent, or for some reason a determined one. In the second case the problem is not a problem and the matter is without interest. One submits.

Modern Western civilization assumes human moral autonomy, or as least it does so as a practical matter since its members act as if they have the power to make choices that will have an effect upon the structures, content, and future of their society. This assumption carries with it a responsibility, recognized since classical times, indeed since human reflection began.

There is an antiutopian tradition of political thought largely neglected in our day. It demands that one look for solutions within, rather than without, in experienced reality rather than imagination about the future, while admitting and accepting the human implication in violence as part of our nature—to be transcended. This is the tradition I defend. It follows from the classical injunction that the human obligation is to cultivate virtue, from which the virtue of society flows—an injunction of reason, as Aristotle held.

This is a formulation that would have been familiar to the educated person of the nineteenth century. It is remote from contemporary advanced society (although it survives in the value systems of many nonmodern social groups). A solid contemporary defense can be made for it, whether virtue is considered in private or public, philosophical or theological, terms. However, it would be mistaken to argue that virtue "pays," since it often does not do so other than in its contribution to the general quality of society.

One can illustrate the argument in art, much more important to human civilization than politics, in the aesthetic commitment that exists, for example, in the classical ballet or in music, where a punishing preparation is accepted in order to achieve perfection in the performance of something of no inherent utility, yet which enriches civilization. Much the same thing can be said of high-level sport.

Another obvious example is found in religion, where virtue pursued for no utilitarian secular purpose can produce unforeseen achievement of social and cultural value. Two individuals who caused fundamental change in contemporary religious consciousness as well as in the conception of religious proselytism, the former with effect on contemporary North-South cultural and political relations, were the hard-living soldier, geographer, and hermit Charles de Foucauld and the philosopher Simone Weil. The latter died in Ashford, England, in 1943, as a consequence of a "revolutionary asceticism" that caused her to eat no more than what she thought would have been her ration had she remained in occupied France.*

Weil today is internationally known and a major influence in sec-

---

* Her death was reported as suicide by starvation ("French Professor Starves Herself to Death"), and the coroner's verdict was that she had indeed done so, "whilst the balance of her mind was disturbed." Always frail, she actually died of tuberculosis, although decisively weakened by her refusal to eat, undoubtedly a combination of a traditional religious self-denial and self-discipline with anorexia, a clinically pathological disposition she suffered during most of her life.

ular as well as religious, philosophical, and literary circles. Foucauld has recently attracted new attention as the result of a joint biography of him and his friend and fellow army officer Henri Laperrine, with whom his career repeatedly crossed course during the years between their graduation from Saint-Cyr and the murder of Foucauld in 1916, in the Hoggar mountains of the Sahara.*

❦

Neither Weil nor Foucauld accomplished anything of particular note in their lifetimes. What they had in common was that both adopted the radical principle of sharing the condition of the oppressed or poor as an act of solidarity and an evidence of the common human condition and destiny.

Nearly all of Simone Weil's writings were unpublished when she died. However, in late 2003, Amazon.com had on sale 136 titles by or about her, and Amazon.fr (Amazon in France) another 46. A Google search yielded 148,000 references to her. Her life became known through her posthumously published notebooks, letters, and essays; and by the interest taken in her by a number of people concerned with philosophy, religion, literature, and feminism, including, in the United States, Mary McCarthy and Susan Sontag. Her most recent biography in English was by Francine du Plessix Gray in 2001.

While she wrote on political, constitutional, social, and philosophical as well as religious issues, her thought was more aphoristic than conventionally analytical, and the power of her thinking was always reinforced by a constant determination to make her life conform with her intellectual conclusions, "to arrive at the truth through experimentation and to remedy oppression by means of physical engagement" (as her biographical note in the *Dictionnaire des intellectuals français* puts it).

A classicist and teacher, she believed that truly radical action is work done for the sake of work well done, defending skilled work

---

* *The Sword and the Cross*, by Fergus Fleming.

and meditative labor and the effort (which she called "revolutionary") to inspire lucidity in how people think. Born in a distinguished and assimilated secular Jewish professional family in Paris, she began from the early 1930s to take jobs in factories and on farms in order to experience workers' lives directly and share those lives. She was inclined toward pacifism, but when the Spanish civil war arrived she went to Spain to support the anarcho-syndicalists (style-POUM). A maladroit warrior, she quickly injured herself in an accident and was repatriated by anxious parents. During the same period she developed Christian religious interests but was put off Catholicism by the institutions and dogmatic apparatus of the Church, which she never joined.

During the Second World War began she managed to reach London and was put to work by the Free French as a writer and editor. She wanted to go on missions to occupied France, but those with responsibility for such operations unanimously believed that she would immediately be killed, captured, and probably be responsible for the capture of those who received her. A plan she had for creating a group of front-line nurses, shown to de Gaulle, caused him to exclaim, "But she is mad!"* She was a kind of pure spirit, character-

---

* These nurses would have accompanied front-line troops to give immediate treatment to the wounded. A close friend, Simone Pétrement, wrote: "She suffered when she thought of all those who were wounded on the battlefields and for whom it was of capital importance to receive speedy assistance. Many of those who died might have survived if they could have been treated immediately, even if the treatment were only rudimentary. As for those among the wounded who were too seriously hurt to be saved, the idea of their solitary, forsaken agony was unbearable to her. So she suggested the organization of a small group of nurses who, having decided to sacrifice their lives, would devote themselves to treating and helping the wounded and dying in the midst of combat. Of course, she would insist on being allowed to join this group; and of course she also realized that most of these women would be killed. . . ." Weil (who probably was ignorant of the front-line medical ministrations that are part of modern military operations) argued in support of her plan that part of the success of the Germans was the existence of special storm and shock troops ready to carry out suicide missions. "We cannot copy Hitler's methods. . . . But . . . we must find equivalents. It is perhaps almost a vital necessity."

istically difficult to deal with. Albert Camus afterwards said she was "the only great spirit of our times." Czeslaw Milosz undoubtedly was closest to the truth when he said that she was "at least by temperament" a Cathar or Gnostic—a theological dualist convinced that purity can be obtained only by abnegation and abstention from fleshly pleasure. Her achievement was in what she wrote, and in her life, which many then and now have regarded as bizarre, affected by masochism (and Christian heresy), yet compellingly, exasperatingly, exemplary. The American short-story writer Flannery O'Connor said, "Weil's is the most comical life I have ever read about, and the most tragic and terrible." Simone Pétrement, who knew her from the time they were together in the lycée and at the École Normale, wrote: "Can one say that she did not desire affliction? It seems indisputable to me that she sought it. Not, of course, because of a taste for affliction. But first of all because of a desire for justice. Since affliction exists in the world, she found it difficult to go without her share of it; and above all she believed that one must share in it so as to understand how one can really remedy it. . . . [She thought] that only through affliction can one come to know the truth of existence, the complete and absolute truth."

Charles Eugène, Vicomte de Foucauld (1858–1916), a rich cavalry officer who had passed out of the military academy of Saint-Cyr as 333rd in a class of 386, was suspended from his first overseas active assignment "for notorious misconduct." (He had arranged to be accompanied by his mistress, posing as the nonexistent Vicomtesse de Foucauld.) He rejoined the regiment on the prospect of active service against an uprising in the Algerian Sahara.* During his Saharan duty he began seriously to learn Arabic, and subsequently the script and language of the Tuaregs, a nomadic Berber people. He

---

* France had invaded formerly Ottoman Algeria in 1830, and in 1848 declared it part of metropolitan France, although there was continuing resistance to French rule.

also began to study Islam and read the Koran, observing that religion had an influence on the lives of Muslims which went much beyond that which Catholicism had for his Catholic contemporaries in France. He was also struck by the intensity of botanical and animal existence in the desert.

Resignation from the army was followed by a yearlong 2,500-mile scientific expedition into the Moroccan Sahara, dressed as an itinerant Jew and accompanied by a Syrian-born Jewish rabbi named Mardochee, himself a noted geographer.* Foucauld's account of the journey won the gold medal of the French Geographical Society (and was used by Marshal Lyautey as a guide during the 1912 French conquest of Morocco). He made a second expedition, to the South Saharan Algerian and Tunisian oases in 1885.

Then came a sudden reconversion to the Catholicism he had left as an adolescent. Three years later he became a Trappist, at monasteries first in France and then in Syria. He stayed with the Trappists for seven years, as a lay brother doing manual labor, then left for the Holy Land, where he found a job as handyman and gardener for a convent of Poor Clares (an order of Franciscan contemplative nuns founded in 1212). There he became convinced that he should become a priest. After theological studies in Paris and ordination, he resolved to go to Morocco, where there was not a single priest. He got as far as Beni-Abbès in Algeria, where he built a mud house and chapel, hoping that others would join him to make the "fraternity" he had imagined. He believed that North Africa was mission territory, and that a mass conversion was possible, "like that of the Franks following [the Merovingian king] Clovis" in the fifth century. He accepted the conventional religious tenet of the time that baptism in the Christian church was essential to salvation. The Muslim poor among whom he lived were indifferent or hostile. He sent to Paris for money to free slaves, and he wrote.

* There then were some half-million Jews in Morocco (as against fifteen and a half million Arabs).

His friend Laperrine, who had become military commander of the region, suggested that Foucauld go deeper into the Sahara, to the Berber Tuareg people. This was not a disinterested suggestion, as intelligence about the Tuaregs and the area was all but totally lacking, and Foucauld, like his contemporaries, was convinced that France's colonialism was a progressive institution. He wanted the Tuareg "naturalized as Frenchmen, so as to be our equals, not our subjects."

The Tuareg experience confirmed a change in his own conception of what he was actually about. In Beni-Abbès there had been a French garrison and contact with Europeans. He had built there thinking others would eventually join him. When he went south, eventually to the village of Tamanrasset, a thousand miles inside the Sahara, all that was finished. He was the only European among a very primitive people, and he realized that his vocation was simply to live among these people on their terms.* He gave them what he had. In extremis, they saved him from starvation. He learned to admit others to his life, gained the humility to accept the gifts of those whom he had considered that he would "save," and came truly to understand reciprocity. He learned the necessity to accept the others as they were. He ceased to believe that formal Christian belief was necessary to salvation. As one of the priests who have since taken his place at the same hermitage has said: "In the world of the Tuareg, a very pure, simple, undogmatic Islam is practiced. You are in the hands of God. There is no revolt but an abandon, a great patience rather than a fatalism." He was accepted as the "white marabout" of Tamanrasset, who happened to know some

---

* Later, among the papers found in Tamanrasset, after his murder, were notes on advice to give to the local nomad chieftain, among them to "make his people learn French, in order to be naturalized French; in order to be, not our subjects, but our equals; so that we may be everywhere on the same footing with themselves and not be bothered by anyone. This will come sooner or later; those who see things coming should take the initiative." He said that the chief obstacle to Christian conversion of the Tuaregs was pride. One of the Tuareg later said of Foucauld to General Henri Giraud: "So you *do* have a religion and priests, and you don't just live like dogs!"

medicine, shared their poverty, recorded their poetry and chants, created a dictionary of their language and grammar which remains a work of reference, gave them advice about dealing with the colonial power, and sent intelligence and advice about them to the French military authorities. What he did was in missionary terms futile. He was eventually murdered, by Tuaregs whom he had known, in an incident consequent on tensions created by the outbreak of the world war.

✺

Fleming, his recent biographer, says "all trace of him has vanished since his death." In 2003, Amazon.com listed fifty-two titles by or about him in English and forty-eight books in French (with more than 21,000 Google references). A book was published about him just a year after his death, and in 1921 the novelist René Bazin published a biography. Groups attempting to live the life he lived came into existence in the 1920s and 1930s. A religious congregation inspired by his life was created in 1936, consisting of small groups of men, and subsequently women, of three to five persons living in conditions equivalent to the people around them, usually supporting themselves through manual labor or other essentially anonymous forms of work, while maintaining a contemplative religious life.* There now are a score of religious congregations or associations that have been formed under Foucauld's influence, by no means all of them Catholic. The members of these groups have held such jobs as miners, drivers, mechanics, factory or refinery hands, street cleaners, herdsmen, and deep-sea fishermen. They make no attempt at religious persuasion or conversion, considering their purpose simply to be present among what Koestler, in another context, had called the scum of the earth. Simone Weil clearly would have approved.

---

* The Fraternities of the Little Brothers (and subsequently Sisters) of Jesus (a title less cloying in French than in English).

❧

You may argue that the virtue of a society can have consequences in its relations with rival states, as the American diplomat and historian George Kennan did in his formulation of American cold war "containment" policy. Kennan was a Niebuhrian "realist" in that he believed that the political order has its own imperatives, and uses power and military force among other means to achieve the general as well as national interest. At the same time he vigorously defended the notion that moral forces exercise great influence and a form of power itself in international relations, and that national power should respect a moral order.

> Any message we try to bring to others will be effective only if it is in accord with what we are to ourselves, and if this is something sufficiently impressive to compel the respect and confidence of a world which, despite all its material difficulties, is still more ready to recognize and respect spiritual distinction than material opulence.
>
> Our first and main concern must still be to achieve this state of national character. . . . In the lives of nations the really worthwhile things cannot and will not be hidden. Thoreau wrote: "There is no ill which may not be dissipated, like the dark, if you let in a stronger light on it. . . . If the light we use is but a paltry and narrow taper, most objects will cast a shadow wider than themselves." Conversely, if our taper is a strong one we may be sure that its rays will penetrate to the Russian room and eventually play their part in dissipating the gloom which prevails there.

This was written in 1951, and forty years later, in the eventual moral crisis in Soviet society that produced glasnost and perestroika, it so occurred.

❧

Virtue in classical thought is connected with tragedy. In drama, tragedy sees virtue confounded by circumstance or by the unforeseen and paradoxical consequences of its own action, producing an outcome that evokes pity and fear, and causes catharsis, or the purging of emotion.

I am not an optimist about history, believing that the evil in history is ineradicable, an evidence, if you are prepared to consider the matter theologically, of what John Henry Newman called the human race's implication "in some terrible aboriginal calamity" for which there is no solution inside historical time. But neither am I a pessimist. I would like to think that what I am offering in this book is a realistic glimpse of where we stand. To conclude a discussion of soldiers, artists, revolutionaries, and terrorists with a defense of individual and national virtue may seem odd, but my intention is to confront ideology with ethic, and to insist that the quality of a society is not determined by power but by the accomplishments and merits of its civilization and its members. It is essential to recognize the possibility that the disordered and morally catastrophic century in which the persons in my book lived might represent our future and not only our past.

There is no serious reason at all to think that a mechanism is at work, or a program is available, to provide us with a future that in essential respects of morality and humanity will be better than the present. We are what we are. To sacrifice living human beings to make "a better world" is an act of totalitarian morality and is also futile. There is no collective solution to the human condition. The only thing we can remake is ourselves. A society's obligation is to concern itself with its own virtue or perfection. There is an intellectual obligation to address what is, not what one wishes might be. That leaves us with the classical contention that only in virtue can we make a positive response to the human predicament.

APPENDIX: "OUT-MÜNZENBERGING MÜNZENBERG"

My account of Koestler (and Münzenberg) is not complete without finishing the story of the creation of the Congress for Cultural Freedom as an American-sponsored postwar version of the kind of thing the prewar "Münzenberg Trust" was responsible for in its time, of Koestler's influence on it, and how the whole affair ended. Had Münzenberg lived, and continued on the course he had begun with his magazine *Die Zukunft*, he might have founded the Congress himself.

The Communists were first onto the postwar political warfare battlefield. In October 1947, in occupied Berlin, a pan-German reunion of German writers was called by an organization formerly banned by the Nazis. Heinrich Mann was the honorary president, and the group included a number of German Communist writers with international reputations, although the majority of members were not Communists, and the conference was held under the patronage of all four Occupying Powers. The announced themes were purely literary.

Shortly before the meeting, a large and previously unannounced Soviet delegation arrived, composed of writers and their presumed political minders. No Americans had been scheduled to take part, as the U.S. military government assumed that the meeting was a German literary affair. However, on the second day a series of attacks began on the United States as a "warmonger" state, and appeal was made to the German participants to join the Soviet-sponsored peace movement.

One of those present was Melvin Lasky, an American journalist and intellectual of German descent, in his thirties, a veteran of the U.S. Army, who wrote from Berlin for the New York social democratic weekly, *The New Leader*, and the intellectual journal *Partisan Review*. His request to address the meeting was granted, and he made a speech dramatically commiserating with the visiting Russian writers whose government lacked democracy, maintained labor camps, censored literature, and imposed a Party line and the aesthetic norms of socialist realism. He closed with a citation from André Gide recalling that every great writer is a nonconformist and résistant.

This created a great scandal, and the text of the speech was reprinted in the Berlin press. It was said, possibly disingenuously, that Lasky came close to being expelled from Berlin by the American military governor, Lucius Clay, for having deliberately disrupted East-West relations. Not long afterwards, however, the Soviet blockade of Berlin began, and the cold war started in earnest. Lasky's fortunes changed.

In December 1947 he proposed to the U.S. military authorities a new cultural publication. "It should be an American review, i.e., American-edited and American-written. Its formula would be to address, and to stimulate, the German-reading intelligentsia of Germany and elsewhere. . . . It would offer not only American views on American problems—and here the unafraid self-critical tone would be a living demonstration of how the democratic mind works; but also American views on European problems. . . ." The result was *Der Monat*, which became one of the more brilliant and successful intellectual reviews of postwar Western Europe.

In March 1949, shortly after former U.S. Vice President Henry Wallace (who, as Arthur Schlesinger observed at the time, "thinks of Russia as a sort of Brook Farm community") had unsuccessfully run for the presidency of the United States as candidate of the Communist-controlled Progressive Party, and when Communists were attempting to take control of other liberal (in the American sense) or left-wing American groups,* a "Cultural and Scientific Conference for World Peace" was called for the Waldorf-Astoria hotel in New York.

The Soviet delegation included the composer Dmitri Shostakovich and A. A. Fadeyev, the head of the Union of Soviet Writers. American participants included Arthur Miller, Lillian Hellman, Clifford Odets, Dashiell Hammett, and Leonard Bernstein among others, some of whom had been close to the Communist Party before the war, while others, as in Miller's case, were favorably disposed to the USSR because of its wartime sacrifices and feared a possible resurgence of Nazism in Germany.

A response to this meeting was organized by a number of American intellectuals with less sympathetic views of the USSR. The inspiration seems to have come from the novelist and critic Mary McCarthy, who in 1948 had tried to start "Europe-America Groups" to promote postwar communication between American and European intellectuals. Not much came of that. She had hoped for intellectual engagement, but when Fadeyev, one of her group's Soviet contacts, said at a World Congress of Intellectuals held in Poland in 1948 (a predecessor of the Waldorf meeting) that "if hyenas could type and jackals could use a fountain pen" they would write like T. S. Eliot, John Dos Passos, Jean-Paul Sartre, and André

---

* These efforts persisted into the early 1950s, one of them the Communists' ultimately unsuccessful effort to take control of a left-wing veterans organization that had emerged from the war, the American Veterans Committee. One of the members of the Committee most effective in resisting the takeover was Michael Straight, years later revealed as the American "fifth man" (or was it sixth?) among the Cambridge spies (or would-be spies). The present writer was later invited onto the board of the AVC as representative of the new wave of Korean War veterans—his first, brief, and terminal encounter with organized political activism.

The battle between Communists and liberals at the time also produced ADA (Americans for Democratic Action, which still exists), an activist group created in opposition to the Progressive Citizens of America, a 1946 merger of two prewar popular front organizations.

Malraux, she and her friends concluded that there was no useful engagement there.

Her group came together again in anticipation of the Waldorf affair. It included the philosopher Sidney Hook and several other belligerently anti-Communist ex-Marxists, including the ex-Trotskyist author of *The Managerial Revolution*, James Burnham, and some of his fellow editors of the *Partisan Review*. There were other former Trotskyists and some (Menshevik) social democratic trade unionists from the Ladies' Garment Workers Union and *The New Leader* magazine. Others came out of a native American radicalism, sometimes blue-blooded, as in the case of the poet Robert Lowell and his wife, Elizabeth Hardwick. Arthur Schlesinger, Jr. (distinguished son of another distinguished Harvard historian), the writers Dwight Macdonald and Richard Rovere, the actor Montgomery Clift, and the composer Nicholas Nabokov were also in the group. Attending the Waldorf congress, their interventions from the floor had a cumulatively devastating effect, particularly in the case of the trapped Shostakovich, who in response to questions was forced into abject recitals of blatant Stalinist propaganda.*

There obviously was official U.S. interest in all this, particularly when the American group, whether with or without official urging, proposed formation of an international committee, initially composed of the philosophers Benedetto Croce, Karl Jaspers, Jacques Maritain, and Bertrand Russell, together with T. S. Eliot, André Malraux, and Igor Stravinsky. Exactly where the crucial initiatives and the money came from is unclear and the question probably irrelevant, since some of the Americans (such as Nabokov and Schlesinger) had served in intelligence or political warfare organi-

---

* In his memoirs, published thirty years later, he said that people commented on his "smile." "That was the smile of a condemned man. I felt like a dead man. I answered all the idiotic questions in a daze, and thought, When I get back it's over for me. Stalin liked leading Americans by the nose that way. He would show them a man—here he is, alive and well—and then kill him."

zations during the Second World War and still had friends if not connections in government.

∾

In 1945 Koestler and George Orwell had discussed founding an organization that would also involve Bertrand Russell and become "a new, broader and more modern League for the Rights of Man."* This project fell apart, and Koestler later joined the planning for a meeting held in Berlin in June 1950, organized by Melvin Lasky and Irving Brown, with sponsorship by the Allied occupation authorities and the city of Berlin. This assembly called itself the Congress for Cultural Freedom, and is described in chapter 9.

Koestler, as we know, proved the star speaker at the meeting but lost out in the subsequent maneuvering to define the character of the organization that was set up to continue its work (and to which Mary McCarthy's American initiative eventually attached itself). Koestler quit the international committee of this new organization after a few weeks in annoyance at its failure to become a "fighting organization." Koestler still had in him the old Münzenberg spirit of "Hit them! Hit them hard! Make the world gasp with horror!"— and when you don't have the evidence, make it up.

The author of the principal hostile history of the Congress for Cultural Freedom, Frances Stonor Saunders, correctly places Koestler at the organization's origins but fails to perceive that the decisive contribution he made to it was to leave it in anger at the liberal or leftist cast it displayed from the beginning.

The French historian of the Congress, Pierre Grémion, writes that "two contradictory conceptions were competing to design the new organization. One wanted an international movement confronting the [organized and Soviet-controlled] Communist peace

* The original such League, founded on noble principles, in reaction to the Dreyfus case, had during the 1930s fallen under Communist control, and defended Stalin's Moscow trials.

movement . . . ; the other wanted a network of high-level influence which, while it would be free to take political positions, would mainly exercise an influence won through the quality of the projects and publications it sponsored." The advocates of the second course won: they had the support of the CIA.

Grémion describes the organizational maneuvers in Paris, Berlin, and Rome among the early leaders of the organization, leading up to a meeting in Brussels in November 1950 in which those invited were not always people who had been part of the Berlin congress, the whole culminating in the summer of 1951 when the international secretariat was taken in hand by Nicolas Nabokov and Michael Josselson, "who had in common that they had been officers of the American military government cultural services in Berlin"—as Lasky had been. The three were to remain the most important figures in the Congress, with Josselson (who actually had been a CIA officer since 1948) the secretary general, until the 1960s, when the Ford Foundation took over the organization following its public disgrace by the revelation that it had been "financed" by the CIA.

Koestler's crucial disagreement with the Congress was that it did not have an aggressive agenda similar to its Communist counterparts (and Münzenberg predecessors). The Congress chose open discussion and intellectual pluralism against the monolithic Party line on offer—and indeed required—on the Communist side. This actually gave it an enormous advantage, which nonetheless had constantly to be defended against more ideologically minded anti-Communists, like Koestler, as well as against a certain manifestation of the bureaucratic mind.*

* At the New York headquarters of the Free Europe Committee in the 1950s, another CIA-controlled organization, a daily bulletin was issued under the authority of one senior officer that provided a running analysis of how each day's events invariably revealed Communist crime and duplicity and demonstrated America's virtue. As no

Edward Shils, an American scholar associated with the Congress from 1953 forward, said in 1999 in a retrospective comment on the organization that it was not its policy

to throw a burning brand into the enemy's camp. It was also not its intention to address an audience of the converted. The audience which it aimed to reach through its conferences and seminars and reviews was the very large part of the intellectual stratum which, although somewhat biased in favor of the Communists, was not rigidly attached to Communist organizations and beliefs. This was a very broad band . . . which the Communists and their most active coadjutors were seeking to attach to themselves as "fellow travelers" . . . they called them "progressive forces." There were also many intellectuals . . . more willing to see the damage which Communism was doing to political and intellectual life, but not yet willing to render a negative judgement because they were inclined to be sympathetic to any idealistic collectivistic tendencies, away from capitalist society. These were the intellectuals at whom the Congress addressed its publications and its gatherings.

The Congress was composed principally of members of the so-called non-Communist Left, or (in the United States) "liberal anti-Communists," or even "cold war liberals," since, as Shils wrote, there "was no one else who had the initiative to create and maintain it. Arthur Koestler, Ruth Fischer [an early leader of the German Communist Party], Sidney Hook, Melvin Lasky, Irving Kristol, Manès Sperber *et al.* were all [then] on the 'non-Communist Left'; of these, only Melvin Lasky and Irving Kristol

---

one working for the Free Europe organization, and virtually no one in the central and Eastern European audience primarily addressed by the Committee's Radio Free Europe harbored much doubt about which side was virtuous, this exercise was not only puerile but redundant, and was the object of general mockery (although it possibly served as calculated reassurance to persons higher in the bureaucratic chain, not always very independent-minded).

had never been Communists or sympathizers. . . . In any case, there were very few conservatives to whom to appeal. I think that [the distinguished French scholar and political commentator] Raymond Aron and I were, perhaps, the only more or less 'conservative' persons in the center of the Congress, and each of us was a composite of liberalism and conservatism."

～

The organization was undoubtedly seen by its CIA sponsors (principally Tom Braden and Cord Meyer of its International Organizations Directorate) as a political warfare operation not unlike the activities of the American Office of War Information, or British intelligence and political warfare groups, during the Second World War, and more generally as part of the long and tangled history of democratic (or other) governments' sponsorship or subsidy of sympathetic or supportive publications and organizations.

While Shils and others involved with the Congress for many years insisted that they never saw evidence of external interference with Congress decisions and initiatives ("the deception [did not lead] me into doing things which I would not have done otherwise") and while it was manifestly to the CIA's advantage that the Congress seem independent and to the greatest extent possible to act independently, it was under direct CIA control (as were the Free Europe organization and a number of other ostensibly independent groups).

Its funding was another matter, as Braden and Meyer had many claims on their fund allocations. Their budgets, like those of the CIA itself, fluctuated over the years, and Josselson's projects were often ambitious, so that he scrambled for money from other sources, including "real" (rather than transmitted) foundation money.

The Ford Foundation was to become the Congress's most faithful foundation supporter. From the 1950s, Ford Foundation grants and CIA funding overlapped. There always was anxiety at Ford over being compromised by the CIA relationship, and controversy over the direction and militancy of some Congress projects. In

1961 the Ford trustees decided to give no more money to groups "whose financial basis had not been made fully public." In 1962 the idea was floated that the CIA give up all support and Ford take over the Congress, but the Ford trustees refused. A memorandum by Shepard Stone of Ford said that the then current Congress budget was $1.8 million, $1.4 million from government sources, approximately $250,000 from Ford, and the rest from other American and European foundations.

In 1964 Josselson talked with the Rockefeller Brothers Fund, the Rockefeller Foundation, the Sloan Foundation, and others. He proposed in 1965 that the Congress be given a new name and made a new organization with publicly audited accounts and totally private financing. His proposal ended by saying that of course "those two or three officers who have hindering connections [i.e., who are officers of the CIA] would sever these connections once and for all before the transformation . . . was made." Finally, after Henry Held was replaced as the Ford Foundation's president by McGeorge Bundy, who had just departed from the Johnson administration, leaving Lyndon Johnson with a Vietnam war of which Bundy had been one of the principal architects, an apparent solution was found. Ford decided in 1966 to give the Congress "a total of $7 million for a period of six years . . . on condition that all ties with the CIA were broken." That of course had always been the problem. Whatever the funding, the Congress had always been controlled by the CIA.*

✧

One can argue that it could not have been otherwise. Just as there never would have been a Münzenberg organization without Soviet sponsorship and money, there never would have been an effective Western response to Soviet political warfare in the 1950s without

* Volker R. Berghahn's *America and the Intellectual Cold Wars in Europe* makes use of the Shepard Stone papers to provide a comprehensive account of the relationship between the Ford Foundation and the Congress for Cultural Freedom.

official financing from Western governments. At the time, to those intimately involved, this seemed self-evident.

Those who managed CIA-controlled organizations employed argument and the independent influence and authority they could command to fend off the efforts of the sponsor to interfere in what they were doing. They also were in some cases having greater influence on the sponsor than the sponsor on them. George Urban, a director of Radio Free Europe from 1983 to 1986, has said that the most remarkable aspect of the relationship between the CIA and RFE (and Radio Liberty, broadcasting to the Soviet Union)

> can be framed in the question: who influenced whom. It was, in my judgement, the two radios that left their imprint on Agency thinking rather than the Agency on the policies of the two radios, and that for perfectly natural and respectable reasons: the specialized personnel of Radio Free Europe and Radio Liberty had wider knowledge, were endowed with finer political instincts, were closer to the scene, and produced more penetrating analyses of all aspects of the communist world than members of the CIA.

Intelligent people in the CIA (and the allied British services) knew they should make the maximum effort to limit interference in the affairs of the organizations they had created. But they had to respond not only to higher authority in their own governments but to the indirect threat of Western public opinion.

Those who criticize the policy of concealment have rarely understood that in the eyes of those involved with the American-sponsored organizations the most urgent reason for secrecy was a domestic political one: to conceal from the U.S. Congress (all but a few selected members) and from the American public the fact that the American government was connected to and responsible for these groups. That may seem very strange, but in the United States in the 1950s it would have been politically impossible to make a successful defense to Congress and public opinion of a policy that spent millions to send foreign intellectuals to conferences discussing academic and literary subjects, or debating political matters in other than hard-line anti-Communist style, or publishing magazines with articles critical of the United States, or expressing other opinions certain to excite populist or fundamentalist outrage.

In a later interview, Braden, first head of the CIA's International Organizations Directorate, said, "In the early 1950s, when the cold war was really hot, the idea that Congress would have approved many of our projects was about as likely as the John Birch Society's approving Medicare."* Many of those involved with the Congress for Cultural Freedom abroad would not even have been admitted to the United States (some were not) in those days of McCarthyism and other manifestations of aggressive congressional pursuit of "un-American" activities and sentiments, visa denials or restrictions on present or former Communists, and private and corporate witch hunts.

The Congress was incidentally responsible for the small and wonderful Fondation pour une entraide intellectuelle européenne, directed by the poet Pierre Emmanuel, and later by Annette Laborey, which mailed books and journals on request to librarians and intellectuals in Eastern Europe, and on the latters' visits to the West arranged for them to meet the people in the Western intellectual community they wanted to meet. It and a similar "mailing project" connected with the Free Europe Committee in New York maintained an intellectual lifeline from the West to Communist Europe despite the cold war.

For a time the Congress also housed a "Fund for Intellectual

---

* The John Birch Society was a politically paranoid extreme-right citizens' group, very active in small-town America, which regarded "socialized medicine" as one of many "Communist ideas" directed at destroying American freedom. Contact with foreign "intellectuals," especially ex-Communist intellectuals, would have been considered scandalously dangerous and an invitation to America's subversion.

Freedom," an old project of Koestler's by which Western writers committed a percentage of their royalties to direct assistance to refugee writers from the Communist countries. Initial members were Koestler himself, Graham Greene, John Dos Passos, James T. Farrell, and Aldous Huxley.

The Free Europe Committee was also created in 1950, also with CIA funding, again ostensibly independent, in Free Europe's case as an American corporation placed under a board of eminent citizens and soliciting public contributions.* The principal influence in its creation was George F. Kennan, although he was never publicly identified with it. He was "the father of our project," to quote an internal memo during the planning period. His wartime service at the U.S. embassy in Moscow had left him with a loathing of Soviet purpose and methods and a conviction, justified in the event, that the brutality and deportations that accompanied the Soviet takeover of power in the states occupied by the Soviet army would in the end prove destructive of the USSR itself.

---

* The board included Lucius Clay, Henry Ford II, Arthur Schlesinger, Jr., Dwight Eisenhower, Cecil B. DeMille (!), and C. D. Jackson, an executive of the *Time* organization who had worked in psychological warfare for SHAPE (Supreme Headquarters Allied Powers Europe) in London during the Second World War and was to become a major figure in American political warfare during the 1950s. The Free Europe Committee was parent organization to Radio Free Europe, broadcasting in most of the central and Eastern European languages on domestic affairs in the various countries, as well as giving international news and discussion, meant as a "home radio" alternative to the official state radio services. The Committee also had a press and publications division which conducted research and analysis, and published scholarly books, a magazine, and other publications on current developments in the region; it carried out other projects meant to use the example of what had happened in the Warsaw bloc countries to influence opinion elsewhere, chiefly in the nonaligned world. It also supported organizations of Eastern and central European political exiles. The author of this book was an executive of the Free Europe Committee in New York for four years in the late 1950s.

The principal moral issue posed by the secrecy about the CIA's control of all these groups was that their challenge to Soviet lies was built on a lie about their sponsorship. They exploited the goodwill of individual participants and placed them in a potentially invidious association with the American government. At Free Europe and certain other organizations of political exiles this was not a problem. Even though knowledge of the CIA tie (referred to as being "witty," derived from being a "witting" collaborator of the Agency) and contact with CIA officials was confined to a limited number of American executives of these organizations, the East European exile staff had not been born yesterday, as the phrase has it. Nearly all had been in influential governmental, intellectual, academic, or political positions in their home countries before Communist occupation or seizure of power compelled them to leave, and many had also spent the war years in anti-Nazi exile, working with the British or American governments. They not only took for granted that Free Europe was funded by the U.S. government (and not by the nickels and dimes collected in the annual fund-raising "Crusade for Freedom") but were delighted that this was so, since this implied official American commitment to the cause of their countries' national independence.*

---

* Radio Free Europe and Radio Liberty (broadcasting to the former Soviet Union) were eventually, in the early 1970s, put together under a single authority, the Board for International Broadcasting, with open congressional financing, which could have been done long before. However, this actually worsened the problem of political interference and partisan manipulation. Arch Puddington, the historian of RFE, writes that interference with broadcast scripts, policy, personnel, and budgets by members of Congress and their staffs became much worse, and that in the Reagan years "the political ideology of top radio management, a non-issue under the CIA, emerged as a source of internal contentiousness." Ralph Walters, head of Free Europe for many years, says that a successor, George Urban, and the chairman of the Board for International Broadcasting in the Reagan period, Frank Shakespeare, "sought to weaken . . . the essential traditions of objectivity and sound sourcing, which had been hallmarks of RFE news practices for uncounted years . . . for opportunistic, shortsighted reasons. To their eternal credit, and at considerable risk to their own job safety, the executives managing the newsroom held their ground."

❦

The Congress for Cultural Freedom was another matter. Shils wrote of the problem created by secrecy: "there were two things wrong. . . . One was its imprudence—it endangered the good name of the Congress and also, which was much more important, the good names of persons like Raymond Aron and Ignazio Silone who were conducting, almost single-handedly [in their countries], courageous and lonely battles for a liberal and humane standpoint against the solid mass of rancorous and unsparing enemies. . . . It is inconsistent to argue for the value of truthfulness while being un-truthful." Aron and Silone angrily quit when the CIA connection was revealed in 1966–67. (Isaiah Berlin, on the other hand, said in 1967, "I did not in the slightest object to American sources supply-ing the money. I was—and am—pro-American and anti-Soviet, and if the source had been declared I would not have minded in the least.") The protestations of a number of others, including former *Encounter* editors Melvin Lasky, Irving Kristol, and Stephen Spender, and Nicolas Nabokov and Michael Josselson, involved with the Congress from its earliest days that they knew nothing about the CIA link were greeted with skepticism by others familiar with such matters. For Lasky, Nabokov, and Josselson, the denial was probably obligatory but was nonetheless grotesque. For some of the others, it seemed pathetic.

❦

The Congress for Cultural Freedom eventually collapsed not only because of the falsehood at the center, corrupting and unsustain-able in the long run (and even eventually unnecessary), but also be-cause the enterprise proved too much of a good thing, too successful for its sponsors not eventually to ruin it by forcing it to abandon its original cause, the support of independent thought and writing, and increasingly to become a vehicle for narrow American propaganda. This development mainly took place in the 1960s, as part of a larger corruption of the CIA, and under pressure of the

Vietnam War, when Washington became desperate to make its case, although there had been premonitory incidents before.

The success of the Congress, while the success lasted, was due fundamentally to the decision not to make it the crusading anti-Communist organization Koestler wanted. There was a genuine belief in the possibilities of political dialogue, and some early efforts were made, which were rebuffed, to include figures from the Soviet bloc in Congress activities. There was a commitment to the values of intellectual and artistic freedom at a time when these were being aggressively suppressed in the Soviet Union and in the central and Eastern European countries under obscurantist Soviet-controlled police regimes. Yet the activity of the Congress in support of these values was increasingly instrumentalized, which is inherent in propaganda and political warfare. The Congress, Free Europe, and other international political initiatives of the CIA in the early postwar years nonetheless had an important influence on how the cold war ended, which is as its founders, officers, and supporters would have wished.

BIBLIOGRAPHY

This book is an essay on history and morals, dealing with several figures from the recent past. As an interpretive reflection on certain events and people, it has been constructed upon the biographical investigations, accounts, and analyses of many others. The author has tried conscientiously, in the text, to acknowledge those works and interpretations to which he is in debt, but in addition he wishes to offer his deep thanks to all of those whose own thought and work, notably as expressed in the books and articles listed below, but in many others as well, have provided the foundation upon which he has built this book.

A special note of thanks is due to the editors of that indispensable publication, *The Journal of Contemporary History*, published under the auspices of the Institute of Contemporary History and the Wiener Library in London.

Because this obviously is not a work of scholarship, and the quotations and references to other works in the text are illustrative, rather than demonstrative of a strict argument, and also because this book is the outcome of reflections and drafts made over a half century of indiscriminate and even capricious reading, footnoted references, even when possible, have seemed inappropriate. However, readers curious to know the source or authority for some statement are invited to inquire of the author, who will do his best to satisfy them.

The books and articles included below are assigned to individual chapters for convenience but also, in many cases, rather arbitrarily, as certain major themes recur throughout the book.

CHAPTER ONE. ROMANTICISM AND VIOLENCE

Acton, John Emerich Edward Dalberg-Acton (Lord Acton). *Essays in the Liberal Interpretation of History*. Edited and with an introduction by William H. McNeill. Chicago: University of Chicago, 1967.

Aristotle. *Politics and the Athenian Constitution*. Edited and translated by John Warrington. New York: Everyman's Library, Dutton, 1959.

————. *Nichomachean Ethics*. Edited by William Kaufman. Mineola, N.Y.: Dover Publications, 1998.

D'Arcy, M. C., S. J. *The Meaning and Matter of History: A Christian View*. New York: Farrar, Straus and Cudahy, 1959.

De Felice, Renzo. *Interpretations of Fascism*. Cambridge, Mass., and London: Harvard University Press, 1977.

Easton, Laird McLeod. *The Red Count: The Life and Times of Harry Kessler*. Berkeley, Los Angeles, and London: University of California Press, 2002.

Eksteins, Modris. *Rites of Spring: The Great War and the Birth of the Modern Age*. London: Bantam Press, 1989.

Falls, Cyril. *A Hundred Years of War 1850–1950*. New York: Collier Books, 1962.

Fussell, Paul. *The Great War and Modern Memory*. Oxford: Oxford University Press, 1976.

Girouard, Mark. *The Return to Camelot: Chivalry and the English Gentleman*. New Haven and London: Yale University Press, 1981.

Green, Martin. *Transatlantic Patterns: Cultural Comparisons of England with America*. New York: Basic Books, 1977.

Howard, Michael. *The Causes of Wars & Other Essays*. London: Unwin, 1983.

————. *The Invention of Peace: Reflections on War and International Order*. London: Profile Books, 2000.

————. *War in European History*. Oxford: Oxford University Press, 1976.

Keen, Maurice. *Chivalry*. New Haven and London: Yale University Press, 1984.

Lambert, Angela. *Unquiet Souls: The Indian Summer of the British Aristocracy*. London: Macmillan, 1984.

Pieper, Josef. *Justice*. Translated by Lawrence E. Lynch. New York: Pantheon, 1955.

Popper, K. R. *The Poverty of Historicism*. London: Routledge & Kegan Paul, 1961.

Schlesinger, Arthur M., Jr. *A Life in the 20th Century: Innocent Beginnings, 1917–1950*. Boston and New York: Houghton Mifflin, 2000.

Spotts, Frederic. *Hitler and the Power of Aesthetics*. London, 2003.

Stromberg, Roland N. *Redemption by War: The Intellectuals and 1914*. Lawrence: Regent's Press of Kansas, 1982.

CHAPTER TWO. OVERTURE

Acton, Harold. *Memoirs of an Aesthete*. London: Hamish Hamilton, 1984.

———. *More Memoirs of an Aesthete*. London: Hamish Hamilton, 1986.

Barzini, Luigi. *The Italians*. New York: Atheneum, 1964.

Burke, Edmund. *Selected Writings and Speeches*. Edited by Peter J. Stanlis. New York: Doubleday Anchor, 1963.

———. *A Philosophical Enquiry*. Edited by Adam Phillips. Oxford: Oxford University Press, 1990.

Clark, Alan. *Aces High*. London: Weidenfeld and Nicolson, 1973.

Coupland, Philip M. "The Blackshirted Utopians." *The Journal of Contemporary History* 33, no. 2 (April 1998).

DeGrand, A. J. "Curzio Malaparte: The Illusion of the Fascist Revolution." *The Journal of Contemporary History* 7, nos. 1 and 2, (April 1972).

Futurismo & Futurismi. Catalog of an exhibition at the Palazzo Grassi, Pontus Hulten, curator. Milan: Bompiani, 1986.

Futurist Manifestos. Edited and with an introduction by Umbro Apollonio. London: Thames and Hudson, 1973.

Gentile, Emilio. "Fascism as Political Religion." *The Journal of Contemporary History* 25, nos. 2–3 (May–June 1990).

Gregor, A. James. *The Review of Politics*. (Summer 1995).

Hibbert, Christopher. *Benito Mussolini: The Rise and Fall of Il Duce*. Rev. ed. London: Penguin, 1965.

Honour, Hugh. *Romanticism*. London: Allen Lane, 1979.

Hughes, H. Stuart. *Consciousness and Society*. New York: Vintage, 1961.

———. *The Obstructed Path*. New York: Harper & Row, 1967.

Joll, James. *Three Intellectuals in Politics* [Blum, Marinetti, Rathenau]. New York: Pantheon, 1960.

Lyttelton, Adrian, ed. *Italian Fascisms, from Pareto to Gentile*. London: Jonathan Cape, 1973.

Maritain, Jacques. *Art and Scholasticism with Other Essays*. Translated by J. F. Scanlan. New York: Scribner's, 1947.

Mosley, Nicholas. *Beyond the Pale: Sir Oswald Mosley and Family 1933–1980*. London: Secker & Warburg, 1983.

———. *Rules of the Game, Sir Oswald and Lady Cynthia Mosley, 1896–1933*. London: Secker & Warburg, 1982.

Mosley, Sir Oswald. *My Life*. New Rochelle, N.Y.: Arlington House, 1972.

Mosse, George L. "The Political Culture of Italian Futurism: A General Perspective." *The Journal of Contemporary History* 25, nos. 2–3, (May–June 1990).

Mussolini, Rachele (as told to Albert Zarca). *Mussolini: An Intimate Biography by his Widow*. New York: Morrow, 1974.

O'Sullivan, Nöel. *Fascism*. London and Melbourne: J. M. Dent & Sons, 1983.

Schenk, H. G. *The Mind of the European Romantics*. New York: Doubleday Anchor, 1969.

Silone, Ignazio. *The School for Dictators*. New York: Atheneum, 1963.

Skidelsky, Robert. *Oswald Mosley*. London: Macmillan, 1975.

Smith, Denis Mack. *Mussolini's Roman Empire*. Harmondsworth: Penguin, 1976.

Talmon, J. L. *Romanticism and Revolt, Europe 1815–1848*. London: Thames and Hudson, 1967.

———. *The Origins of Totalitarian Democracy*. New York: Praeger, 1960.

Tisdall, Caroline, and Angelo Bozzolla. *Futurism*. London: Thames and Hudson, 1977.

Vansittart, Peter. *Voices from the Great War*. London: Jonathan Cape, 1981.

Wiskemann, Elizabeth. *Fascism in Italy: Its Development and Influence*. 2nd ed. London: Palgrave-Macmillan, St. Martin's Press, 1970.

Wohl, Robert. *The Generation of 1914*. Cambridge, Mass.: Harvard University Press, 1979.

Woolf, S. J., ed. *European Fascism*. New York: Vintage, 1969.

CHAPTER THREE. THE FALLEN HERO

Aldington, Richard. *Lawrence of Arabia: A Biographical Enquiry*. Chicago: Henry Regnery, 1955.

Armitage, Flora. *The Desert and the Stars: A Portrait of T. E. Lawrence*. London: Faber and Faber, 1956.

Asher, Michael. *Lawrence, the Uncrowned King of Arabia*. London: Viking, 1998.

Boyle, Andrew. *Trenchard*. London: Collins, 1962.

Fromkin, David. "The Importance of T. E. Lawrence." *The New Criterion* 10, no. 1 (September 1991).

Griffiths, Robert. *Fellow Travellers of the Right: British Enthusiasts for Nazi Germany 1933–39*. Oxford: Oxford University Press, 1983.

Hyde, H. Montgomery. *Solitary in the Ranks: Lawrence of Arabia as Airman and Private Soldier*. London: Constable, 1977.

Lawrence, T. E. *Seven Pillars of Wisdom: A Triumph*. New York: Doubleday, 1935.

———. *The Mint: 352087 A/c Ross*. London: Jonathan Cape, 1955.

The Essential T. E. Lawrence. Selected and with a preface by David Garnett. New York: E. P. Dutton, 1951.

The Home Letters of T. E. Lawrence and His Brothers. New York: Macmillan, 1954.

The Letters of T. E. Lawrence. Edited by David Garnett, with a foreword by Captain B. H. Liddell Hart. London: Spring Books, 1938 and 1964.

Liddell Hart, B. H. *"T. E. Lawrence": In Arabia and After*. London: Jonathan Cape, 1934 and 1948.

Mack, John E. *A Prince of Our Disorder: The Life of T. E. Lawrence*. London: Weidenfeld and Nicolson, 1976.

Monroe, Elizabeth. *Philby of Arabia*. London: Faber and Faber, 1973.

Rougemont, Denis de. *Dramatic Personages*. New York: Holt, Rinehart and Winston, 1964.

Stewart, Desmond. *T. E. Lawrence*. London: Hamish Hamilton, 1977.

Tabachnick, Stephen E., and Christopher Matheson. *Images of Lawrence*. London: Jonathan Cape, 1988.

Tabachnick, Stephen E., ed. *The T. E. Lawrence Puzzle*. Athens: University of Georgia Press, 1984.

Thesiger, Wilfred. *The Life of My Choice*. London: Collins, 1987.

Weintraub, Stanley. *Private Shaw and Public Shaw: A Dual Portrait of Lawrence of Arabia and G.B.S.* New York: George Braziller, 1963.

Wilson, Jeremy. *T. E. Lawrence*. Catalog of an exhibition at the National Portrait Gallery 1988–89. London: National Portrait Gallery Publications, 1988.

Young, Gavin. *Eye on the World*. London: Penguin, 1998.

———. *Return to the Marshes*. London: Collins, 1977.

CHAPTER FOUR. THE WARRIOR

Banine. *Ernst Jünger aux faces multiples*. Lausanne: L'Age d'Homme, 1989.

Bloy, Léon. *Pilgrim of the Absolute*. Selection by Raissa Maritain, introduction by Jacques Maritain, translated by John Coleman and Harry Lorin Binsse. New York: Pantheon, 1947.

Cornut-Gentille, Giles, and Philippe Michel-Thiriet. *Florence Gould, Une américaine à Paris*. Paris: Mercure de France, 1989.

Heppenstall, Rayner. *Léon Bloy*. New Haven: Yale University Press, 1954.

Horne, Alistair. *Death of a Generation: Neuve Chapelle to Verdun and the Somme*. New York: American Heritage, 1970.

Jünger, Ernst. *Jardins et Routes: Journal 1939–1940*. Paris: Christian Bourgois, 1979.

———. *Premier Journal Parisien, 1941–1943*. Paris: Christian Bourgois, 1980.

———. *Second Journal Parisien, 1943–1945*. Paris: Christian Bourgois, 1980.

———. *La Cabane dans la Vigne, Journal 1945–1948*. Paris: Christian Bourgois, 1980.

———. *Soixante-dix s'efface: Journal 1986–1990*. Paris: Gallimard, 2002.

———. *Ernst Jünger*. [August von Kageneck and others]. Dossier conçu et dirigé par Philippe Barthelet, Les Dossiers H. Lausanne: Editions L'Age D'Homme, 2000.

———. *Le Problème d'Aladin*. Paris: Christian Bourgois, 1984.

———, avec Antonio Gnoli et Franco Volpi. *Les Prochains titans [I Prossimi Titani, Conversazioni con Ernst Jünger]*. Paris: Grasset, 1998.

———. *On the Marble Cliffs*. New York: New Directions, 1948.

———. *Orages d'acier [Im Stahlgewittern]*. Paris: Christian Bourgois, 1970. (New translation into English by Michael Hofmann published in 2003 as *Storm of Steel*, London: Allen Lane)

Kinser, Bill, and Neil Kleinman. *The Dream That Was No More a Dream: A Search for Aesthetic Reality in Germany, 1890–1945*. New York: Harper Colophon, 1969.

Koch, H. W. *The Origins of the First World War: Great Power Rivalry and German War Aims*. London: Macmillan, 1972.

Kohn, Hans. "Romanticism and the Rise of German Nationalism." *The Review of Politics* 12, no. 4 (October 1950).

Kracauer, Siegfried. *From Caligari to Hitler*. New York: Noonday Paperback, 1959.

Mosse, George L. *The Crisis of German Ideology: The Intellectual Origins of the Third Reich*. New York: Grosset & Dunlap, 1964.

———, ed. *Nazi Culture*. New York: Grosset & Dunlap, 1966.

Nevin, Thomas. *Ernst Jünger and Germany: Into the Abyss 1914–1945*. London: Constable, 1997.

Nietzsche, Friedrich. *A Nietzsche Reader*. Selected and translated with an introduction by R. J. Hollingdale. Harmondsworth: Penguin, 1977.

———. *Thus Spoke Zarathustra*. Translated and with an introduction by Walter Kaufmann. New York: Penguin, 1954.

Nolte, Ernst. *Three Faces of Fascism: Action Française, Italian Fascism, National Socialism*. New York, Chicago, and San Francisco: Holt, Rinehart and Winston, 1966.

O'Neill, Robert J. *The German Army and the Nazi Party 1933–39*. London: Cassell, 1966.

Polimeni, Emmanuela. *Léon Bloy: The Pauper Prophet*. New York: Philosophical Library, 1951.

Reck-Malleczewen, Friedrich Percyval. *Diary of a Man in Despair.* New York: Collier Books, 1970.

Saint Marc, Hélie de, and August von Kageneck. *Notre histoire (1922–1945): Conversations avec Etienne de Montety*. Paris: Editions des Arènes, 2002.

Salomon, Ernst von. *The Answers* [to the 131 questions in the Allied Military Government "Fragebogen"]. Translated by Constantine FitzGibbon. London: Putnam, 1954.

Steiner, George. "Hitler's Vienna." *Salmagundi*, nos. 139–140 (Summer–Fall 2003).

Stern, Eritz. *The Failure of Illiberalism: Essays on the Political Culture of Modern Germany*. New York: Knopf, 1971.

Theweleit, Klaus. *Male Fantasies*. Vol. 1. Minneapolis: University of Minnesota Press, 1987.

Thurlow, Richard C. "The Guardian of the 'Sacred Flame': The Failed Political Resurrection of Sir Oswald Mosley after 1945." *The Journal of Contemporary History* 33, no. 2 (April 1998).

Venner, Dominique. *Histoire d'un fascisme allemand, Les corps-francs du Baltikum et la révolution*. Paris: Pygmalion/Gérard Watelet, 1996.

Viereck, Peter. *Meta-politics: The Roots of the Nazi Mind*. New York: Capricorn Books, 1965.

Wachsmann, Nikolaus. "Marching Under the Swastika? Ernst Jünger and National Socialism, 1918–1933." *Journal of Contemporary History* 33, no. 4 (October 1998).

Woolf, S. J., ed. *European Fascism*. New York: Vintage, 1961.

CHAPTER FIVE. THE HAPPY MAN

Cohen, Eliot A. *Commandos and Politicians: Elite Military Units in Modern Democracies*. Cambridge, Mass.: Harvard University Press, 1978.

Cooper, Artemis. *Cairo in the War, 1939–1945*. London: Hamish Hamilton, 1989.

Cowles, Virginia. *The Phantom Major: The Story of David Stirling and the S.A.S. Regiment*. London: Collins, 1958.

Gray, J. Glenn. *On Understanding Violence Philosophically & Other Essays*. New York: Harper Torchbooks, 1970.

———. *The Warriors: Reflections on Men in Battle*. Introduction by Hannah Arendt. New York: Harper Torchbooks, 1967.

Kennedy Shaw, W. B. *Long Range Desert Group: The Story of Its Work in Libya 1940–1943*. London: Collins, 1945.

Maclean, Fitzroy. *Escape to Adventure*. Boston: Little, Brown, 1951.

Marshall, S.L.A. *Men Against Fire*. New York: William Morrow, 1947.

Peniakoff, Vladimir, Lt.-Col., D.S.O., M.C. ("Popski"). *Private Army*. London: Jonathan Cape, 1950.

Swinson, Arthur. *The Raiders: Desert Strike Force*. London: Pan/Ballantine, 1974.

Vagts, Alfred. *A History of Militarism*. New York: Meridian, 1959.

Vigny, Alfred de. *The Military Necessity*. Translation by Humphrey Hare of *Servitude et Grandeur Militaires* (Paris, 1835). New York: Grove Press, 1953.

Wavell, A. P. [Field Marshal Earl Wavell]. *Soldiers and Soldiering*. London: Jonathan Cape, 1953.

Willett, John. *Popski: A Life of Vladimir Peniakoff, D.S.O., M.C.* London: MacGibbon & Kee, 1954.

CHAPTER SIX. THE MEDITERRANEAN SUPERMAN

Alatri, Paolo. *Gabriele D'Annunzio*. Translated into French by Alain Sarrabay-rouse. Paris: Fayard, 1992.

Andreoli, Annamaria. *D'Annunzio (1863–1938)*. Paris: Museé d'Orsay, Editions de la Réunion des Museés Nationaux, 2001.

James, Henry. *French Writers, Other European Writers and the Prefaces to the New York Edition*. New York: The Library of America, 1984.

Ledeen, Michael A. *The First Duce: D'Annunzio at Fiume*. Baltimore: Johns Hopkins University Press, 1977.

Londres, Albert. *D'Annunzio, Conquérant de Fiume*. Edited and with a preface by Francis Lacassin [including "Fiume: Imagination in Power," by Jacques Benoist-Méchin]. Paris: Julliard, 1990.

Rhodes, Anthony. *D'Annunzio: The Poet as Superman.* New York: McDowell, Oblensky, 1960.

Woodhouse, John. *Gabriele D'Annunzio: Defiant Archangel.* Oxford: Clarendon Press/Oxford University Press, 1998.

Wiskemann, Elizabeth. *Fascism in Italy: Its Development and Influence.* London: Macmillan, 1969.

Zapponi, Niccolò. "Fascism in Italian Historiography, 1986–93: A Fading National Identity." *Journal of Contemporary History* 29, no. 4 (October 1994).

CHAPTER SEVEN. THE CONFIDENCE MAN

Aron, Raymond. *The Opium of the Intellectuals.* Translated by Terence Kilmartin. New York: Norton, 1962.

Carr, E. H. *Twilight of the Comintern, 1930–1935.* New York: Pantheon, 1982.

Caute, David. *The Fellow Travellers.* London: Quartet, 1977.

Conquest, Robert. *The Great Terror: Stalin's Purge of the Thirties.* New York: Macmillan, 1968.

Journal of Contemporary History, special issues on "Left-Wing Intellectuals Between the Wars," vol. 1, no. 2 (1966); and "Popular Fronts," vol. 5, no. 3 (1970).

Koch, Stephen. *Double Lives: Stalin, Willi Münzenberg and the Seduction of the Intellectuals.* Rev. ed. London: HarperCollins, 1995.

Malia, Martin. *The Soviet Tragedy: A History of Socialism in Russia, 1917–1991.* New York: Free Press, 1994.

Schalk, David L. *The Spectrum of Political Engagement.* Princeton: Princeton University Press, 1979.

Seton-Watson, Hugh. *From Lenin to Khrushchev: The History of World Communism.* New York: Praeger, 1960.

Tuominen, Arvo. *The Bells of the Kremlin: An Experience in Communism.* Edited by Piltti Heiskanen; translated by Lily Leino. Hanover, N.H., and London: University Press of New England, 1983.

CHAPTER EIGHT. L'HOMME ENGAGÉ

Courcel, Martine de, ed. *Malraux, Life and Work.* London: Weidenfeld and Nicolson, 1976.

De Gaulle, Charles. *The Complete War Memoirs, 1940–1946*. New York: Simon & Schuster, 1964.

Friang, Brigitte. *Petit tour autour de Malraux*. Paris: Editions du Félin, 2001.

Godard, Henri, ed. *L'Amitié André Malraux, souvenirs et temoignages*. Paris: Gallimard, 2001.

Howe, Irving. *Politics and the Novel*. New York: Horizon & Meridian, 1957.

Lacouture, Jean. *André Malraux*. Translated by Alan Sheridan. New York: Pantheon, 1975.

Langlois, Walter G. *André Malraux: The Indochina Adventure*. New York: Praeger, 1966.

La Nouvelle Revue Française. "Hommage à André Malraux," various authors, no. 295 (Juillet 1977).

Lewis, R.W.B., ed. *Malraux: A Collection of Critical Essays*. Englewood Cliffs, N.J.: Prentice Hall, 1964.

Lottman, Herbert R. *Camus: A Biography*. London: Weidenfeld and Nicolson, 1979.

Malraux, André. *Anti-Memoirs*. Translated by Terence Kilmartin. New York: Holt, Rinehart and Winston, 1968.

———. *Felled Oaks: Conversation with de Gaulle*. New York: Holt, Rinehart and Winston, 1971.

———. *Lazarus*. Translated by Terence Kilmartin. New York: Holt, Rinehart and Winston, 1977.

———. *Oeuvres complètes*. Paris: Bibliothèque de La Pléiade, Editions Gallimard (vol. I, 1989; vol. II, 1996).

———. *The Metamorphosis of the Gods*. Translated by Stuart Gilbert. Garden City, NY: Doubleday, 1960.

———. *The Voices of Silence*. Translated by Stuart Gilbert. Garden City, N.Y.: Doubleday & Company, 1956.

Malraux, Clara. *Memoirs*. Abridged and translated by Patrick O'Brian from *Le Bruit de nos pas: Apprendre à vivre* (1963) and *Nos vingt ans* (1966), both published by Bernard Grasset, Paris; Farrar, Straus & Giroux, New York, 1967.

"Passion and the Intellect, or André Malraux," by various authors, *Yale French Studies*, no. 18 (Winter 1957).

Picon, Gaëtan. *Malraux*. Paris: Éditions du Seuil, 1953.

Roy, Jules. *Mémoires barbares*. Paris: Alban Michel, 1989.

Speaight, Robert. *Georges Bernanos: A Study of the Man and the Writer.* London: Collins and Harville Press, 1973.

Todd, Olivier. *André Malraux, Une Vie.* Paris: Gallimard, 2001.

CHAPTER NINE. THE ANTI-COMMUNIST

Carr, E. H. *Twilight of the Comintern, 1930–1935.* New York: Pantheon, 1982.

Cesarani, David. *Arthur Koestler: The Homeless Mind.* London: William Heinemann, 1998.

Grémion, Pierre. *Intelligence de l'anticommunism: Le Congrès pour la liberté de la culture à Paris 1950–1975.* Paris: Fayard, 1995.

Hayman, Ronald. *Sartre: A Biography.* New York: Simon & Schuster, 1987.

Koestler, Arthur. *Arrow in the Blue: An Autobiography.* New York: Macmillan, 1961.

———. *The Invisible Writing: An Autobiography* [Part Two]. New York: Macmillan, 1954.

———. *Dialogue with Death.* New York: Macmillan, 1960.

———. *Janus: A Summing Up.* London: Hutchinson, 1978.

———. *Oeuvres autobiographiques.* Edited by Phil Casoar. Includes the posthumously published *L'Étranger du Square*, a collaboration with his wife Cynthia Koestler, found among his papers after their death and edited by Harold Harris, published in London by Hutchinson in 1984 as *Stranger on the Square.* Paris: Robert Laffont, 1994.

———. *The Act of Creation.* London: Pan Books, 1964.

———. *The Call Girls: A Tragi-Comedy with Prologue and Epilogue.* London: Hutchinson, 1972.

———. *The Case of the Midwife Toad.* New York: Random House, 1971.

———. *The Heel of Achilles.* London: Picador (Pan Books), 1974.

———. *The Sleepwalkers: A History of Man's Changing Vision of the Universe.* London: Hutchinson, 1959.

———. *The Trail of the Dinosaur & Other Essays.* London: Collins, 1955.

———. *The Yogi and the Commissar, and Other Essays.* New York: Macmillan, 1945.

Lendvai, Paul. *The Hungarians.* Translated by Ann Major. Princeton: Princeton University Press, 2003.

CHAPTER TEN. CODA

Chambers, Whittaker. *Witness*. New York: Random House, 1952.

Crozier, Brian. *The Rebels: A Study of Post-War Insurrections*. Boston: Beacon Press, 1960.

Eisenstadt, S. N. *Fundamentalism, Sectarianism, and Revolution*. Cambridge: Cambridge University Press, 1999.

Furet, François, Antoine Liniers, and Philippe Raynaud. *Terrorisme et démocratie*. Paris: Foundation Saint-Simon, Fayard, 1985.

Guevara, Ernesto Che. *Passages de la guerre révolutionnaire: le Congo*. Paris: Editions Métailié, 2000.

Hardt, Michael, and Antonio Negri. *Empire*. Cambridge, Mass.: Harvard University Press, 2000.

Kedward, Roderick. *The Anarchists: The Men Who Shocked an Era*. New York: American Heritage (Library of the 20th Century), 1971.

Mishima, Yukio. *Mishima on Hagakure: The Samurai Ethic and Modern Japan*. Harmondsworth: Penguin, 1977.

Mongin, Olivier, ed., "Terrorismes" (special issue), *Ésprit*, Paris, October–November 1984.

Rojo, Ricardo. *My Friend Che*. New York: Dial Press, 1968.

Scheer, Robert, ed. *The Diary of Che Guevara: The Secret Papers of a Revolutionary, Bolivia: November 7, 1966–October 7, 1967*. New York: Bantam Books, 1968.

Sorel, Georges. *Reflections on Violence*. Translated by T. E. Hulme. New York: Collier Books, 1961.

CHAPTER ELEVEN. PROGRESS

Auchincloss, Louis. *Woodrow Wilson*. New York: Penguin/Viking, 2000.

Cohn, Norman. *The Pursuit of the Millennium*. New York: Harper Torchbook, 1961.

Fleming, Fergus. *The Sword and the Cross*. New York: Grove Press, 2003.

Foucauld, Charles de. *Lettres et carnets*. Paris: Éditions du Seuil, 1966.

Fremantle, Anne. *Desert Calling: The Life of Charles de Foucauld*. London: Hollis & Carter, 1950.

Gray, Francine du Plessix. *Simone Weil*. New York: Viking, 2001.

Julliard, Jacques, and Michel Winock. *Dictionnaire des intellectuels français.* Éditions du Seuil: Paris, 1996.

Kennan, George F. *American Diplomacy 1900–1950.* Chicago: University of Chicago, 1951.

Knox, Ronald A. *Enthusiasm: A Chapter in the History of Religion.* Oxford: Oxford University Press, 1950.

Levi, Peter. *The Frontiers of Paradise: A Study of Monks and Monasteries.* London: Collins Harvill, 1988.

Lukacs, John. *Historical Consciousness, or the Remembered Past.* New York: Harper & Row, 1968.

Moorhouse, Geoffrey. *Against All Reason: The Religious Life in the Modern World.* London: Weidenfeld and Nicolson, 1969.

Pascal, Blaise. *Pensées.* Translated and with an introduction by A. J. Krailsheimer. Harmondsworth and Baltimore: Penguin Library Edition, 1966.

———. *The Provincial Letters.* Translated and with an introduction by A. J. Krailsheimer. Harmondsworth and Baltimore: Penguin Library Edition, 1967.

Pétrement, Simone. *Simone Weil: A Life.* Translated by Raymond Rosenthal. New York: Pantheon, 1976.

Six, Jean-François. "The Conversion of Charles de Foucauld." *The Life of the Spirit* 14, nos. 158–159 (August–September 1959).

Steiner, George. "The Muses' Farewell." *Salmagundi,* nos. 135–136 (Summer–Fall 2002).

Voillaume, René. *Seeds of the Desert: The Legacy of Charles de Foucauld.* Translation by Willard Hill of *Au Cour des masses* (Paris, 1952). Chicago: Fides Publishers, 1955.

APPENDIX

Berghahn, Volker R. *America and the Intellectual Cold Wars in Europe,* Princeton: Princeton University Press, 2001.

Puddington, Arch. *Broadcasting Freedom: The Cold War Triumph of Radio Free Europe and Radio Liberty.* Lexington: University of Kentucky, 2001.

Spender, Stephen. *The Thirties and After: Poetry, Politics, People (1933–75).* London: Fontana/Collins, 1978.

Stonor Saunders, Frances. *Who Paid the Piper?: The CIA and the Cultural Cold War.* London: Granta, 1999.
Urban, George R. *Radio Free Europe and the Pursuit of Democracy.* New Haven: Yale University Press, 1998.

INDEX

ABOUT THE AUTHOR

William Pfaff is a political columnist for *The International Herald Tribune*, London's *The Observer*, and other newspapers. He was a political essayist for *The New Yorker* from 1971 to 1992. He is the author of seven previous books, including *Barbarian Sentiments: How the American Century Ends*, a National Book Award finalist. He lives in Paris.